Best Wishes
Jim Thom...

"*A straight-forward tale of a young college graduate in his first job, immersed in Pan American Clipper Glory on Guam in 1941. Suddenly four years of his life were stolen by a ruthless enemy. Writing from the heart about the despair, boredom, uncertainty, and lack of communication with the outside world, as well as starvation, he never loses his sense of humor. On his return home he describes with candor the universal challenge of adjustment to civilian life. Definitely a page-turner.*"
—Capt. David P. Marin, USNR Ret., Communication Intelligence Officer, Veteran of WWll and Korea.

"*As a B-29 Aircraft Commander in World War II who fire-bombed Kobe on the night Jim describes, I find this true story of a civilian POW's 4 years in hell in Japan totally enthralling and riveting.*"
—Capt. Stan Pierce, PanAm Ret., Jim's brother-in-law

"*Some of the details of our internment had left me until I read Jim's "Trapped With The Enemy". Now I have re-lived those details with Jim's excellent and accurate narrative of four years of despair, uncertainyt and loss of liberty, with his unique touch of humor—even under such circumstances. The impact to me is overwhelming, as it will be to every reader.*"

—Dick Arvidson, Jim's cellmate

D1601341

TRAPPED WITH THE ENEMY!

Four Years a Civilian P.O.W. in Japan

James O. Thomas

To order additional copies of this book, contact:
Xlibris Corporation
1-888-7-XLIBRIS
www.Xlibris.com
Orders@Xlibris.com

CONTENTS

Dedication

To all prisoners of war who have experienced the debilitating torture of hunger, the hopelessness of confinement and the agonies of despair in the hands of a strange and ruthless enemy.

The passage of time has warped my impressions of things that happened fifty nine years ago. This story comes from many sources: personal notes and mementos, historical facts, my memory and diaries of my buddies. I am deeply indebted to Bob Vaughn, Roy Henning, Grant Wells, Jack Taylor and Dick Arvidson. for their notes and recollections.

I am beholden to Polly Tooker, my patient and talented copy reader, to Carole Davis for her professional analysis and suggestions, to Colleen Watson for her encouragement. They helped make this book possible. Many thanks, also to Ted Hatrack for demystifying the enigma of my computer and Roger Mansell for guiding me through the pitfalls of publishing.

I'm also thankful to my wife, Barbara, who carried on so nobly while I was bent over the keyboard.

FOREWORD

There are thousands of World War II stories of combat, bravery, treachery, love, and pain that line the bookshelves and fill the movie houses. But none are more intimate with boredom, hunger, isolation, melancholy, and despair than this one. As a civilian prisoner-of-war, we had few choices but to comply, starve, seek solace as best we could in daydreams, memories, loneliness and deprivation while tolerating chafing regulations, obnoxious guards, and quirks of fellow cellmates. We missed love, country, freedom, involvement, and the chance to contribute to America's victory. We sat out the war behind enemy lines and watched the defeat of Japan from a ringside seat. But admission to this spectacle wasn't free. Those four years were the best years of our lives as far as health, enthusiasm, love, and action are concerned but in a sense they were wasted. But In a larger sense, they were years of testing, maturing, learning, and survival. Not many people can boast of experiencing these things so intimately during their lifetime. If Shakespeare's lines, *Sweet are the uses of adversity*, are true, then things came out pretty much even after all.

This story was written for the benefit of my descendants. It might satisfy their curiosity as to what I did during World War II. Assuming of course, they care what I did. Maybe a few of my old cronies will read it if they can still see the print. Otherwise, I leave it to posterity.

PROLOGUE

America, 1941. New Buicks sold for fifteen hundred dollars and a gallon of gas cost fifty cents. A man's suit cost twenty-five dollars, and bread was a nickel a loaf. Glenn Miller's band was in the groove and *Elmer's Tune* was number one on the Hit Parade. *Gone with the Wind* was still packing the theaters. Saturday night dances competed with *Bank Night* at the movies for a place to take your best girl. Traffic jams, smog, and free-ways had not been invented. Neither had computers, microwaves or television, so people read more and snacked less. Fashion dictated short hair and long skirts. The exploits of baseball great Joe DiMaggio, super athlete Babe Didrickson and heavyweight champion, Joe Louis, filled the sports pages.

James O. Thomas, 1941

But parts of the world were in turmoil: World War II raged in Europe while Japan lurked in the shadows of the far East. Charles Lindbergh, the famed pilot, the first to fly solo over the Atlantic in 1927, wrangled with President Roosevelt over America's role in the conflict. Town meetings, newspapers, and politicians debated the issues of war, peace, and neutrality. The country was confused, insular, naive, divided. For better or worse, 1941 was the year America changed its course and lost its innocence. Fate played a hand in this change and swept me along with it.

Unknowingly, in 1941, I, too, was at a crossroads; and when the year ended, nothing in my world would ever be the same again. Armed with a diploma from the University of California at Berkeley, I was twenty-four, optimistic, aspiring. Talk of rearmament was heavy and I was "1A" in the draft; the perfect candidate to serve in the Armed Forces. I was also broke and needed a job until they drew my number. If I couldn't find a job, I would enlist in the Army's Signal Corp to make use of the professional photographic experience I had gained earlier.

Pan American Airways, the famous airline that once spanned the Pacific, had a contract to help deliver a dozen Catalina Flying Boats (PBY's) to the Dutch East Indies for patrol duty in the south China seas. PanAm was beefing up its Pacific bases and searching for personnel to fill the slots. Though my aviation skills were nil, I decided to take a "flyer" for a job in their ground operations department. This might be my big break. Perhaps I could hitch a ride on the wings of an exciting profession.

My first interview filled me with PanAm's unique bi-product—*Clipper Glory*—a hypnotic state about south sea romance on palm covered beaches, hula girls, and moonlit nights. After a month of intensive training, I was assigned to Guam as Assistant Station Manager for a six-month hitch. To my surprise, PanAm got me a six-month deferment from the draft. I was to report back to my draft board in January 1942. War in Europe seemed too remote to worry about and Japan was talking peace. Like everyone else, I felt uninvolved and anxious to do other things. As it turned out, I was listening to the solacing rhythm of my heart instead of the distant pounding of drums.

By July, the training was over. We were going to our assigned locations and had one week to get ready. I shopped for clothes, got my shots, packed my bags, and called mother to say good-bye. We were booked first class to Honolulu on Matson Line's luxury liner S.S. Mariposa, a trip only the socially privileged had ever enjoyed. That was my preliminary taste of *Clipper Glory*. I was headed for an adventure that would alter my life—one that I wouldn't have taken for a million dollars and one that I would never forget.

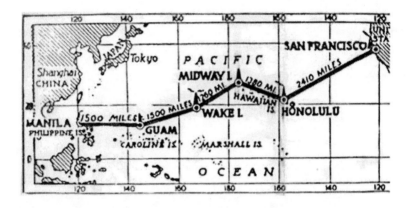

Boeing 314 Clipper leaving the Golden Gate

CHAPTER 1

Clipper Glory

Mariposa's crowded dock was a melee of bustling porters, honking horns, paper ribbons, champagne, and singing to the music of a honky-tonk band. Waving farewell from the railing to the shouts of 'Bon Voyage', the heavy whistle moaned a signal for all visitors to go ashore. Tugs grunted the liner into the bay and pointed her prow towards the open sea. The ship shuddered as the propellers took hold. Silently, I watched from the stern as the Golden Gate faded into the distance. I would remember that scene many times over the next four years.

Treaure Island (center) within the Golden Gate Berkeley in foreground, San Francisco-Oakland Transbay Bridge on left.

Dozens of pretty, chaperoned coeds, strolled the decks and splashed in the pool. A hundred or so patriotic prostitutes, stiffly decorous, were on their way to raise the morale at Hickam Field and redistribute the wealth of Honolulu. Their raucous language proved Dorothy Parker was right when she said, "You can lead a whore to culture (horticulture) but you can't make her think." Scores of new PanAm employees were aboard: radio operators, mechanics, meteorologists, cooks, carpenters, elec-tricians, all reporting to various stations. Dancing, swimming, shuffleboard, movies and eight course meals left little inclination to study our manuals. Clear weather, smooth seas and a steady deck added to the luster.

On the morning of the sixth day, as the sun peeked through billowing clouds, we entered Pearl Harbor. The sights and sounds of Hawaii in motion made me dizzy. Outrigger canoes filled with laughing natives diving for coins and 'hula girls', swaying to the strains of *Blue Hawaii*, draping fragrant pakaki leis around our necks as we came down the gangplank, made *Clipper Glory* a new word for heaven.

The Moana Hotel, on Waikiki beach, was waiting. So were cool Mai Tais under the famed banyan tree in the flowered court-yard. The next three days were a whirl of girl-watching, body-surfing, exotic dining, looking at the spectacular view of a sample of Hawaiian paradise from the Pali, and dancing to Polynesian rhythms. *Clipper Glory*, that exclusive fringe benefit of Pan American Airways was a form of rapture experienced once in a lifetime.

Our departure from this Pacific paradise came too soon. With engines idling, the Honolulu Clipper waited in Pearl Harbor. Seat belts were tightened, as the Boeing B-314 taxied into position. Wind from the spinning props on the four 1500 horsepower engines rippled the water as the Clipper gathered speed, bounced twice and lifted off. We were headed for Midway Island 1304 miles to the northwest.

This was my first flight over water. Sights of bulging cumulus towering thousands of feet above and cloud shadows on whitecaps six thousand feet below turned the world into a fairy land. Half-way out, French Frigate shoals slid beneath us. In mid-afternoon, a tiny dot appeared on the horizon. It was Midway, a coral atoll halfway around the world from Greenwich, England. We lost a day by crossing that imaginary dateline so we joined the exclusive 'Short Snorter' club. I still treasure my membership card, a dollar bill autographed by the passengers and crew. The initiation fee was a round of drinks for the passengers.

The touchdown in Midway's lagoon was smooth and gentle. We taxied to the PanAm pier. A neat, one story hotel occupy-ing the highest point on the island, (eight feet above sea level) was ready to host us. Thousands of gooney birds amused us and a white sandy beach invited us to dip in the warm, clear water.

At sun-up the next morning we left for Wake Island, three tiny atolls, 1182 miles to the southwest. We moved about in the comfortable cabin, played cards, read, talked and enjoyed the hot meals prepared in a tiny galley up front. Five hours later we skimmed into Wake's lagoon. Since Guam was bend-ing under a typhoon, Waiting for clearance, we snorkeled, swam and goofed off for three days. We were now well-tanned beach bums.

On the fourth day, we lifted off Wake's lagoon and turned the clipper's nose towards Guam 1508 miles further west. The weather was CAVU (ceiling and visibility unlimited) all the way. Seven hours later, the dark speck of Guam appeared on the skyline. Dur-ing the next hour it grew into a green tropical island. On the down-wind leg, the plane skimmed over a jungle of lush under-growth speckled with coconut palms, banana trees, and isolated huts. In the near distance, waves curled around inviting beaches. Agaña, the capital, slid out of sight under the wing. We circled low for a gentle landing in Apra harbor, the four engines roared triumphantly as we taxied to the landing barge in mid-bay. A launch carried us ashore where a colorful crowd of natives shouted its welcome. This island, with its rich historical background, Hollywood setting, and friendly people, would be my home for the next six months. Feeling as though I had grabbed the brass ring, I stepped out on Guam's shores on July 15, 1941. We were thirteen days, 6382 miles and seven time zones west of the Golden Gate.

Apra Harbor

Sumay, Guam

CHAPTER 2

Paradise Won

A whisper of a breeze slipped by looking for something to cool, but missed my dripping brow. I scanned the strange tropical scene. Widely spaced palm trees, bent from the recent typhoon, dotted the flat PanAm compound. Off to the right, two massive oil tanks stood ready to feed high octane to hungry clippers. On the left, a modest, white stucco airport office guarded the end of the launch slip. Nearby was a large, corrugated tin maintenance shop. This friendly compound would be my work station until I left in January.

"Hi Jim, welcome to Guam, paradise of the Pacific," a friendly voice shouted, and a slim figure in a pith helmet and cotton shorts detached itself from the crowd. "Shake the hand of Bob Vaughn, the world's greatest lover, mechanic and jack-of-all-trades. Besides that, I'm your roommate, advisor and tour guide. Let me show you to our palace. We'll have to walk — the station wagon is for paying passengers not for peons. We'll get your bags later. On the way I'll show you the high points of interest. Grant, you and Dick might as well come along." An ex-sailor, Bob had acquired his social skills and lingo from wild, unchaperoned shore leaves. Vivid, funny, and practical.

Past the shop we took a hard left and immediately found ourselves in the center of Sumay. Squatting on the inside shore of the Orote peninsula, Sumay, a village of about a hundred natives and assorted hybrids, was a case study in tropical simplicity. Two short, rutted streets formed a "T" at the village center. A hodgepodge of

nipa huts, wooden shacks, a few odd stores and two scruffy saloons
shouldered for space on the narrow streets. Rosie's Bar looked halfway respectable but Ben Cook's tavern was the dirtiest, noisiest,
most run-down joint I've ever seen. "We'll check that out later,"
Bob muttered out of the side of his mouth.

Panam Hotel

Thatched-roofed, clapboard houses mounted on stilts were
scattered among palm trees and bougainvillea. Wide-eyed, bare-
footed children in cotton shorts peeked shyly from doorways as
they hid behind smiling mothers in casual gingham dresses. Pigs,
chickens and dogs milled about underneath to eat table scraps
dropped through cracks in the floors. Indoor privies contributed
to the atmosphere. Suntanned men in ragged shorts gave us friendly,
betel-toothed grins from under tattered straw hats. Many of the
people were barefoot but some covered their callused feet with
sandals made from worn tire treads. Nondescript dogs wandered
about, listlessly. Dozens of rangy, chickens meandered through
foot traffic. "Dogs, cats, chickens, and pigs don't adapt to the tropics," Bob commented. "Their offspring are runty and weak. Every
new generation of animals has to be imported." I appreciated his
lesson in genetics.

Two blocks further down we turned right onto a cascajo (decomposed, crushed coral) road. Neat, white bungalows, housing the PanAm staff, lined both sides. The familiar PanAm single-storied hotel stood nearby on a gentle, landscaped slope overlooking the company compound.

"There's the hotel, the center of our life on this island and our home away from home." Bob said. "It's our restaurant, our library, our social center and a place to shoot the breeze. We have a special dining room away from the passengers. Dinner is from six to eight in the evening and breakfast from six to eight in the morning. Lunch is catch-as-catch-can around noon. No dress code, but no slobs either. The best part is, it's all free. Dick, since you're a radio operator you're bunking with the other "Sparks" in that shack over there. Grant, Jim and I are bunking in this one up the road." Bob pointed to a neat bungalow overlooking the harbor. Higher on the slope sat the sturdy, ferro-concrete compound of the Pacific Cable Company, whose undersea cable had linked America to the Orient since 1906.

Our three-room "snake ranch", as Bob proudly called it, (borrowing the local slang for a house of ill repute), was tidy and clean but the heat was oppressive. "How do we cool it so we can sleep at night?" I asked.

"See those ropes stretched catty-cornered near the ceiling? We hang wet bed sheets over them and turn on the portable fans. They work fine. Drops the temperature twenty degrees and keeps the mosquitoes off at the same time. They call 'em "Swamp Coolers" . You'll get used to the noise. You guys flip for bunks. Your bags will be delivered soon. If you want to explore a bit, go ahead. I've got to check in with Max Brodofsky, my boss, before he tears me apart. See ya at dinner."

Grant, a mechanic, was a bit older than I, happily married and already missing his wife. Handsome, quiet in a pleasant way, he fit like a glove. He and Bob would be good roomies. We meandered through the hotel and headed for the compound. He went to the shop and I to the airport office.

Manuel Calvo, the brown skinned Chamorran clerk on duty, jumped up to shake my hand. His warm smile lighted his round, intelligent face. His short, chubby physique reflected a placid interior and long, happy moments at the dinner table. He'd be easy to work with.

"Welcome aboard, Mr. Thomas. We have been expecting you. Our station manager, Mr. Gregg, is busy with the passengers. He asked me to show you around. He'll be here soon." His clipped, Guamanian accent was pleasing to the ear.

After he sent messages concerning the current flight, we toured the office and compound. He carefully pointed out my desk, the supplies, the reference books, a drawing board for weather map making and flight-watch, the radio-telephone and the water cooler. Outside were the meteorological post with reporting devices, the launch, and two station wagons. Turning his body like a weather vane, he indicated north, south, east and west. Good thing, for I was completely disoriented. We then returned to the office to meet the station manager.

Chuck Gregg bounded in, dressed in his naval finery and looking like a Boy Scout up for a merit badge. Cordial, but with a touch of loftiness, one could readily see he was enjoying his role. He wasted no time in briefing me on company protocol: dress codes, no socializing with the natives, no absenteeism or tardiness, and no hanky-panky with females. I'd start my duties tomorrow at 5:30 A.M. sharp regardless of the jet-lag. The Honolulu clipper was scheduled to leave for Manila at 8 A.M. and we needed a couple of hours lead time to get ready. He wished me a good evening and disappeared. I bid Manuel goodbye and went to the hotel.

Our small dining room was filled with company personnel: radio operators, mechanics, carpenters, and clerks, some stationed here, some in transit. Introductions were informal. There were Dick Best, Chief Radio Operator, a humorous, friendly chap; Max Brodofsky, Chief Mechanic, a burly man of action; Everett Penning, a radio operator, red-headed, quiet-spoken, funny; and Alfred

Hammelef, an efficient, dedicated, Port Steward. A practical and friendly bunch.

So far so good. I had a good station, on a beautiful island, an amiable gang to work with, and a feeling of pride and elation with Pan-American. The courses taken at Treasure Island covering meteorology, navigation, radio-telephone, air and sea emergencies, airplane statistics and personnel policy would help me do my job with confidence.

Weather forecasting was vital to all who sailed the seas or flew in the air, especially PanAm. Since the airline covered such long and hazardous distances, weather and winds could make a flight successful or turn it into a failure by returning to the place of departure.

All stations were equipped with weather instruments: theodolites for upper-air readings, barometers, thermometers and hydrometers. There were also anemometers, rain gauges, balloons and tanks of helium. We were required to report winds aloft with helium filled balloons at 1000-foot intervals to 20,000 feet, also surface winds, temperature, humidity, dew point, cloud cover and rainfall twice daily. This information was transmitted at specific times to Honolulu and Manila weather centers. The data were collated by meteorologists who relayed their maps and forecasts on special channels at specific hours for everyone's use. International law required such information from all bases, planes, and ships at sea. It was exciting to see my report recorded on the international weather map only a few hours after it was sent.

Personnel for different operations were as essential to the airline as were the pilots and flight crews. Mechanics kept the planes airworthy; radio operators furnished vital communications; and the port steward and his staff catered to the passengers and station personnel. We in Ground Operations assisted the flight crews and acted as the "pilots" on the ground. Armed with weather forecasts, we selected the plane's best routes and altitudes to the next station and gassed the plane accord-ingly. Everything going aboard was weighed, including the passengers, and proper plane balance was found with slide rules and formulas. Sometimes cargo and bag-gage had to be shifted to meet this requirement. A flight plan, cargo manifests, and passenger lists were provided for the captain.

Whenever a plane was in the air, continuous flight watch was necessary. On "howgozit" curves, we plotted the flight path, weather, and remaining fuel load by hourly fixes from the plane to our radio shack on the hill. Lack of alternate landing harbors added to our worries. Wind directions and storm fronts might require a change in altitude and heading to avoid gas consuming headwinds and dangerous air currents. A new storm front might force a re-turn to base (REW–return weather). ETAs and ETDs (estimated times of arrival and departure) were posted in the airport office for the public and press. Schedules called for one flight a week in each direction. That meant two arrivals and two departures every seven days. The PBY's had not yet started their shuttle.

Though the climate was generally pleasant, some adjust-ments were required. On the second night, as we lay in bed, Bob Vaughn clued us in on a few facts. "The humidity here is a bitch on cloth-ing, shoes, and things like cameras. Mildew will eat them up in a week if they're not protected. So we stash them in the closet with the electric light on day and night. This helps dry them out. We wash our clothes regularly and shine our shoes weekly. Spraying them with powder helps to keep them dry."

"Also," he continued, "only drink the water that's served in the hotel. Everywhere else you drink only coke, beer, coffee, tea or bottled water. The tropical trots are hell. Wash your hands before you eat anything." Having dispensed those words of wisdom, Dr. Bob, M.D., PhD, from the College of Hard Knocks, immediately started to snore. We knew six A.M. would come early so we knocked off the bull. We were going to Agaña in the morning.

The capital city of Agaña, twelve miles north of Sumay, was reached by a narrow paved road that twisted between the shore-line and the jungle. Small "ranches" (plots of land with house on stilts) poked their heads out from the tangled undergrowth. Farm-ers, plowing rice paddies with water buffalo (or caraboa) up to their bellies in mud, could be seen on either side of the road. Two-wheeled carts, filled with bananas, palm fronds or pineapples and drawn by shuffling caraboa, would slow auto traffic to a crawl, causing a Guamanian gridlock. Sometimes the crushed bodies of hundreds of poisonous toads, victims of auto traffic, littered the road.

A typical street scene in Guam

Airport Office, Guam, 1941, Shop in background

Agaña was the political, financial, merchandising and social center on the island. Spanish influence was evident everywhere. Tiled roofs, adobe stores and government offices bordered the zocalo (town square) and its central bandstand. The Catholic church, a single storied stucco building with a tile roof and a cross, commanded a strategic spot so did the Bank of Guam and the Governor's mansion, a dignified wooden structure. Except at siesta time, the town bustled with activity. A cool beer on a hot day in a noisy bar was like a Coney Island sideshow.

Other Americans were living on the island. The Marine barracks, on the hill behind our compound, housed a hundred or so of these gallant warriors. They manned the ramparts with rifles and held parades but off duty, they were hell-raising brawlers. After a few dollops at Ben Cook's bar, they'd invite us up to the base to see a movie or play poker, providing we bought the next round.

A small group of naval personnel—officers, medics, nurses, and orderlies—were stationed in Agaña. Maintenance crews manned the Piti naval yard near Sumay. A score of white American businessmen with Chamorran wives enjoyed cloistered lives. Some were retired military men who had "gone native" and settled in Guam. They were fondly referred to as "Bamboos" and I enjoyed their friendship.

J.H. Pomeroy Construction Company had a government contract to build a causeway from the mainland to Cabras Island bordering Apra harbor. It had something to do with America's attempt to rearm Guam. Some eighty or so construction workers were housed in special barracks near Sumay. Cat-skinners, shovel operators, and pile drivers worked their machines with skill. Welders, surveyors, and carpenters followed behind to ply their trade. This was a rough-hewn and hardy bunch.

Our days settled into a pleasant routine. PanAm's arrivals and departures came and went on time. Tropical sunrises and sunsets competed daily in heavenly beauty contests. Rainstorms raced across the island every afternoon, cooling the air. The weather was predictable and, except for the humidity, pleasant. A couple of fresh-water showers a day kept us comfortable.

Apra harbor lay flat and peaceful between Cabras Island and our boat slip. Its coral bottom, which could tear open a ship's hull or lacerate an exposed foot, lay four feet beneath the surface at low tide. Channels for seagoing traffic had been blown open with dynamite by the U.S. Navy years before. A dazzling garden of colorful coral and tropical fish made it a snorkeling paradise.

Off duty, we explored the island, snorkeled in the harbor, beered-up in the bars, read, sunbathed, and hiked. Sometimes, we played with coconut crabs, bet on cockfights and swam in the fresh water caves.

Around the first week in August, the PBY's started coming through, two at a time for safety sake. Their three man crews did not have the experience nor the spit and polish of the PanAm uniformed demi-Gods. Despite their casual appearance, they were competent airmen and knew how to fly. By October all the flying boats had been safely delivered to the Dutch East Indies.

On a plane-free weekend, Bob and his Chamorran assistants organized a fandango, a Guamanian mixture of the New Orleans Mardi Gras, the Munich Oktoberfest, and a wild Texas barbecue thrown together on the 4th of July. Wheedling permission from Max by promising no hanky-panky, he invited thirty or so native guests to our cabin for an evening of feasting and music, dancing, drinking and a mixed menu of native niceties. The main course was two pigs on a spit and twelve fried chickens. These were accompanied by fresh pineapples, and wild bananas. All this was to be washed down with six cases of beer and two kegs of Aggie, a fermented concoction of coconut milk and dead flies, strong enough to kill a mule. A wind-up phonograph with a dozen scratched 78s provided the music, which everyone with a drink in their hand ignored. Things started slow and easy, but as time went on and the drinks flowed faster the decibels increased exponentially. Except for the dogs fleeing in terror, the attendance of party-goers increased likewise. We discovered that fandangos, one of the most popular events on the island, outdrew the Catholic church. Party-crashers flocked in from miles around with friendly grins, food, and sacks full of drinks. Around 2:00 A.M. when supplies ran out, the party broke up. The next day, Gregg sent a stern memo out-lawing company fandangos forever.

PanAm was the only air route between America and Asia. It was the fastest transit across the Pacific. It catered to those who wanted to travel in style and who could pay the fare. Guam was one of their most pleasant stops. We talked to world-famous pas-sengers on their overnight layovers: Claire Booth Luce, writer and wife of the editor of Time magazine, chic in black slacks and high heels; Leland Stowe, famous war correspondent, cordial and dig-nified; Maxim Litvinov, Russia's ambassador to the United States, pudgy, pallid, and inscrutable; and countless others. We were an important stop in that exclusive highway in the sky.

PanAm was also the quickest link to the outside world. Ships took months, while PanAm delivered a letter from San Francisco in five days. Every arrival was a newsworthy event and made head-lines in the *Guam Eagle*, a local paper. Landings from each direc-tion turned the office into a miniature Grand Central station. Lo-cal businessmen and messengers crowded the lobby an hour be-fore an arrival. Chauffeured military officers came to read the pas-senger lists, check the manifests, and ask a thousand questions. A pompous Marine officer, sporting a pith helmet, khaki shorts, and a swagger stick, always showed up. His hobby was hosting lady passengers in need of his special talents and charm—the horny, old goat.

CHAPTER 3

Special Memories of Guam

As mentioned before, on dull afternoons in Sumay we'd watch coconut crabs splitting coconuts. These weird crustaceans, measuring six inches across the back, had a gigantic claw that could split a coconut in two with one pinch. Angered, they would snip off the end of a broom handle. Our tin roofed bungalow, where they performed their nightly mating rituals, sounded like a kettle drum filled with rocks as they skittered around flirting and fighting. We gave them the 'hot foot' with a blow torch to get them off the roof so we could sleep. They'd disappear for awhile until their claws cooled off and their urges brought them back.

The freshwater caves were hidden in a cavern in a cliff near the ocean about two miles south of Sumay. To get there, one followed a trail hacked through a heavy undergrowth of bamboo, brambles and vines. The ten-foot deep, twenty-by-forty-foot pool was circled by a convenient shelf to sit on. The cool, spring water was refreshing. Dozens of lighted candles, perched on the walls of this grotto, gave the interior a cathedral-like glow. These caves were a bit of our secret tropical heaven.

If one could stand the blood, Sunday afternoon cockfights, were popular pastimes. Bred for fighting and equipped with razor-like blades strapped to their legs, the cocks were bundles of killing fury. Rowdy fans, drinking warm beer or unstrained aggie, placed their bets with bleary-eyed bookies. Yelling spectators, with mouths dripping beetlenut juice, sprawled in a circle to form the arena, as the owners teased their feathered fighters into a frenzy. When the whistle blew, the two bristling combatants, squawking defiance, plunged into a raging brawl of slashing claws, flying feathers, and flapping wings. With a lucky stroke the fight could end in two seconds or it could last until both birds were bloody and exhausted. The ringmaster would then announce the winners. As assistants cleaned up the gory mess bets were settled and money collected for the next fight. Though illegal, the cops placed their bets and looked the other way.

Ben Cook's Hangover Haven

Architecturally, Ben Cook's bar, in Sumay, Guam was a mess. It resembled a pile of warped lumber, rusty tin, and splattered mud thrown together by a raging typhoon. Its stucco walls were flaking from a terminal case of tropical psoriasis and its paint job appeared to have been applied from a distance of thirty feet. Rotting palm fronds, harboring rats and coconut crabs, covered its corrugated tin roof. The L-shaped structure had only two rooms—a 15 by 25 foot barroom bordering the street and a small storeroom with a lavatory in the rear. The whole tired shebang leaned southwesterly on a compass course between the south pole and the Marine Corps barracks, a half mile up the hill.

Ben Cook's bar was a major part of the social center of Sumay in the fall of 1941. This cluttered village housed a mixed population of five hundred or so native Chamorros, U.S. servicemen, stateside company employees and a scattering of transplanted, intermarried Americans deprecatingly called 'Bamboos'. A crazy pattern of streets and alleys ran off in all directions. The main drag followed a rutted cascajo street that turned left 90 degrees at the edge of the PanAm compound and disappeared southward into the boondocks. Small shops, edged between tin-roofed shacks, lined both sides of this one block long metropolitan thoroughfare. Halfway down the street, Ben's place squatted between two establishments, occupied by a couple of merchant princes selling cheap bric-a-brac on one side and warm soda-pop on the other.

Due to the ever-present heat and humidity, business practices were slow and easy before and after the mid-day siestas. The pace quickened in the cool of the evening. Friendly people ambled up and down main street listening to canned music and idle gossip until bed time. The two busiest places in town were the Catholic church and Ben Cook's bar, especially on weekends. The church would have had an unlimited source of converts if it could have canonized Ben Cook and had him hold revival meetings at closing time. But such a miracle never happened.

Ben Cook's stocky, muscular body teetered on bow-legs that ended on gnarly feet strapped into open-toed sandals with soles made of sections of automobile tires. His tanned, wrinkled face displayed a warm, gapped tooth grin exposing a mouth-full of gold teeth. His cauliflowered ears evidenced an earlier career of professional wrestling, Ben was of Japanese ancestry. He had arrived in Guam during the nineteen-twenties as the ship's cook aboard a Japanese freighter. He jumped ship the night before it sailed. Under interrogation by the local constabulary he answered every question with the only English words he knew, 'I been cook', whether they were referring to his nationality, profession, or his name. Therefore, 'Ben Cook' was the American moniker they gave him.

Everyone thirsty enough to enter his exclusive establishment was welcome. His merchandise and services were simple and direct. He scoffed at fancy drinks like Mai Tais or Gin Fizzes. They were complicated and slowed the action. He stuck to bourbon and water, beer, straight gin, soda pop, peanuts, and pretzels. His regulars were a boisterous bunch of friendly natives; a polyglot group of construction stiffs; a few adventurous PanAm employees in search of native lore and a short beer; sailors looking for local beauties in grass skirts resembling actress Dorothy Lamour; and a band of wild, disheveled U.S. Marines who had skipped the Enlisted Men's Club and were there to raise hell and blow their loot. A few girl friends and ladies of the night giggled over drinks. The joint was beneath the dignity of supervisors, construction bosses, military officers, priests, intimidated husbands, and shy civilians. Some of these upstanding citizens discreetly cadged their drinks elsewhere.

The cocktail hour started around 4 P.M. except on pay day or Saturdays when it was well underway by noon. Entering through a sagging door, one was dazed by swirling clouds of cigarette smoke smothering the faint glow of two bare, sixty-watt bulbs hanging over the bar. Several more bare sixty-watters, partially covered with fluttering moths, cast shadows in the cocktail lounge at the far end of the room, furnished with six wobbly tables decorated with torn oilcloth and stinking ashtrays. A dozen or so rickety chairs, wobbly benches, empty beer barrels, and produce crates were scattered about for the tipsy, tired, and tousled. Holes in the wooden floor made a hazard course for those already into their third drink. However, these potholes served as handy places to sweep away spilled drinks, broken glasses, and cigarette butts. The proverbial smell of the Orient from the adjoining lavatory, mixed with the stench of sweat and stale cigarettes, did not smell like gardenias in the moonlight. Actually, it brought tears to eyes not fortified with a few beers. Two screened open windows barely kept the revelers from suffocating. A flashing jukebox, blaring the latest hits, competed with the din of raucous laughter and colorful four-lettered words of wisdom uttered in sincere and confidential tones by rheumy-eyed customers hovering over their drinks.

The lavatory, set apart by a rickety, swinging door, consisted of a concrete floor and one clogged stall. The latrine was a cement wall with a drainage trough in the floor leading to a hole where the contents flowed into the back yard. Every once in a while Lucy, the cocktail waitress, (secretly nick-named ' The Rock Ape' for obvious reasons), would slosh out this fancy powder-room with a bucket of dishwater, sometimes filling the shoes of the nearest occupant busily engaged at the wall. Having sanitized the place, she'd toss the empty bucket into the corner, wipe her hands on her dirty apron and go back to serving drinks.

A trusting man, Ben stationed himself next to the cash register. With the help of lovely Lucy, he managed to serve drinks, sell cigarettes, make change, and bang the register without moving more than three feet in any direction. The bar itself was two warped planks from the deck of a wrecked schooner, engraved with initials of dedicated drinkers, leaving their marks for posterity. The original bar-stools had disappeared long ago. Ben wouldn't replace them for two practical reasons. He didn't want barflies obstructing his view of the lounge and the stools seemed to splinter easily in a brawl.

Ben preferred cash but gave credit when a guy's wallet went flat. He had three long wire spindles, about a foot high, standing on the shelf behind the bar, out of reach of the customers. He'd spear the drink chits on these spindles as a method of bookkeeping: One spindle for enlisted men, one for local Chamorros, and one for state-side civilians. A stranger paid cash on the barrel-head. If a regular customer, short on cash, wanted to keep his credit rating intact, he settled with Ben on payday. Sometimes the spindles would fill to the top but the chits never came off until paid. Standard and Poors would have rated Ben's operation triple A-plus-plus as far as the ratio of income to expenses were concerned. If he had incorporated and sold stock, I would have bought a hundred shares and retired.

I frequented Ben's a few times and made friends with some nice fellows. I was there in the evening of December 7, 1941, the night before the war started (remember, we were on the other side of the International dateline). A marine friend had escaped from the brig and was feeling no pain. I tried to get him to report back to his outfit before being caught but to no avail. He just took another snort and roared, 'Nobody can hurt me for I'm 180 pounds of romp-stompin' hell.' He never served time in the brig for the Japanese air force changed his world and mine at eight o'clock the next morning with their sneak attacks on Pearl Harbor, Guam, the Philippines, and other bases in the Pacific.

One of the Jap's first 200 pounders hit smack-dab in the middle of Ben Cook's barroom. The entire structure, including the juke-box, beer kegs, glasses and the empty cash register, was blown to bits. The wooden bar cart-wheeled in the air and landed on the roof of the house across the street. Because the joint hadn't opened that Monday morning, no one was killed or injured. Witnesses say the bar chits fluttered down like confetti on New Year's eve in Times Square. Thus, for the first time in the history of Ben Cook's enterprise, all drinking debts were canceled. But, it took a war to do it.

The only things remaining of Ben Cook's and the village of Sumay are my memories. When the U.S. armed forces recaptured Guam in July 1944, the U.S. Navy blasted and bulldozed Sumay into oblivion and turned the entire area into a major naval base to carry on the war against Japan. Now, the area is off-limits and surrounded by a cyclone fence topped with barbed wire. Except for the church's cross and the PanAm slip, not a single clue remains of this shaggy but wonderful place in the tropics.

I hope Ben Cook's bar has become part of that great, festive, glittering gayway in the sky and he's still serving drinks to friendly souls with empty pockets and stacking their chits on his spindles.

Rainstorms, Rainbows, and Rapture

As a child, I cowered under the blankets while streaks of lightning and thunderclaps shredded the night in the high mountains of Idaho. As cold winds whipped around the corner of our log house and rain pellets rattled the windows, I heard ghosts moaning in the darkness. To my great relief, however, the storm would pass and the next day would find friendly skies turning on their charm and beckoning me to join them in a game of floating fantasy. I often lay on the shady lawn with Old Sport's head on my shoulder as we watched imaginary horses, Indians, castles and dragons roll in and out of floating cumuli sweeping across the sky high above the trees. A good dog, a shady lawn, fleecy clouds and happy fantasies filled many blissful hours on lazy, sunny afternoons. As years passed and Old Sport went to dog heaven, I continued to watch weather patterns: rainstorms, blizzards, rainbows and golden sunsets.

Now, from a perspective of several decades, I can think of no single weather phenomenon that impressed me as much as one particular tropical sunrise I witnessed on October 3, 1941. In the early dawn, I was at the pier helping passengers board the sputtering launch which would deliver them to PanAm's China Clipper, already anchored in mid-harbor with motors idling. The seaplane was ready for its scheduled 6 A.M. departure for Wake Island 1508 miles to the east. The passengers, having overnighted on their flight from Manila, were anxious to leave on the next leg of their journey to San Francisco. The forecast was favorable, the harbor calm, the water rippled by a gentle breeze. Scores of small cumuli dotted the sky as the morning sun, about an inch high, warmed the tropical air.

Though busy with pre-departure duties, I occasionally glanced at the fluffy clouds building on the eastern horizon. One cloud, directly in front of the sun, seemed to dominate the rest. It was growing rapidly. Like a giant magnet, it seemed to entice, then embrace and finally devour the smaller clouds hovering nearby. Its bulk nearly filled the eastern sky. As the plane lifted off the water, we watched it bank to the right and skirt around the cloud's base before disappearing from sight.

Back on the pier, I was entranced by the unfolding of this meteorological phenomenon. Even the native Chamorros, who had seen thousands of tropical sunrises, were moved to watch in silence. The anvil-shaped top of the darkening cumulus now towered over 40,000 feet as its bulk hid the sun from our gaze. Dozens of tiny holes punctured the roiling mass, allowing sunbeams to peek through and turn each opening into a rainbow. A narrow strip of sunlight encircled the upper perimeter like a golden crown. Shafts of light streaking downward from its base resembled stiffened legs of a gigantic monster striding towards the equator. Swirling air currents inside its belly added a kaleidoscopic effect to the tumbling vapors and caused dozens of tiny rainbows to flutter, vanish, and reappear. At a discreet distance, smaller clouds, imitating the master, wore rainbow ribbons and golden halos. Finally this visual symphony ended, to my disappointment, with flashes of lightning splitting the air and smashing into the sea.

Slowly, a shadowy curtain drew across the celestial stage. As the cloud drifted closer and the sun's angle changed, an invisible hand seemed to flip a switch and turn off the skylights. The darkened mass, now overhead and angry, discarded its heavenly charm and proceeded to exact payment for this special showing by drenching us in a tropical downpour.

In silent awe, I dashed inside the airport office reflecting that Old Sport would have wagged his tail in approval of what must surely be one of the most beautiful scenes in creation.

A Short History Lesson

One afternoon, Roy Henning, a friendly cable station technician, stopped by the hotel to shoot the breeze and enjoy a cool drink. Having been on Guam for more than a year, he was knowledgeable about the flora and fauna, the people, the weather and history of this beautiful island.

"What about the Chamorrans? Where did they come from and what is their ancestry?" I asked over a beer. He quickly launched into a capsulated version of their history.

"The origin of the Chamorros is shrouded in folklore. Ancient burial sites marked with latte, or monument stones, are scattered in the jungle and hold the mystery of their antiquity. Anthropologists generally agree their seafaring ancestors probably migrated from the Malay Peninsula thousands of years ago. Various plagues have decimated their numbers but 20,000 hardy souls remain. Most natives claim a strong blood strain of the Spanish rulers who occupied this island for 200 years. Others are mixed breeds with German, Scottish and English blood. Some laughingly say their grandfathers were American sailors on shore leave. Their language is a creolean-like mixture of Chamorran, Spanish, Tagalog, and English salted with American slang. The Catholic Church dominates their lives—marries their lovers, christens their children, and buries their dead. They are friendly, intelligent, and loyal to the United States." He paused to sip his coke.

"What about Guam itself, is it volcanic in origin or did it grow out of the ocean as a coral reef?" I asked.

"It's a dormant volcano perched on the edge of the Marianas trench, one of the deepest spots in the Pacific." He continued, "Don't worry we won't fall in. On his voyage around the world, Magellan stopped here for supplies in 1521. When hostile natives stole one of his boats, he named the place, Islas de Los Ladrones, 'The Island of the Thieves'. Under the rule of Spain, the islands were later named Marianas, after the Spanish queen in 1668."

"The island is kidney-shaped and measures about thirty miles long and ten wide. Its only thirteen degrees above the equator. It's 1589 miles east of the Philippines and about 4300 miles west of Hawaii. A long ways to anywhere.

The weather pattern is generally pleasant but it has its extremes—gentle breezes or raging typhoons. Cooling showers seem to fall from giant cumuli every afternoon. The nearly uninhabitable jungle, we call the boondocks, covers most of the interior and is said to be filled with snakes, lizards, flying foxes or fruit bats and a variety of pestiferous insects. Bananas, pineapples, coconuts and mangoes grow wild. In fact, coconuts, in the form of copra, are one of Guam's biggest exports. You've noticed that steep cliffs dominate the shoreline. Most people say its white, sandy beaches are better than Waikiki. Orchids, hibiscus, bougainvillea, and jasmine grow everywhere." He paused for another sip. Roy was warming to his subject.

"Historians claim that during the Spanish-American War of 1898, the United States captured Guam from Spain by firing a single shot over fort Santa Cruz on Cabras Island.

"The U.S.S. Charleston, with all flags flying, had steamed into Apra harbor, ready for battle. Because of poor communications, the Spanish general was unaware of war between their two countries. Mistaking the shot as a friendly salute, the general invited the ship's captain ashore as his guest. After the ceremonial toasts, the US Navy captain demanded the surrender of Guam. I can imagine the startled general spewing his drink across the table."

A humorous story, indeed, but the irony of a similar situation repeating itself was hidden in the ominous future. For now, the pleasant interlude was over. There was work to be done.

PAA Fueling Barge

CHAPTER 4

Delayed Departure from Guam

At low tide, the water in Guam's Apra harbor on this bright October morning in 1941 was glassy smooth, not a ripple broke the surface. The air was still and heavy. A tropical sun blazed in a cloudless sky. PanAm's Honolulu Clipper, poised in the ship channel, waited for take-off on its scheduled flight to Wake Island, 1508 miles to the East. Captain Chase, a wild character and veteran overseas pilot, rechecked the instruments in the cockpit. His four crew members sat at their work stations and the twenty-two eager passengers were buckled in and ready. Chuck Gregg, the station manager, stood by in the launch with radio-telephone mike in hand. Chief mechanic, Max Brodofsky, and his two assistants Bob Vaughn and Grant Wells, were securing the refueling barge anchored in mid-harbor before returning to the PanAm base a half mile away. In the airport office with my radio-telephone on alert, I worked on the departure routine. Captain Chase finally finished his pre-flight check.

"There's no headwind but time's a wastin'. Let's get the hell outa here." Chase blurted into his mike in his usual salty language. Slowly he pushed the throttles forward. As the four 1500-horsepower Wright-Cyclone engines roared in response, the plane shuddered a moment then began its run. Clutching the arms of their seats, the passengers watched the spray lift from the harbor surface. Gradually, the giant seaplane gathered momentum. A half mile down the channel the trailing rooster-tail of spray shot high in the air. At the mile mark near the open sea, the Boeing was still unable to lift off, so Chase cut the engines. The passengers relaxed their grips as the forty ton behemoth slowed and settled in the water.

"Damn it." Chase cursed. "We need a headwind and choppy water for lift off. Gregg, don't just stand there, get out some kitchen fans and stir up a breeze. If that doesn't work, we'll off load some cargo or dump the fattest passengers overboard. He sighed heavily. "Instead of that, let's give her another try."

Following the ship channel, the clipper headed in for a second run. On a 180 degree turn to get into starting position, tragedy struck. Like the Titanic on the iceberg, the Honolulu Clipper ran headlong onto an unmapped coral head that sliced through the aluminum bottom like a massive can opener. Water gushed into her ruptured belly and, like a punctured balloon, the wounded seaplane crunched down on the reef, dead in the water.

It took a moment for the magnitude of the disaster to register on the thunderstruck witnesses.

Honolulu Clipper Stranded on a Reefhead

"Oh my God, we've hit bottom." Chase cried as he cut the engines. This cry echoed through the crew, the men on the launch, the men on the barge and the terrified passengers. Later, a similar cry sped through every PanAm base across the Pacific, into the Pacific-Alaskan Division headquarters on Treasure Island in San Francisco Bay and PanAm's boardrooms in New York City. I grabbed a pair of binoculars and dashed outside for a better look. There, in mid-harbor, this beautiful silver bird sat silent and still, impaled and helpless, cocked at an angle with her belly full of water. I, too, mumbled "Oh, my God."

The crackling radio pulled me back into the office. Everyone with a radio-telephone was hollering at once—screaming orders, asking questions, canceling orders, barking directives and cursing the heavens. The launch rushed to the plane's side to rescue passengers and crew. Luckily, no one was hurt and the forward baggage compartment was undamaged. Three shuttles brought the confused passengers with their baggage onto the refueling barge a hundred yards away, and another relay delivered them safely onto the pier.

Max yelled, "Bob, dive under the plane and see how bad its damaged."

Bob, part ex-sailor and part sea lion, stripped to his waist and dove in. A minute later, he emerged spewing sea-water and gasoline. After a series of dives, he climbed back in the launch, red-eyed and gagging.

"There's an eight foot gash in the cargo compartment near the prow." He sputtered. "There's four shorter gashes near the big one and the fuel tank in the right sea wing is punctured. She's sitting on a coral head. Water around the head is about six feet deep." He took a long, shaky breath and added, "Max, tell everyone to douse their cigarettes—the water is covered with gasoline and could blow if a spark hit it."

Local sailors, monitoring the situation, rushed to the scene. Unaware of Bob's fire warning, their dilapidated, coal burning tug, not unlike the African Queen, came snorting and chugging towards the plane with sparks flying from its smokestack and good intentions from the minds of its crew. Bob jumped on top of the fuselage and waved them off with his skivvy shirt fluttering like a semaphore flag. Confused, they nevertheless obeyed his signal and turned away.

Max, a burly ex-wrestler who had earned his master's degree on the rough and tumble streets of San Francisco, took charge. As head of aircraft maintenance, this crisis was within his realm of responsibility and he proved highly qualified to do the job. As word of the accident spread ashore, every employee on the base stood by to help. The plane's crew, the port steward, the radio operators, the native carpenters, mechanics, and truck drivers waited for orders. Even the U. S. Navy offered to help. The home office in San Francisco, confident that Max and his crew could do the job, gave him its vote of confidence.

Max recognized the urgency of getting the Clipper off the coral head before high tide could swamp it. He had twelve hours to act, "come hell or high water." He called the nearby Piti naval yard asking for all the empty gasoline drums and heavy lines they could spare. His plan was practical and ingenious — to lace strands of manila lines alongside and under the hull to form a cradle, much like a spider web, on which to lash the empty drums. If everything held, the drums might provide enough buoyancy for the plane to float off the coral head with the rising tide.

Meanwhile, Gregg and I carried on with the operation of the airline, maintaining uninterrupted schedules. PanAm's traffic department canceled bookings on the following week's flight from Manila, so our stranded passengers could be rescued from their plight. Besides running the airline, Gregg and I spent the next week helping the port steward entertain twenty-two disgruntled passengers with guided tours around the island, shopping trips to Agaña, the capitol city twelve miles away, and exhausting happy-talk. This assignment alone almost did us in. Our thoughts, however, were seldom far from the Clipper's problems.

Besides the heavy load of operational messages, long detailed

TRAPPED WITH THE ENEMY

inquiries and status reports flew back and forth across the Pacific, taxing the energies of our communications staff.

Within half an hour after Max's call, three Navy trucks loaded with drums, lines, diving masks, and an air pump swept into the compound. The sailors tied a dozen drums in tandem to our two launches that towed them to the aircraft. Since the spilled gasoline had dispersed, six native Chamorros, with Bob instructing, began making the cradle. Diving back and forth under the plane with lines around their waists or in their mouths, they interlaced the lines and attached them to the heavy hawser that now girdled the hull. They cinched the girdled drums tightly to the underwater strands to get maximum lift. Sometimes the drums slipped out of their harnesses to the consternation of the exhausted swimmers. With practice, their efficiency increased and soon fifteen empty drums were bobbing along each side of the fuselage.

Word had spread throughout the area of the need for empty drums. Looking towards the mainland, Max and his gang were astonished to see the flashing paddles of an approaching flotilla of canoes, outriggers, and rowboats, each towing drums, and resembling a tribe of friendly Tahitians greeting the H.M.S. Bounty. Within half an hour, fifty drums were lashed to the plane. Racing against time, they managed the last strand as the new tide began its surge.

Everyone held their collective breath as the tide rose. The lines creaked and tightened. The plane began to ride higher. It floated free except for that devilish coral head stuck in the gashed bottom. Lines were quickly tied from the tail assembly to the two launches, which managed to back the floating plane off the coral head. The plane was now free and could be moved to a safer more practical place for repair.

The captain tested the controls and started the engines. To everyone's relief, everything worked. With Max shouting orders, the two launches were tethered to the prow and the plane's engines set at idle. Slowly, with drums bobbing along side, this Rube Goldberg assemblage wallowed into position. Max guided them

towards a small island nearby with a sloping sandy beach. They
planned to beach the plane as far in as possible by releasing the
launches and the front drums a moment before the final run at full
throttle. They gambled on the prow being strong enough to with-
stand the shock without collapsing. With split second timing, the
plan succeeded. Tethered in place, the Boeing sat on the beach
with the dignity of an eagle, despite its sore belly and undignified
gas drums tied to its rear end. As hoped, the slope of the beach left
proper depth for men to work on the damaged hull regardless of
tidal changes. Tired but satisfied, everyone returned to base except
Bob and Grant who stood watch all night aboard the Clipper.
They ate cold sandwiches for dinner that night. It would be another forty hours before they fell into bed, exhausted.

Since there were neither blueprints nor a manual of instructions for such an emergency, plans for the next phase of repair were
made and canceled, suggestions added and discarded, advice given
and rejected during dinner hour and far into the night. Through
the haze of smoke and the stench of stale coffee, "final" decisions
were adopted only to be modified the next minute. However, with
pluck, tenacity, Yankee ingenuity, plus a mixture of skill, patience,
and providential guidance, they made it through each day. Andy
Miravelli, a good sheet-metal man, was flown in from Manila. A
couple of mechanics arrived from Wake and Honolulu to service
the scheduled flights, freeing Bob and Grant to work on the crippled
ship.

Opening the floor panels behind the cockpit revealed the damaged hatch full of water, fish, seaweed and saturated cargo. The
ugly gashes had to be closed immediately. Water-soaked cargo was
sent ashore and the inquisitive fish gently herded out of the compartment. A hand operated bilge pump from the emergency locker
was set up for operation. A water proof coffer-dam, designed to
cover the damaged bottom, was made from pine 2x4's and heavy
aluminum sheeting. Rubber inner tubes attached to the wooden
frame served as a gasket. This contraption was held in place by
hand under the belly. With a bucket brigade and the bilge pump

in full swing, the hatch began to empty. As the hatch emptied, pressure from the sea water held the coffer-dam in place, limiting the inflow of water. When the bottom of the hatch was exposed, Grant flattened the curled aluminum back into place. Heavy coal tar and plaster of Paris were spread inside and around the coffer-dam's gasket to further close the gaps. But the bilge pumps couldn't keep up with the seepage. With Bob and Grant holding vigil, a chain gang of strong natives manned the pumps in twenty minute intervals all night.

Another council of war was held that evening. The bottom had to be reinforced and further waterproofed. A call to the Navy produced a half dozen 2'x 6' sheets of steel plating, an air-driven drill with steel bits, sharpening files, a sack of bolts and an electric air pump mounted in a launch.

Max began issuing orders. "Bob, you're a good water man. Put on one of those snorkel air masks and attach it to the air hose. The pump in the launch will furnish the air. We'll start at the rear of the gash and work forward. Cap, you're strong and smart, you put on a mask too. You guys work as a team. Take off the coffer-dam first. We're going to bolt these steel sheets in its place. You guys hold the sheets in place against the hull while Andy drills holes through the aluminum bottom and the steel. Then you guys shove a bolt through from the underside and Andy can turn the nut tight from the top. Get the sheet lined up and hold it in place. We'll work in one-hour shifts with ten minute breaks, except for the bilge pump handlers. The punctured wing tank can't be fixed here so we'll fly it home empty. They can fix that in San Francisco. Grant, you inspect and overhaul the hoses, valves, electrical switches and cables that control the airfoils and gas transfer pumps. As you know they are assembled behind the middle bulkhead. If they don't work, we're in real trouble." Five days later, Grant found, to everyone's relief, this vital control center undamaged.

Attaching the steel sheeting to the bottom was a gut-wrenching job. It took over a week to bolt the four sheets in place. Drill bits were dulled, bolts lost in the sand, tools knocked overboard, knuckles scarred and tempers frayed. Buckets of tar were smeared along the edges inside and out but water continued to seep through. Tar and plaster of Paris were added inside, to no avail. Since the bottom had to be reinforced from within, angle irons were cut and welded into a grid-like form to fit the contoured hull, then bolted to the frame. Still the seepage continued. What was to be done? The bilge pumps couldn't handle heavy leakage and any accumulated water would reduce the fuel load required to cover the distance to the next harbor.

**Honolulu Clipper beached on Islet for repairs.
Barge in background**

Again the Navy personnel came up with the answer. They suggested salt-water cement and they had a warehouse full. Following directions written on the sacks, our men poured the mix into the V shaped hull, covering the angle iron frame and the entire bottom. Soon the concrete was rock-hard and the damaged fuselage reinforced. The seepage stopped! Victory! There were drinks and steaks for everyone that night. For the first time in three weeks of worry, strain, and frustration, the entire base relaxed and enjoyed a full night's sleep.

Before the Clipper's departure for Wake Island, the drums were detached and the pumps stowed in their locker. The plane was pronounced seaworthy and airworthy. Since the former crew had been returned to San Francisco a few weeks before, a skeleton crew arrived to fly the Honolulu Clipper home.

**Honolulu Clipper beached on Islet for repairs.
Jim Thomas watching from left.**

Despite a ton of concrete and steel in her belly the plane became airborne on its first run. With salt water spewing from the ruptured wing tank, the captain radioed that all was well and thanked us for a job well done. Everyone, including the natives, the Navy, and all the tired—but happy PanAm employees, wished her Godspeed as she disappeared from sight, three weeks behind her scheduled departure.

PanAm personnel along the way were awestruck at the innovative and successful repair job which held together through landings and take-offs at Wake Island, Midway, and Honolulu. When the Clipper miraculously arrived in San Francisco, every employee on the base and half the reporters in the Bay Area went down to the landing slip on Treasure Island to greet her. After she was wheeled on shore in her cradle, bulbs flashed as welding torches cut open her bottom. Out poured 2000 pounds of tar, concrete, plaster of Paris, three dead fish, a hammer, a crescent wrench, seaweed, and a strange, dead creature of unknown species. A cheer went up and congratulations from PanAm's president were sent to the good men on Guam. Max strutted a little thereafter, as well he should, and we all felt a sense of pride for having experienced a minor miracle. The Clipper lived to fly four more years and earn her colors in World War II.

Looking back, I salute that gang of unsung heroes who saved the Clipper's life on a giant coral head in a small harbor on a tiny island in middle of a wide ocean. With minimum equipment and unlimited dedication, these otherwise ordinary men rose to the challenge. Without sleep or food for hours on end, without overtime pay, union rules, hoopla or T.V. cameras, they went about their work in that hot, humid hold of that crippled ship and added luster to the term, *Clipper Glory.*

I salute Bob Vaughn, the flamboyant underwater expert and master mechanic, who led the natives through strange and challenging assignments.

I salute Grant Wells, the quiet, talented technician who tackled seemingly impossible tasks with calmness and aplomb.

I salute the U.S. Navy and the native Chamorros for their cooperation and response to our call for help.

Last but not least, I pay a special tribute to Max Brodofsky, the gentle giant, whose ingenuity, resourcefulness, and leadership saved the Clipper. This was Max's finest hour.

The Honolulu Clipper played an important role in my life. She flew me to Guam in July 1941, she survived the episode on the coral reef, and coincidentally, flew me home from Honolulu after my rescue from the Japanese prison camp in September 1945. She met an undeserved, inglorious end a few months later in November 1945. On a flight from Honolulu to San Francisco, she lost two engines and tried to limp back to Honolulu but had to ditch short of her goal. Again, the U.S. Navy rushed to the rescue. Luckily, there were no fatalities and all personnel were saved. Unsalvageable and a hazard to navigation, the Navy ordered her destroyed. Heavy gunfire from a destroyer finally sent her to a watery grave. She was a tough old girl and I loved her.

**Honolulu Clipper Leaving Apra Harbor
after repair, Sumay, Guam.**

CHAPTER 5

Hints of War

As the summer turned into fall, the war in the Pacific was the farthest thing from our minds. It couldn't intrude into our pleasant little world. Company personnel came and went. George Blackett, a small town radio operator from Wells, Nevada, joined us around the first of November. Fred Oppenborn a tall, slender radio technician from Fort Lauderdale, Florida arrived and waited for further assignment.

In October, PanAm and the U.S. Government ordered the evacuation of all American wives and dependents from Guam, an ominous sign and the first indication of increasing tension in the Pacific. All the American women left except Mrs. Charlene Hellmers, an expectant mother, and five naval nurses. We went on about our business in happy ignorance.

Late in November, the nightly over-flights increased into regular *milk-runs*. However, PanAm crews seemed calm and unworried. Letters and mail from the States gave no hint of war in the Far East. Europe was grabbing all the headlines. The company's calm lulled us into a false sense of security. Since I was due to leave Guam in a few weeks to report to my draft board, I felt confident of keeping the appointment.

In mid November, word came that Saburo Karusu a special envoy from Japan, was passing through to help Ambassador Nomura maintain peace with the United States. He looked like an innocent Japanese businessman, short, tidy, pleasant, wearing horn rimmed glasses and a homburg. He spoke excellent English and made a good impression in the hotel. He was cordial and friendly as I drove him to the boat ramp the next morning. Little did I realize that his mission was nothing more than an act of duplicity.

On December 5, rumors circulated that three Chamorrans from Saipan had braved the open sea in an outrigger canoe and landed on the northern coast of Guam to warn their relatives that Japan was planning to attack America in early December. Some of the natives took heed and headed for the boondocks—bicycles and carts loaded with supplies. The Americans ignored them. If that information had been relayed to Washington and properly used, the tragedy at Pearl Harbor might have been avoided. Instead, the military police threw them in jail.

On the afternoon of Sunday, December 7, Nick Gumetaotao, our faithful driver, loaded the station wagon with box lunches and soda pop for a picnic. We were driving to the village of Umatac where Magellan landed in 1521. The weather was clear and our spirits high. My good friend, Roy Henning was joining Dick Arvidson, Grant Wells and me for the ride. We passed colorful flowers, graceful palms, caraboa carts, happy children and pounding surf. After picnicking on the beach and examining the monument commemorating Magellan's landing, we meandered slowly back to Sumay, happy with the day. After a short beer in Ben Cook's bar, dinner at the hotel was a T-bone steak with all the trimmings. Then we shuffled off to bed. It would be a full day tomorrow, a plane from Wake was due in the afternoon.

CHAPTER 6

Pearl Harbor

Jesús Rivera, the airport clerk, shook me awake. Groggily, I saw his somber face in the beam of his flashlight. I sat up and watched as he moved across the room and awakened my two roommates.

"Mr. Gregg wants to see all of you in the PanAm office immediately. There's trouble," he whispered. Then he disappeared into the night to awaken the rest of the station personnel. Shuffling to the light switch, I looked at my watch: 6 AM. Monday, December 8.

"We'd better shake a leg—must be something big." I grunted.

"What in hell's up?" Bob muttered as he tucked in his shirt. "The plane ain't due from Wake 'til this afternoon."

"Beats me. Maybe there's an accident or something." Grant mumbled.

We dressed and stumbled into the dim dawn. A pale moon flitted through the light overcast. We made our way on the gravel path past the hotel now shrouded in flickering shadows. The diesel generator rumbled in the compound's corner. A rooster crowed in the distance. A dog barked an answer as the nearby village of Sumay began to stir. The rest of the station's staff, including the Chamorran personnel, made faint shadows as they quietly converged on the lighted office a hundred yards away. The two massive Standard Oil tanks stood alone next to the shoreline, silhouetted against the sky. We quietly entered the office. Manuel Calvo and "Sus" Rivera, looked grim and distracted at the flight-watch routine on the Philippine clipper that had just left Wake Island.

Chuck Gregg sat at his desk, ashen faced. He looked up as we entered and waited for him to speak.

"The governor's office just called. The Japs bombed Pearl Harbor about an hour ago, without warning. We're at war with Japan."

Looking at each other in stunned silence, we were unable to grasp the import of this devastating news. Finally, Bob blurted, "Well, those dirty, little, yellow-bellied, slant-eyed bastards! I hope America kicks the hell out of the goddam, slope-headed, sons-o-bitches." Bob never was one to mince his words.

"Now we know the reasons for the recent Jap overflights at night. Spy planes on photographic missions." Grant interjected. "What do we do now?" I heard myself saying.

Gregg spoke again. "Here's the situation. All we know is that Pearl Harbor was bombed. No other particulars. We don't know what's going on anywhere even in Agaña. Some of our fleet might be near Guam or four thousand miles away. If there's a carrier or a destroyer nearby we could be rescued. If not, and if the Japs immediately attack in force, we're in a helluva shape." He let us absorb this before continuing. "As you know, Guam has no defenses. Its handful of Marines, Navy and militia have only Springfield rifles, Browning Automatic Rifles and .45 caliber pistols, all useless as squirt-guns against the heavy artillery they might bring ashore. However, some of our military here feel the Japs may bypass Guam since it has little military value. Any suggestions ?" (As it turned out, the military strategists who made that remark must have been drunk.)

"I'm thinking about the Philippine Clipper." I said, "Manuel says it has already left Wake and is scheduled to arrive here at 3:30 this afternoon. It's our only chance to escape if it gets here. But the Japs could easily shoot it down. I wonder if it's crew is aware of Pearl Harbor? Maybe we should advise it to turn around."

"Jim, send a top-priority message to the Clipper advising it to return to Wake immediately. Copy Wake, Manila, Honolulu, and San Francisco." Gregg ordered.

I composed the following message and relayed it to Dick Arvidson at the radio station through our direct telephone line:

"PHILIPPINE CLIPPER STOP EMERGENCY REPEAT EMERGENCY JAPS BOMBED PEARL HARBOR THIS MORNING STOP GUAM UNSAFE STOP SUGGEST RE-TURN WAKE REPEAT RETURN WAKE STOP COPY WAKE MANILA HONOLULU SAN FRANCISCO. signed: Operations Guam.

I asked Dick if there was anything on the air about Pearl Harbor. He said there was nothing but static. I briefed him on our meeting. "We're probably surrounded by Jap subs right now. There's no way anybody could rescue us." Bob interjected.

"I bet the Japs will attack from Saipan." I said, "but we don't know when. It could be tomorrow or a week from now. Our small launch is useless. If we head for the boondocks, we can hold out for a few days hoping our navy comes to get us. At least we can play for time there."

Grant said, "If it's the boonies, we'll have to have food, cloth-ing, blankets, prayers, guts and luck."

"It could be surrender or death or maybe both." Max added. "That's a helluva choice!"

That about sums it up." Gregg agreed. "We don't have many choices so let's take a vote. All in favor of sitting tight and surren-dering here if they attack, say yes." Silence echoed in the stark office. "All in favor of heading for the hills." The vote was unani-mous. "I'm sticking around the office for now in case we get more messages." Gregg added. "You guys can check your emergency gear and talk it over. Let's meet here in an hour."

"Chuck, I think we ought to send all the Guamanians home to their families."

"Good idea, Jim." Gregg replied. Thankful, they quickly left the office. Only Manuel and Sus decided to stay.

I checked the weather map, Manuel's "howgozit" chart on the clipper, and noted the secret codes in the office safe. Satisfied, I suggested someone to relieve Dick. It was about 8:00 A.M.

Seven of us shuffled towards the hotel each lost in his own thoughts. This was no time for levity. The sun was up–the stars had disappeared. Light cumulus dotted the morning sky. Sumay was awake and happy family noises floated out of the village. A soft breeze swept off the bay, cooling the morning air. A lone car rattled by on its way to somewhere. Though we were informed of war and were making plans, we had not fully absorbed the gravity of the situation and didn't realize that this moment could be the last peaceful interlude in our lives.

The kitchen staff, unaware of the situation, was waiting in the dining room.

"I suggest we pig-out and shoot the works." Dick said. "I'm ordering two of everything." Though he didn't want to say it, I sensed the feeling of futility in his voice.

"If we can't do anything else, we can at least eat," I agreed. "For now, one order of fresh pineapple juice, bacon, scrambled eggs, hash browns, and toast is enough for me."

"What did you hear on the circuit, Dick, anything about Pearl Harbor?" someone asked.

"Nothing, absolute nothing. All the circuits but one were jammed. I think the Japs were doing it. There was a lot of gobble-dygook I couldn't understand. Jap talk." he added. "I think I got our message through to Wake though."

Tense, we indulged in small talk. "I just realized that my message turned around the plane that was scheduled to take me back to the states on its return trip to San Francisco. I screwed myself on that one," I joked, dryly.

"I should have mailed a letter to my wife a week ago." Grant mumbled.

"Me, too," added Max, whose thoughts were in San Francisco, six thousand miles away. Fred stared at the table. Penning, said nothing.

Finally Bob spoke up. "I hope Hirohito's white horse gets constipated and throws the bastard off. If I was there I'd stick a burr under his saddle to make sure he turned a somersault before his fat ass hit the ground."

My hot breakfast was served. It looked good but had no taste. I ate perfunctorily. I was concerned more about my mother than I was about myself, not knowing what was happening to me. Halfway through my bacon and eggs, we heard the faint sounds of airplanes. Everyone looked up. The sounds grew louder.

We listened with forks poised in mid-air." I wonder whose planes they are? Maybe from one of our carriers? I jumped to my feet. Stepping outside, I realized immediately how foolish I was to think American forces were coming to our rescue.

To my horror, a small squadron of single-engine biplanes, with red circles on their sides, coming in our direction. Our peaceful world was blown apart in less than ten seconds at 8:30 A.M. on December 8, 1941, Guam time.

CHAPTER 7

Guam Attacked

"My God, they're Jap planes." I screamed. "They're headed straight for the hotel. Get the hell out of here!" Everyone scrambled in different directions, knocking over furniture as they went. For some unknown reason, I dashed towards the lobby. The planes dipped low with guns blazing. Bullets tore through the roof, splintering the lobby desk barely eight feet from me. As I opened the front door, the lawn in front of me erupted from a five-hundred pounder that blew a crater ten feet deep. The explosion, rocked the hotel, showering me with grass, shrapnel and gravel. My survival instinct took over. Sprinting around the corner, I dove headlong into a shallow trench partially hidden in the weeds. No sooner had I hit the ground than the kitchen and dining room exploded from a direct hit. Frying pans, plates, utensils and the rest of my scrambled eggs were blown sixty feet in the air. Fifty-caliber bullets swished through the weeds, missing my head by inches. Terrified, I gritted my teeth and clutched the ground, willing myself to disappear like a mole into the safety of the earth. I imagined the pilot had me in his sights and the next round would blow me apart. I murmured a prayer, wondering if I'd just entered the depths of hell.

The slow, antiquated, biplane dive-bombers, about eight in all, were sufficient for the job. Unopposed, they maneuvered freely. As they banked for another pass, I could see the helmeted, mustached faces of the pilots.

Evidently, their assigned targets were all on or near the Orote Peninsula where many vital island complexes were clustered: Sumay village, PanAm's compound, Marine barracks, Piti Naval yard, contractor's quarters, and the Pacific Cable station. Knocking these out of commission would cripple communications, military counter-attack, chances of escape, and any effort to repair war damage. Bombing and strafing indiscriminately, they hit everything in sight and everything that moved: men, women, children, schools, hospitals, houses, and churches. Ugly sounds of roaring engines, machine-gun fire, exploding bombs, mingling with screams of terrified victims tore into my ears and brain.

My first rational thought, was to get the codes in the office safe. Dodging my way through machine gun fire, I dashed for the main street of Sumay. The street was in pandemonium. Smoke billowed from burning houses. Shrieking parents and crying children dashed madly about to escape the holocaust. While the wounded cried for help, the dead sprawled where they had fallen. A tear drenched two-year old, covered with dirt and blood, was screaming for its dead mother.

A bare-headed marine, shouting encouragement to everyone, was going from door to door offering help to the wounded. I joined him.

Hearing moans in the rubble of a partially destroyed house, we found our PanAm driver, Nick Gumetaotao, crying on the floor. He had taken some shrapnel in the back. He kept wailing that he was paralyzed. We found a shogi screen leaning against a wall. Folded, it made an acceptable stretcher. I hailed a pick-up to take Nick to the hospital. Suddenly a bomber dove in with guns blazing. Nick jumped off the stretcher and beat us into the house, demonstrating that one possible cure for paralysis is a volley of machine gun fire.

Ben Cook's bar was demolished from a direct hit. The bar itself had been blown across the street. The shattered jukebox was leaning against a scarred girder. Unpaid drink chits still fluttered in the air. The Catholic church was blown open. Its twisted cross lay on the ground. The bitter smell of smoke and burnt gunpowder floated in the air.

The PanAm compound had taken several hits. Debris from bomb craters littered the yard but the buildings though pock-marked with bullet holes, were intact. Black smoke poured from flames flickering at the top of the nearest Standard Oil tank. The trigger-happy Japs had stupidly bombed a priceless oil supply.

I saw Bob struggling to lift a wounded Chamorran into a pick-up to take him to the hospital. I stopped to help. We ducked under the car as a plane made a pass, with machine-guns chatter-ing. We were trapped between gun-fire from the sky and a burn-ing tank of high octane that could blow any minute. Somehow, we were spared. Bob managed to speed out of the compound with his wounded charge and head for the Agaña hospital.

Bullet holes dotted the stucco walls of the office. Inside, desks, typewriters, and chairs were strewn about from concussions of near hits. As I bent over the safe and fiddled with the combination lock, a bomb hit the estuary next to the rear window above my head. The explosion blew out the glass pane and drenched me with seawater. Despite three attempts to twirl the dial, my shak-ing hand failed to open the safe. Dripping wet and cursing, I steadied my right wrist with my left hand and spun the dial again. This time it opened. Stuffing the codes and $3000.00 in greenbacks into a manila envelope, I dashed out in time to hit the dirt as the building was raked with gunfire. The pilot must have seen me go inside the building and was determined to get me. Bullets tore through the pitched roof, shattering everything inside. Sweeping in low he hit his target. The entire office disintegrated.

Like a halfback headed for the goal line, I zigzagged across the battered compound towards the Marine barracks on the hill. Too intent to be scared, I still held papers and money in hand. Think-ing I should get permission from a top military officer before de-stroying the codes, I searched the grounds for the marine com-mandant. I finally found him wild-eyed behind a tree. He brusquely told me to destroy everything including the money, then turned on his heel, and disappeared into the din, riding-crop in hand. Burning the codes was easy, but it was traumatic to light a match to a bundle of crisp greenbacks. I quivered with emotion as the flames died. I'd squandered money in my time but I'd never burned hundred dollar bills before. Nor have I, since. In retrospect, I think it was a mistake. We should have taken a chance on smuggling them through the war.

Some Marines were blasting away at the swooping planes with Springfields and Browning Automatic Rifles. Others were running in panicked circles.

Suddenly there was a lull in the attack. As the planes disappeared over the northeastern horizon, a Marine yelled, "They're probably returning to Saipan to reload and refuel. They'll be back in about three hours."

Working my way to the PanAm compound, I found grief stricken natives wandering about begging for the help I couldn't give. I found Gregg, Max, Conklin, Blackett, and Grant waiting near the village center. Fred Oppenborn, Dick, and Al Hammelef were missing but had been seen alive. Everyone present had hair-raising stories to tell but we had no time to listen. We had to hurry and run for the boondocks, before the next attack. Bob had returned from the Agaña hospital after a rip-roaring ride under fire. Max's Chevy sedan and the pick-up was ready to go. Escaping Chamorrans passed us with children on their backs and sacks of rice on their bicycles. Some had "Ranches" in which to hide. Others had relatives to help them. Some, like us, had no particular place to go but into the hills.

CHAPTER 8

Jungle Hell

In our confusion, we forgot to pack even the minimum necessities for the tribulations that lay ahead. Except for a case of Campbell's vegetable soup, we had overlooked blankets, food, clothing, knives, machetes, tents, and insect repellent. The trudging refugees were better equipped than we to survive in the jungle.

Thankfully, the rest of the PanAm gang was waiting at the end of the road thus all eleven of the PanAm Americans were safe. Stashing our cars in the high brush halfway up Mt. Almagosa about four miles from Sumay, we grabbed the soup and fled into the dank jungle. Twisted vines tore our clothes; piercing thorns lacerated our faces; and tangled undergrowth tripped our feet. The smell of rotting vegetation stung our nostrils. Scorpions, centipedes, tarantulas, giant cockroaches and what seemed like fifty million mosquitoes per cubic inch bade us a foreboding welcome. This was our first taste of what hellish conditions awaited us.

That night turned into a dripping nightmare. Intermittent showers soaked us to the skin. We slept uncovered on beds of soggy leaves and slippery mud. My arms flailed in vain at the hordes of voracious mosquitoes chewing on my face, hands, and ankles. They crawled through my hair, pierced my scalp and sucked blood through my wet clothing. Their high-pitched whine sounded like a screeching violin stuck on high C. Like hyenas on a downed gazelle, they were eating me alive. Slapping to kill the swarming pests, my hands became red with my own blood. The next morning, debilitated and nearly delirious, I could hardly open my swollen eyes. My face felt like a festering piece of raw meat. At sunup, squinting through distended eyelids, I shared a can of our cold soup with Max. Someone, thank God, had brought a can-opener. Having no utensils, we used flat sticks as spoons. We wolfed down the soup and licked the can lids. We looked like escapees from Devil's Island—muddy, unshaven, hungry, wet, scared and miserable.

Panic-stricken, we crawled and staggered through the underbrush, trying to hide from an enemy we didn't know and couldn't see. Max carried the case of soup on his broad shoulders, harboring it like a box of precious diamonds. After an hour, we lay on the ground, exhausted. Eventually, reason returned and we took stock of our situation. We needed blankets, shoes, food, clothing, and most of all, mosquito repellent. A call was made for volunteers to return to our barracks after dark to scrounge supplies and send a final message to the states. Bob, Dick, Gregg and I decided to go in Max's Chevy. Without lights for security purposes, we drove down the mountain in a cloak of semi-darkness.

In the misty moonlight and the flickering glow of burning buildings, Sumay was empty and silent, occupied only by ghosts, shadows and two lonely dogs. Our hotel was smoldering but the friendly diesel still hummed in the distance. The Pacific Cable Station on the hill was empty and burning. By some miracle, our cottage was intact and my flashlight was still on the wooden apple box that had served as a night stand. We worked quickly and silently. I stuffed a pair of pants, a shirt, shoes, shorts, and a pith helmet into a pillow case. Blankets were in the closet. I paused a moment to pick up a silver dollar, my "short-snorter" card, and Band-Aids from the dresser. While Gregg kept a lookout at the car, Bob and I rummaged through the other cottages, some of which were burning and giving off an eerie glow. All the garments and blankets we could find were stashed in the car. There was no mosquito repellent and no food—the commissary had been blown up with the hit on the hotel kitchen.

Dick Arvidson had fired up the generator at the radio station and sent the last message from Guam to PanAm, San Francisco, reading "GUAM UNDER ATTACK STOP SO FAR NO COMPANY CASUALTIES STOP LANDING IMMINENT STOP GOOD-BYE." Then he smashed the equipment.

"I think we'd better get out of here." I whispered. "I feel queasy about this place. I smell Japs." As it turned out, my nose was right: We later learned that a Jap patrol was only a few hundred yards away from our salvage operation in the cottages. Sitting amidst our paraphernalia, we drove out of Sumay for the last time and back to the hills in the dark.

Emboldened by their success on Monday they started bombing and strafing Agaña and nearby villages at sunup on Tuesday. More planes and wild pilots filled the skies and more death and devastation lay in their wake. Each explosion cut deeper into our souls. Peeking through the underbrush, we searched the sea in vain for an American ship. We saw nothing but whitecaps and a flat horizon.

CHAPTER 9

Paradise Lost

The second night was worse than the first—more mosquitoes, more mud, more hunger pangs, more misery, more despair. Unable to sleep, I sat on a rotten tree trunk with my blanket draped over my head in a useless attempt to shield myself from the mosquitoes and the rain. Equally restless, Bob, Grant and Dick joined me. I raised my head and focused on the scene below. Silently, we watched silhouettes of enemy ships zigzagging near the shore in the flitting moonlight. Sometimes a glistening gun turret highlighted its bristling intentions.

"What a helluva thing to be watching." Dick muttered. "It's like having a lodge seat in the middle of a stinkin' lion pit."

But we have mosquitos, rain, and scorpions for added attractions." Bob added.

I buried my head in my arms to block out the scene. The blanket filtered out the rambling dialogue. My thoughts drifted backward to happier days, to my boyhood in Idaho when everything was peaceful and serene. There was our warm log home in beautiful, green Malad valley in the Wasatch range of the high Rockies. Mother was laughing as she served us kids hot toast and scrambled eggs. My dog, Sport, was wagging his tail outside the kitchen door. Toosie, the cat, slept in the sun on the kitchen porch. I worried about mother. She's had a sad life and here I am neck deep in Japs.

Bob interrupted my reverie, "A week ago we were on top of the world, tonight everything's turned to shit."

"Look at that Jap fleet, "Grant said. "Must be at least half a dozen destroyers and cruisers and twenty or so transports. They must mean business. They're ready to fight. I wonder how long we can hold out in this Godforsaken place surrounded by Japs?" Dick grumbled.

"Things couldn't be worse," Bob muttered. "No food, no hope, no nothing but these goddam' mosquitoes. I think Hirohito's little yellow bastards have got us whipped. Right now, I'd trade a thousand pounds of *Clipper Glory* for a one way ticket to hell."

As the sun rose in the eastern sky, landing craft hauled soldiers of the Empire of the "Rising Sun" ashore near the village of Agat directly below us. Guns on the cruisers pounded Agaña and Sumay. We watched the smoking barrels and waited to hear the thumps and feel the reverberations. Too numb to think and too tired to care, I closed my eyes and dreamed of home.

The mosquitoes were still on the attack, reminding us that we had two battles on our hands. We cursed both adversaries and cowered under the blankets. Soon, our breakfast of a cold can of soup was passed out sans waffles, eggs, bacon and coffee. Scraping the last bite from my last can with my makeshift wooden spoon, I thought of the bacon and eggs that blew up when the hotel was hit. I'd think of that breakfast and the steak dinner the night before for the next forty-six months.

Sporadic gunfire could be heard in Agaña. A brave attempt by a handful of ill-equipped U.S. Marines and Navy personnel proved futile against six thousand crack Japanese troops armed with cannons, grenades, flame-throwers, tanks, horse cavalry and filled to their slanted eyeballs with *Bushido*, (the code of the samurai, stressing unquestioning loyalty and valuing honor above life). After half an hour, the sound of gunfire ceased. Fourteen noble Americans had given their lives in one of the first military encounters of World War II in the Pacific.

Early captives had informed the Japs of the refugees in the hills. About noon, a car flying a white flag slowly climbed the rutted road honking its horn for all to hear. Scores of tattered refugees appeared at the roadside. We came out of hiding, suspicious and afraid. When the car stopped, a smart looking U.S. Marine officer stepped out and gave a snappy salute.

"The Governor has surrendered the island." he said. "I've been sent here by the Japanese general to ask you to surrender immediately and come down under a white flag. He says you'll be treated as prisoners of war by the rules of the Geneva convention. If you cooperate, you'll be eligible for a prisoner exchange. He hopes you'll see your homeland and families again. If you don't surrender, you'll be hunted down and shot on sight."

The ultimatum was curt, clear, and complete. With no choice but to surrender, we discussed the situation anyway as a matter of pride. We were well aware of our predicament: no hope of rescue, and no place to hide. With no food, water, or supplies we wouldn't last a week on bananas, while being eaten by relentless mosquitoes and hunted by angry Japs. It was a question of trust: we didn't believe the little, yellow bastards. I remembered the Japanese army's notorious "Rape of Nanking" in 1937 when 250,000 men, women and children were slaughtered in cold blood. I knew our chances of being exchanged as prisoners of war was remote and probably impossible. I felt we wouldn't get home until the war was over, if ever. Even so, I had faith in our survival, despite the odds against it, and I didn't question an American victory whether the war lasted six months or six years. It was still a morbid choice—imprisonment with its inherent risks, certain death in the jungle, a slow death by starvation or a quick death by a Japanese firing squad. Imprisonment, with a chance of survival, however agonizing, seemed the least of all the evils.

Bob put the clincher on the situation. "It's either the goddamn Japs or the goddamn mosquitoes. I'll take the Japs any day. At least we can talk to the Japs but all we can do is swear and swat these goddamn mosquitoes. The Japs can shoot us, starve us to death, or maybe let us live. The mosquitoes will eat us alive or leave us anemic targets for Jap sharpshooters. Let's give up and trust to luck."

"I agree with Bob. If we surrender we'll at least have hope to live on and maybe hope will pull us through." I added. "Frankly, I'll be relieved. We can't take this crap much longer." The marine agreed.

"What are the other Americans doing?" I asked.

"Everyone else is giving up." he added. That settled it.

We tied a skivvy shirt on the radiator cap as a flag of surrender and crawled into the car. I sat in the back seat with Bob and Grant. Gregg, Max, and George were up front. Dick, Al, Fred, Penning, and Blackett followed us in the pickup. I'd kept a pillow case with a few belongings, a shirt, a blanket, and a pair of pants. Since mildew had rotted my shoes, I slipped my silver dollar and short-snorter dollar bill between the cracks in the soles. The ride down the mountain was the longest and saddest journey I've ever taken. Filled with dread, we drove slowly down the road. We tried to make small talk .but couldn't. So we started to sing *America the Beautiful*. Imagine, singing on the way to surrender. But it helped us relax.

We shook hands and wished each other good luck. We made a promise that if any of us didn't make it, the survivors would contact our families and tell them our story. I had often wondered how I would act when facing death. I found out that day.

CHAPTER 10

Surrender to Japanese

Rounding a bend in the road, we came upon a squad of Jap soldiers marching four abreast downhill away from us. Instantly, fears and forebodings were mixed with hopelessness and trepidation. Short in stature and marching in quick rhythmic steps, they looked like toy soldiers in bubble-top helmets. Their light brown uniforms were camouflaged with webbing and interwoven vines. Leggings were wrapped up to their knees. Their bayoneted rifles looked as tall as the soldiers themselves. Instead of being tiny and fragile, we soon learned they were tough, sadistic, ruthless, noisy, impatient, and cruel. Startled as we drove up behind them, they squatted, leveled their guns and barked unintelligible gibberish. We stopped the car and raised our hands in surrender. Jumping on the fenders and pointing forward toward the military compound, they screamed for us to drive on in a strange, unfathomable language. They seemed to yell constantly, even at each other, with mouths full of sputum and yellow teeth.

Bellowing orders we didn't understand, they shoved and kicked us into an open, heavily guarded area (the military golf course) filled with 500 or so haggard and unshaven prisoners. New groups were straggling in under guard. There were no women. The few naval nurses and Mrs. Hellmers with her baby must have been imprisoned elsewhere.

Wandering through the crowd, I spotted Roy Henning, my buddy, sitting with the other befuddled cable-station personnel. He had a sad story to tell. Mr. Perry, one of his colleagues, had been crippled by shrapnel and was in the Agaña hospital, paralyzed below the waist. Roy and the rest of the station gang had fled to the fresh-water caves for shelter but had been turned away by a contingent of brave Marines who had commandeered the place for themselves. Returning to their shattered quarters, the group had no choice but to wait to surrender.

Learning we were PanAm employees, an officer singled out Max Brodofsky to show them how to drain gasoline from the huge oil tanks. Soon Max returned with a Jap noncom driving his beautiful Chevy. We PanAmers were told to get in the car. They must have been satisfied with Max's performance, for we were driven pell mell into Agaña and housed in a wing of the hospital. On the way through the empty streets, we saw the Japanese "Rising Sun" flag, a red circle with streaking sunbeams, waving on the flagpole in place of Old Glory. It was a sickening sight. It told us we were now in Japanese territory—an unbearable thought.

Rummaging in closets and store rooms, I found a canvas hammock, a beer mug, a spoon and fork. These stolen treasures served me well, and my conscience remained clear for the theft. This situation was too good to last. We enjoyed our last shower and full dinner that night. Five hours later, three hundred tattered prisoners moved in with us.

Some prisoners were kept in the jail, others in various buildings in the center of town. Mrs. Hellmers and her baby stayed with the five naval nurses in a separate wing of the hospital. Four days later, all prisoners were mustered on the golf course.

After six sweltering hours in the burning sun, they herded us into the Catholic church and parish hall, our home for the next thirty days. Spying the Jap flag fluttering on the flagpole, a guy next to me muttered, "That f—ing flag reminds me of a flaming A—hole." "Flaming A—hole", caught on and soon became a single word in our lexicon. We would see this ugly rag every day for the next four years.

Wooden benches and a silent organ gave the church a barren atmosphere. Even the alter was stripped of its usual charm. The picture of Christ, himself, looked saddened as he gazed down on the misery below. After the umpteenth role call, (*tenko* in Japanese) we sought relief in any place available. Limp forms sprawled on and under benches, in doorways, in pews, or any space big enough for a human body. I found a spot on the parish stage next to a window along with seven other guys.

An interpreter read a declaration from the commandant warning us that if anyone tried to escape the rest of the prisoners would be shot. This was a warm note to hear. The warning forced us to patrol ourselves. No one wanted to be responsible for the death of his buddies nor was anyone willing to let others be responsible for his death.

Since this was not a country club, social manners were unnecessary and scarcely practiced. Seldom did anyone bother to introduce themselves and shake hands. Eye contact was sufficient for starting a conversation. Except for small groups of friends clustered together, everyone else sat or wandered in silence, struggling alone with their dilemma.

Our starvation diet of watery rice-gruel, served on plates and bowls taken from stores and the hospital, began that night. Two bowls a day of this tasteless slop equaled about eight hundred calories—far short of the minimum necessary to stay alive. Sometimes a boiled potato or a small piece of bologna was added to the empty dish. We devoured it all and then licked our plates. Hunger gnawed at our innards night and day. Wooden floors bruised our bones and bent our spines as we tried to sleep, fully clothed, under glaring lights kept on all night for security purposes. Noisy guards covered every exit with guns and *kendo* sticks (split bamboo clubs used for riot control) at the ready. Two water taps quenched our thirst. We soon learned that flush toilets, toilet paper, and privacy had been a western luxury. Only six or so latrines, open holes dug by Chamorran prisoners, served the entire complex. One had to bow for permission to stand in line to use them. Dignity had died in the gunfire.

There were tall tales to tell. The sinking of the U.S.S. Penguin, a small mine-sweeper, the island's entire naval force, was one of them. The crew claimed a Jap plane before sinking from torpedoes and gunfire out side Apra harbor. The little ship had put up a gallant fight. One sailor had been killed, some injured, but everyone alive made it to shore.

At five A.M. Bill Hughes, a government employee, was shot in his hand by a squad of Jap marines as he rounded a corner in his pickup with his family in the back. In an effort to escape, Bill gunned the car and sped through the group, nearly killing a Jap on the way. The Japs speared at the exposed occupants. His wife was wounded and his sister-in-law killed by thrusting bayonets as he flashed past the screaming soldiers. He was the first American to encounter the enemy and so notified the governor that the Japs had landed.

Everyone relayed stories of sadism and savagery. Women and children had been slaughtered while begging for their lives. Dogs and cats were shot for target practice. The "Rape of Nanking" had been reenacted by the these benign, intrepid, emancipating soldiers of the Emperor of the Rising Sun.

Despite being heavily outnumbered and out gunned, fourteen brave United States marines and naval personnel had fallen in the short, futile battle of Agaña.

Crowded and miserable, it became apparent that many things we had taken for granted had died on the first bomb run—freedom, happiness, shelter, food, and sleep in a comfortable bed. Supplies of whiskey and American cigarettes were suddenly cut off and some heavy drinkers were forced to chew their fingernails to cure the shakes and demean themselves to drinking water. Privacy, cleanliness, clothing, and soap had disappeared when the gates to freedom slammed behind us.

Simple necessities had become luxuries and these, in turn, had been replaced by fear, hunger, anxiety, and despair. Isolation cut us off from news of home, America, and the world. How was America responding to Pearl Harbor? How was the war going and how was it going to end? Not knowing our fate was almost unbearable. The future reflected nothing but hopelessness and gloom. Were we to live in this stinking place for the rest of our lives or until we were mercifully shot?

Our fate was in the hands of a brutal enemy filled with *Bushido* ("the way of the warrior"); an enemy with no respect for human life and an eagerness to die in *Banzai* charges for their Emperor. If we were to believe their propaganda of never surrendering, would America have to annihilate the entire Japanese race to win the war? Would the Japs take us prisoners with them as they charged into the machine guns? It was a bleak future with little chance for survival. We had to rely on hope, tenacity, and good luck.

CHAPTER 11

The Church—Our First Compound

Roll calls and boredom filled our days, rasping snores, and garrulous guards filled our nights. In the mornings rifle butts, baseball bats, and *kendo* sticks slamming the floor next to our heads, awakened us into a nightmarish world.

Each miserable day was the same: wake up, go to the john, line up for *tenko*, stand in line for a bowl of rice soup, sit around and make small talk, exercise the best you could, or take a nap on the hard floor. Our only escape was in sleep and dreams. Even day-dreaming was a luxury.

Rumors lifted our hearts or rent them in despair. Scuttlebutt of all kinds filtered into the camp: Manila was about to fall. Hongkong and Singapore were surrounded. Washington was in panic. San Francisco, Seattle, Los Angeles, San Diego and the Panama Canal had been bombed. Our merchant fleet was sunk and our entire Navy blown up at Pearl Harbor. Some Chamorros passed notes that our Navy was coming to our rescue and Germany was suing for peace. To taunt us, the Japs had planted these sadistic tantalizing rumors.

The three Saipan Chamorros, who had braved the ocean to warn their Guamanian friends of an impending Japanese attack, only to be thrown in jail by the shore patrol for spreading false information, were dragged out and shot as traitors.

With no means to bathe or wash our clothes, fleas took over where the mosquitoes had left off. Itching wasn't much fun but scratching became a pleasant pastime. As hunger pangs roiled our guts, food became the main topic of conversation. Exotic dishes like pancakes dripping with syrup, fried eggs, roast beef and chocolate sundaes were conjured up and salivated over in idle conversation.

"I think the agony of hunger is the worst form of torture," Conklin confided. "Starvation would be the slowest and most miserable kind of death." His listeners agreed.

Our benefactors, in a benevolent mood, allowed wives and girl friends to bring food to their loved ones. Devout Catholics brought food to the priests. Sometimes notes were buried in a piece of cake. Despite being surrounded by famished inmates, of which I was one, the recipients ate with relish not sharing their food with fellow prisoners. That was the price I had to pay for having led a puritanical life. Next time around, I vowed to live it up.

Occasionally, the Japs themselves broke the daily monotony. We stood in the hot sun for two hours to witness their marksmanship and military prowess. Having attached an American flag to a buoy in mid-harbor about two miles away, they proceeded to blast at Old Glory with a five-inch cannon. The roar of the cannon startled us civilians who stood only fifty feet away. The acrid smell of the gunpowder mingled with the sweet aroma of grass and pineapples, reminding us that nature still existed. They hit the beautiful, fluttering target after the tenth try. Ironically, that was the last American flag we'd see in nearly four years.

The sadistic bastards made some of us watch an execution by firing squad of two small boys who had stolen a pair of shoes from a warehouse. Their tearful parents were forced to stand beside them while being executed and then compelled to cover their son's graves. We had the luxury of covering our eyes.

On a Sunday afternoon, three trucks filled with kimono clad, giggling, teenage Korean "Comfort Women" rumbled by the camp. These cute, little innocents, were here to satisfy the sexual urges of the filthy, stinking soldiers of His Majesty's Grand Imperial Army of Liberation. What a cruel and demeaning fate for these poor little girls. Death would have been sweeter.

Frightened natives wandered by unable to help. Every gesture of friendliness toward us put them at risk. If they didn't bow when approaching a Jap, they were slapped and beaten. Their lives, too, had been ruined.

One redeeming feature in the Japanese character showed itself in an unexpected way. They believe in the benefits of exercise. They set aside a half-hour a day for calisthenics under the guidance of an instructor in the plaza across the street. Despite hunger, these moments to smell the earth, see billowing clouds, and stretch my muscles were antidotes to my misery.

Like everything else, the beautiful plaza had suffered the pain and humiliation of the occupation. It had become a junkyard of wrecked automobiles. The Japs had gone wild with the joy of driving American cars. Side-swipes, missed turns, and head-on crashes proved the drivers were careless, unskilled, or drunk. Some cars were junked for only a flat tire. In another month, there wouldn't be an auto left on the island fit to drive. It was sad to see the commanding officer and his entourage drive by in Max's Chevy, apparently the best car left on the island.

Soldiers found some whiskey in a warehouse. Thinking the booze might be poisoned, they forced a dozen or so prisoners to act as tasters by taking a healthy horn out of each bottle. Needless to say, volunteer tasters stood in line.

Catholic and Protestant Christmas services were held on a saddened note. Later, to show some respect to these Christian holidays, the Japs unloaded a pickup full of wild bananas into the parish hall as a Christmas present. I had never liked bananas since had become deathly sick from gorging a sackful as a child, but managed to grab one and devour it, skin and all. This was my Christmas present for 1941. It was one of the sweetest things I've ever eaten.

CHAPTER 12

Leaving Guam

Apparently, the island was too small to accommodate such a large prison population. On January 9, 1942, the camp was buzzing with rumors of our impending evacuation from Guam.

"I guess they're not going to shoot us after all," I deduced to Bob. "The fact that we're leaving Guam is encouraging. They probably feel we are worth more as hostages. Maybe things are looking up. But that depends on where we're going. If it's a tropical jungle and forced labor, God help us."

Was our destination the Philippines, China, Korea or Japan? The next day, January 10, 1942, thirty days after capture, we were ordered to gather our belongings and line up for a count. I wrapped my pillow case and spare clothing in the hammock. Somehow, my valuable drinking mug and helmet had mysteriously disappeared in the crowded church. The tropical sun blistered our skulls as we marched towards the Piti Naval Yard four miles down the road. Dozens of armed guards lined the route as we stumbled along, weakened by lack of food. Some of the older men had to be carried. The priests, Mrs. Hellmers, her baby, and the nurses were driven to the dock. Except for the short distance, the trek had all the earmarks of a pending death march.

The Argentina Maru, a beautiful ship of the line, floated in mid-harbor. Recalled from a South American trip, it had been diverted to Guam to pick up us prisoners. Lurching scows and puffing launches carried us to the ship. From the deck, I managed to get a last glance of our little cottage hiding on the hill, a sad but satisfying sight. I know the curtains were waving us good-bye.

For an hour we milled about on board while the victorious benefactors loaded the ship with war booty: appliances, tools, and warehoused supplies. Soon the island would be stripped of everything valuable, showing the citizens of Guam, newly freed from American's shackles of imperialistic slavery, the munificent benefits of Japan's "Greater East Asia Co-Prosperity Sphere".

While waiting on deck, we smelled, for a precious moment, the sweet aromas of jasmine wafting across the harbor. It seemed to be saying farewell and Bon Voyage like the well-wishers at the dock in San Francisco had done eons ago. Then, amid threats and screams of the armed guards we were ordered below decks. I peeked a last look at the beautiful Guamanian horizon as I stepped onto the ladder leading to the deep, dark hold of the ship.

CHAPTER 13

Cruise to Japan

In the darkened hold, five hundred scruffy prisoners were jammed together like canned sardines. Eight average-sized men occupied cubicles built for four small Japanese. Gasping for fresh air, we squirmed for space to lie down. Claustrophobia was both inevitable and unthinkable. Body odor, mixed with the stench of diesel fuel, curled our nostrils. Several PanAmers and I were squeezed into a cubbyhole in miniature bunks along the walls with tatami mats for mattresses. My six-foot-two frame was tight in the five-and-a-half-foot bunk. Luckily, I was next to a small porthole so I had daylight and an ocean view at eye level. In the darkness, the ship weighed anchor and quietly slipped out of Apra harbor. We were leaving our beloved island forever.

The Argentina Maru was pleasant in comparison to the jungle and the church, supporting the adage that everything is relative, even misery. We had sufficient latrines, faucets, and lights to make life bearable.

Buckets of steamed rice and dried fish were lowered into the hold through skylights on deck. Twice a day, we devoured a scoop of rice and a small piece of dried fish, with water for dessert. But, after our church diet, this stuff tasted like French cuisine. We even had the luxury of a personal rice bowl and a spoon, both of which we guarded jealously and washed in the latrine. The hum of the diesels and the slosh of the propellers lulled us to sleep. Good weather and a calm sea gave the ship a steady course.

On the first day, a huge pile of tangled clothing and shoes, was dumped through the hatch onto our deck. What a welcome surprise! Our clothes from Guam! I spotted my gabardine suit, minus my lapeled fraternity pin. I grabbed for the suit and was shoved back by an burly guard who, ignoring my pleas, claimed it for himself. The clothing pile was circled by five hundred raggedy-assed prisoners. When the go-ahead signal was given, it was catch-as-catch-can. Clothing flew in all directions. I grabbed a woolen GI overcoat that later saved my life in the coming Japanese winter—a far better deal than the suit. Like a proverbial sale in Macy's basement, pants were torn apart by tugging contestants. I managed to grab a pair of shoes that were too small. Afterward everyone wandered about trading for stuff that fit. I traded my shoes with Blackett for a pair that were too large for him. We both gained by the exchange.

I found an old copy of Reader's Digest amongst the rubble. An article on the probability of war between America and Japan caught my eye. An American admiral was declaring that war would never come between them. He claimed America could lick Japan in a week and the Japs knew it, so they'd avoid a fight. Besides, Honolulu and Manila were impregnable. Moreover, the Japs were too small to be good soldiers. He capped his article by saying the Japs were near-sighted and therefore couldn't shoot straight or fly airplanes. I wondered what in hell I was doing in the hold of an enemy Jap ship, on my way to Japan? If he were America's chief strategist, we'd be in a worse mess than we are in now.

Settled in, I tried focusing on guys around me. The military personnel, though carefully cordial, kept pretty much to themselves but the civilians turned out to be a diverse and congenial bunch.

The seventy or so contractors were professional journeymen. Their talents covered every skill needed to finish a major project—supervisors, engineers, cooks, machine operators, semi-skilled laborers and roustabouts. Some were men on their first job, but most were veteran construction stiffs known as "boomers", since they moved from one construction site or boom town to another following their jobs. They came from cities, towns, farms and villages, from every point of the compass—Florida, Maine, North Dakota, California, Hawaii and a thousand places in between. As workers of different ages, education, and dreams—they were a composite of Americana.

Twelve Capuchin priests, a dozen civil servicemen, a score of Guam residents, six cable-station personnel, fourteen government workers and eleven of us PanAm employees rounded out the civilian group. About a hundred and forty five in all.

In the afternoon of the first day, we were allowed on the main deck for a splash of sun and exercise. Emerging from the dark belly of the ship, our eyes were blinded by the sunlight. The good weather was holding and the deck was steady. It was good to stretch our legs and flex our cramped muscles. Sun and shadow showed we were sailing north.

I found myself strolling the deck with Fred Oppenborn and Bob Vaughn, instinctively talking in whispers so others could not hear. This was the first opportunity we had to be alone in six weeks.

Things were going better than expected. We agreed that, so far, no one was hurt, sick, or dead and best of all, there were no mosquitoes. We were getting two scoops of rice, seaweed, and dried fish every day. We were still hungry, hairy, filthy, and despondent but alive. Not knowing how much damage the Japs had done to our fleet at Pearl Harbor, we worried about American submarines torpedoing an unmarked ship in the open sea.

Fred, a cynical soul, was giving us a lesson in survival. "It looks like it's every man for himself in this mess. If anything unattached is available, take it. Grab anything belonging to the Japs that's not nailed down. If you don't need it, take it anyway and use it for trading material."

"I agree," added Bob. "And we should hide everything we've got, especially from the Slopes. Play it safe until we get to know the guys we're locked up with. This is going to be a scratch for survival so let's take care of ourselves."

"You guys have a point." I said. "But, cooperation amongst us is also important. So far, our real enemies are the Japs, not each other. Someday, we may have to kiss ass for a kernel of rice but let's leave that as a last resort. We're amateurs at this stuff now but we'll be professionals in a month. God only knows how or when this stupid war is going to end, so we'd better plan for the long haul."

When the officer blew his whistle, we returned to our rabbit warren below.

My small bunk became a torture chamber at night. I couldn't turn over or change position because my long legs hung over the side. Bob Vaughn had also purloined a hammock and was equally uncomfortable. Without permission we strung our hammocks between stanchions, amidships. If the Japs didn't like it, they could order us to remove them. Nothing was said. We enjoyed the comfort of a swinging bed that eliminated the pitch and roll of the ship and allowed us to stretch in luxury.

I soon learned that "bitching" is a hearty American pastime. It reflects robust animosity towards discomfort, tastes, personalities, whether fictitious or real. When overdone, it can be a pain in the neck but in proper doses it can be constructive. That's what makes wars, laws, rules, and revolutions. Some say, only the sick and cowardly suffer in silence. Unresolved frustrations breeds hatred.

With healthy American resilience, most everyone bitched about the "goddamn Japs" . In fact, those two words also merged into one like "Flaming asshole" . Our vocabulary had now enlarged to include "Nips", "Slopeheads", "Gooks", "Slants", and "Little-Yellow-Bastards" . Things were looking up. Maybe the improved diet was helping.

Little character hints showed themselves in subtle ways. On deck the second day, Neil Campbell, a friendly accountant with the contractors showed me a unique trait for a healthy attitude. He was sitting on deck, reading an article from a dog-eared magazine about boats and ships. His flaccid appearance reflected a leisurely life in a swivel chair or hours at a poker table in Vegas. My shadow distracted him. Without hesitation, he looked up and started talking.

"It sez here that ships are built assbackwards. They've got sharp prows and a big sterns like some women I know. They should be built like fish with blunter prows and pointed sterns. This ship we're on would be twenty-five percent more efficient if it turned around and went backwards. A scientist has proven this theory in the laboratory and I think he's got something."

"Sounds good to me too. I wonder why they haven't done this before now?" I queried.

"Beats me." he said. "Maybe they'll change around after they read this article. I'll call Washington and bring it to their attention. Ha-ha." He returned to his reading and I continued my walk.

This told me a lot about the man. His thoughts were outside of himself. He was interested more in facts and ideas than in self pity or personal discomfort. He had risen above his present predicament and was in control of the situation. His was a rare quality worthy of emulation.

CHAPTER 14

Zentsuji

As days passed the weather grew colder. We were headed to Japan or maybe Korea or north China. The sea was calm and the wake of the ship bubbled out of sight. We were racing against the clock and the American submarines.

By the fourth day, the temperature had dropped to near freezing. As darkness fell, we smelled the earthy pungency of land and saw white mountaintops in the distance. At sunup on the fifth day, January 15, 1942, we were anchored in the Inland Sea off the harbor of Todatsu, on the island of Shikoku, Japan. Our "pleasure cruise" was over. We were now prisoners in enemy country.

Our destination turned out to be the Zentsuji War Prisoner's camp, a few miles inland from the city of Todatsu. The city's port facilities were too small for the Argentina Maru so we anchored off shore all day while our fate was debated between the captain and the authorities ashore. Evidently, the personnel at the camp were surprised to learn of our arrival. The captain was trying to get rid of 500 irksome prisoners and the camp wasn't ready to take us. On deck the cold air, whipped by a Siberian storm, plunged the wind-chill temperature to a paralyzing sub-zero. Huddled below decks, we wolfed down a luke-warm cup of tea and a slice of crusty bread.

Finally, at ten that night, after much jabbering and screaming, they loaded us aboard a "lighter" and, with water lapping at the gunwales, we wallowed to the docks. Thus began one of the longest and most miserable nights in my life. Hundreds of curious, inscrutable civilians, in quilted cassocks, crowded the streets to catch sight of these strange, haggard foreigners. Unshaven, ragged, and ugly, we must have looked like refugees from outer space. Hunched against the cold and nearly at the end of our rope, we were certainly non-threatening. Fresh out of the tropics, we shuddered and trembled in arctic misery. Some of the prisoners were nearly barefoot—dressed in torn shirts and tattered pants. My GI coat eased the agony in my body but my arms and legs were stiff and numb from the polar bite. While guards counted and recounted and quarreled over our numbers, we shivered silently in the darkness. What few words were spoken seemed to freeze in mid-air and shatter on the ground.

We shuffled, under bayonet, through dimly-lit streets filled with more inquisitive, impassive civilians clothed in quilted cottons and wearing wooden clogs on single-toed stocking feet.

While waiting for transportation, some of us lucky ones in front were flabbergasted with the kindness of a small group of smiling, kimono-clad women serving us tea and rice cakes while bowing and muttering "*Dozo*" (please) with each friendly offering. This was the first compassionate word we had heard since capture. It was so unexpected, so humane, so kind.

Finally, we boarded a rumbling, narrow-gauged trolley and headed towards the Zentsuji camp a few miles southwest of town. We passed through small villages, silhouetted in the darkness. Every dimly lit station was filled with similar people: curious, placid, silent, colorless.

The Zentsuji camp, a cluster of wooden barracks surrounded by high, brick walls topped with barbed wire, loomed in the darkness. Watchtowers gave the place a foreboding look. We bailed out of the cramped cars and stood robot-like to be counted. Our fears were overpowered by misery. Our brains were too numb to think. Guards barked orders for us to enter and the iron gates slammed behind us. We filed into a large, dimly lighted, unheated barracks, our bedroom for the night. A small cup of soup and a piece of dry bread were bedtime snacks. A *sufu* blanket was passed to each prisoner. (S.F., meaning "staple fiber" was pronounced *SOO-foo*. Staple fiber was a wood byproduct with very little softness or warmth).

To sleep warmer, everyone found a bed-partner to share two blankets and exchange body heat. Hard tatami mats of woven rice straw served as mattresses. Grant Wells was my partner. We slept in spoon-fashion and soon learned to roll over simultaneously. Fortunately, I had my woolen army blanket to reinforce our bedding. As I lay there, I realized it had been nearly five-weeks since I had shaved, bathed, or taken off my clothes. I must have looked awful and smelled worse. No wonder I was itching and scratching in secret, unmentionable places.

As dawn broke over Japan, we were awakened by banging gongs, whistles, and brutish shouts. Again, rifle butts and baseball bats slamming the floor, punctuated the wake-up call. It was sad to see the tired and disheveled inmates, scratching and mumbling, as they stirred to life. Little was said. We'd almost forgotten how to talk through our despair.

Huddled around an open fire in a central pit, we whipped our arms and jumped about to stir circulation. After *tenko* (muster and roll-call) we filed past the soup barrels for a hot bowl of watery, rice soup, a piece of cold fish and a hard biscuit.

After breakfast, I scanned the outside of the barracks to see how this mysterious land of heaven looked in daylight. There were trees, fences, dogs, clouds, sunlight and air just like in America. Days followed nights like my world at home, only it had a tainted smell. Strange odors filled the air, some sweet and enticing, emanating from tea leaves and cooking pots; some mixed with rotten fish and sour trash; some carrying the obnoxious stench of "honey buckets" filled with "night soil". Yes, Japan was a mysterious country with an alien culture, overrun by peculiar, energetic, little, yellow people speaking a strange, guttural, choppy language and bowing from the waist.

There seemed to be no sanitary facilities like running water, gutters, and sewers. Instead, massive iron-pots were collection basins for human wastes. Bacterial action turned this solid waste into a liquid fertilizer to be spread on vegetable gardens and rice pad-dies by Korean coolies. With a full bucket of night soil swaying from each end of the pole balance on his shoulders, the coolie would pace smoothly along without spilling a drop. There, he'd ladle out a portion to each plant. Downwind, one's nose would burn. This simple procedure was an example of oriental efficiency—disposing of human wastes by recycling them into fertilizer through cheap labor, a honey pot, two buckets, and a bamboo "yo-yo" pole. However, this procedure required all vegetables to be thoroughly cooked before eating.

"*Benjo*" was the Japanese word for toilet. Benjo rooms were attached to the end of each barracks. A urinal trough, attached to the wall, drained into one of the enormous pots under the floor. Slots, four inches wide and sixteen inches long, were cut in the floor directly over the pots that acted as catch basins. There was little waiting. Just find a vacant slot squat, set aim, and let go. Thin toilet paper hung on a peg, one piece to a customer. Modesty was a luxury we lost in Guam.

During morning chow time, we met six Australian prisoners from the south China Sea. As look-outs stationed on remote Ma-laysian islands to spot enemy activity, they were captured early on by the Japanese navy and brought to Zentsuji. These guys were a delight to meet—happy, buoyant, hilarious and optimistic. They brought us up to date on the pessimistic progress of the war—the sinking of the British battleships, Repulse and Prince of Wales, the fall of Hongkong, the devastation at Pearl Harbor, the immi-nent fall of Singapore and the Philippines. Despite the bad news, we reveled in their enthusiasm. These new faces reminded our-selves we weren't alone in this mess.

At mid-morning, we were herded into the center of the com-pound. Shafts of sunlight glistened through the frosted branches of trees hunkered in the cold January air. The winter chill sunk into our bones. Apparently, something big was about to happen, but no one seemed attentive or interested in anything except their own wretchedness.

After a long wait, the camp commandant arrived to speak to us. His squat, bow-legged, be-medaled presence would, no doubt, add joy to the occasion.

He mounted an elevated platform, papers in hand. Looking down on his subdued audience, he read the following speech, copies of which were passed around to read again in our leisure. "I am Major General Mizuhara, superintendent of the Zentsuji War Prisoners Camp. Receiving you American Marines here, I should like to give some instructions to you all." (Hell, we civilians weren't marines but why quibble over details.)

"You were faithful to your country; you fought bravely; and you were taken captive, unfortunately. As a warrior belonging to the Imperial Army, I could not help expressing the profoundest sympathy and respect towards you. I hope you will consider how this Greater East Asia War happened. To preserve the peace of the Pacific had always the guiding principle of Japan's foreign policy and the Japanese government conducted patiently and prudently for eight long months diplomatic negotiations with the United States, endeavoring toward a peaceful settlement, while America and Britain increased military preparations on all sides of the Japanese Empire to challenge us. The very existence of our nation being in danger, we took up resolutely with unity of will strong as iron under our Sovereign to eliminate the sources of evil in East Asia. The rise and fall of our Empire that has a glorious history of 3,000 years and the progress or decline of East Asia depend upon the present war. Firm and unshakable is our National resolve that we should crush our enemy, the United States of America and British Empire.

"Heaven is always on the side of justice. Within three days after the war declaration our navy annihilated both the American pacific fleet and the British far eastern fleet. Within one month, our army captured Hong Kong and the Philippine Islands; and now the greatest part of the British Malaya have already been occupied by our army. Singapore being on the verge of capitulation and the Dutch East Indies too, having been suffering several surprise attacks by our landing forces since the 11th of the month. In the Pacific arena there is left not a single battleship belonging to the allied powers. Above our land there has appeared not a single aircraft belonging to them since the outbreak of the war, their air forces having been entirely crushed elsewhere. Who can doubt this is the most brilliant success that has been recorded in the world history of war?

"About the significance of the present war, I hope you will reconsider deeply with clairvoyant calmness of mind that you must have acquired after the life and death struggle.

"What I would like to explain are some principles as to how we shall treat you and how you should behave yourselves.

1. Though treating you strictly in accordance with the regulations of our army, we will make every effort to maintain your honor of being warriors and your persons shall be fully under fair protection.

2. You should behave yourselves strictly in accordance with the discipline of the Japanese Imperial Army. Otherwise you will be severely punished according to Martial Law.

3. As far as Japan is concerned, you must do away with the false superiority complex idea that you seem to have been entertaining towards the Asiatic people. You should obey me and the other officers of the Japanese Army.

4. Prejudice against labor and grumbling over food, clothing and housing are strictly prohibited. Because we are now launching death-defying attacks on the Anglo-American military preparations in East Asia, all the nation with a unity of will, strong as iron. There is not a single man or woman who is idling about in this country; everyone is working as hard as possible I order to attain the aim of the present campaign. Therefore you must regard it as natural that you should not be allowed to be loose and reckless in your living. You ought to worked as hard as the people of this country do.

5. Don't be demoralized and do take good care of yourselves. As long as the war continues, your present mode
of living will remain as it is. In order to endure this
mode of living you should encourage each other in
avoiding demoralization and taking good care of yourselves. Don't fail to hold the hope that peace will be
recovered in the future and you will be allowed to
return to your homes. I have ordered our medical officers to offer enough medical treatments to you in case
you should be taken ill.

6. Among you officers and men of the American Marines
you must attain discipline. Be obedient to your seniors;
be graceful to your juniors. None of you must bring
disgrace upon the American Navy's Glory.

7. If you should have any troubles in you personal affairs
don't refrain from telling our officers of them.^

"With the deepest sympathy with you as captives, I and our
officers will be pleased to be consulted with and will make every
effort to alleviate your pain. Trust me and our officers.

"Closing my instructions, I advise you all to study the Japanese language. I wish you to master it in a degree that you will not
feel much difficulty in understanding instructions and I hope you
will be able to establish friendly relations between Japan and
America when peace is restored in the future."

"That was a pretty stiff speech." Bob muttered. "Sounds like
America ought to throw in the towel. If the Aussies hadn't con-
firmed it all, I'd say bullshit to the little, bow-legged bastard."

"It sounded like a badly written grammar-school play." I replied with false bravado. "I know this is going to be a long war. It
may take a year for America to rearm and take the offensive. Dammit!
In the meantime, we'd better shape up."

Later in the day, the commandant learned there were a hundred or so civilians in the group. No wonder he had addressed us
the kindness of his Majesty and his subjects. If cooperative, we
would be treated well otherwise, we would pay dearly. Hopefully

we would be exchanged as war prisoners if such an exchange were arranged. Again, we were cautioned to take care of our health. He wished us well. He strutted off and we shuffled back to quarters.

Despite our hunger, our hopeless predicament, and the cold January air, we resented the tone of his speech. He failed to mention that they had put us into this predicament by bombing Pearl Harbor, capturing Guam, and bringing us to Japan as prisoners. His country and his Emperor had created this mess and yet he had the temerity to lecture us on the standards of behavior and how wonderful they were to offer us a modicum of hospitality.

CHAPTER 15

Life in Zentsuji

A few days after the commandant's lecture, the most welcome news of the new year played a sweet tune in our ears. We were going to have a bath. A real Japanese bath! Tub, water, soap and all.

The bath turned into a delightful oriental experience. In a nearby building three fifteen by twenty feet recessed concrete bathtubs were filled with clear, warm water about three feet deep. Concrete coping and drainage gutters circled the edges.

The guards whistled us into three long lines inside our building. The first ten in each line were to bathe first—ten to each tub. However, there was protocol to follow. The prisoners had to wait till last. To start, the commandant was ceremoniously bathed by his orderlies in private. Off-duty guards came next. To learn the routine, we were allowed to watch. Dipping a bucket of the eighty degree water from the tub, they soaped themselves as they squatted on the coping. They rinsed off by pouring the clean bucket of water over themselves. Cleansed, the guards stepped into the warm tub for a few minutes until whistled out to towel off. Our turn was next.

We were furnished a towel, soap, and a fundoshi. (Japanese version of boxer-shorts) This garment was nothing more than a piece of white cotton cloth about one foot in width and three feet in length sewn to a string to be tied around the waist like a belt. With the cloth hanging down in back, it was easy to pull it up between the legs and lap it over the string in front. Practical, comfortable and easy to clean, they automatically fit everyone thus eliminating tailoring problems. They served us well for the duration.

Naked, we worked our way towards the tubs. On signal, I soaped, scrubbed, and rinsed twice to make sure I had washed off the various layers of accumulated crud. In the bath, of the warm, clean water on my sore, itchy, drought-stricken body was rapture soaked in ecstasy immersed in bliss.

Whistled out, we drip-dried our way back to the dressing area, to towel off, don our new skivvies and dress.

"I hope the fleas and bugs I left in the tub will gag as they go down the drain." I said. "I forgot to say good-bye to the little "bastards". After all, we'd become well acquainted over the past sixty days."

The best was yet to come—Hollywood style. Lights! Action! Camera! Hooray! We were going to be actors in a movie masterpiece with a cast of thousands. As a director, a cameramen, actors, lighting assistants, and pompous military supervisors milled about, production began in earnest.

They issued us (temporarily, it turned out) safety razors and told us to shave and spruce up the best we could. We were directed to stand in a long line facing the sun. The director shouted for us to smile and move slowly forward. Midst grinding cameras and grinning guards, we shuffled past a pretty, kimono-clad girl who handed each of us a bar of soap and a towel. Moving on, a friendly looking guard thrust an orange in our hands. What a delightful surprise. We were told to keep moving so the rest of the men in line could be served. As soon as we passed out of sight of the camera, a sullen corporal grabbed our gifts and sent us back to our quarters empty handed, disappointed, and angry. The items were then returned to the girl for a repeat performance. It was a massive production all right, better than a DeMille masterpiece, showing the world how the beneficent Nipponese treated their hapless captives.

Meanwhile, Fred Oppenborn was busy manipulating. Somehow, he had wormed his way into the kitchen routine. He was one of the volunteer mess gang serving food and stoking fires. He whispered that a job was available and that it meant more chow and perhaps a chance to steal a slice or two on the sly. I quickly volunteered. It was a cozy assignment with happy prospects. However, I lost my appetite when I saw the hairless hind-quarters of a horse with no hooves floating in the soup pot. The next pot was even worse. A bare horse's head, with its tongue hanging out lay in the bottom of the pot. Its bulging eyeballs kept staring at me. We never mentioned this salubrious cuisine to anyone until months later. Food was precious and nothing would be gained by our repulsive reports on boiled horse flesh. By talking, we would have lost our jobs, and moreover, we weren't dining at the Ritz. Although the recipe remained a secret, the soup was nutritious and nobody died or even had a bellyache.

Despite my extra kitchen rations, I was weak from the gnawing agony of chronic hunger. A thousand calorie daily diet, dropped thirty-five pounds from my aching bones and my clothes hung in odd angles like a tattered scarecrow in an Idaho cornfield. Hunger is hard to adopt as a friend.

CHAPTER 16

Transfer to Kobe

On January 22, 1942, seven days after our arrival, we civilians were told to pack and get ready to leave Zentsuji the next afternoon—destination unknown.

We were not surprised about the move. We knew we'd eventually be sent to a new camp somewhere in this wonderful land of OZ. At 600 PM we boarded the trolley and rumbled toward Todatsu. A chilly overcast with a north breeze whipping up a storm added a somber tone to our departure. Little was said as the trolley bounded along. Small farms and tiny cottages with industrious farmers bending to their tasks filled the landscape. Todatsu, a small town of bustling streets and unpainted wooden buildings, hugged the north shore of Shikoku Island in the Inland Sea. The Kogane Maru, a ferry boat, waited at the dock.

"From the size of the boat, we're not going very far", I surmised to Dick as we stepped off the trolley.

"I heard a rumor it might be Kobe, wherever the hell that is" he replied.

With a final tenko, the military officer handed over the papers and fate of the group to the civilian police awaiting at dockside. Then, without ceremony, the officer and his assistants turned on their heels and disappeared.

The second class quarters on the *Kogane Maru* were reasonably comfortable with tatami mats and miniature bunks The breeze had worked its way into a storm. Plowing through the cold, lapping waters of the inland sea, the little boat groaned and shud-

dered all night long. Our new guards wakened us at 4:30 A.M. A
small rice cake with tea in the dining area completed our breakfast. We docked in Kobe, an industrial city on the shore of Honshu
Island, at 6:30 A.M. on January 23, 1942—the end of our journey that started thirteen days ago in the tropics and zigzagged
1800 miles northward over the China and Japanese Seas.

Postcard of Street Scene, Kobe, Japan—1941

Kobe's waterfront, busy with the logistics of war, was mind-
boggling. So was the noise. Toots, whistles, clangs, and bellows
added to the bedlam. Ships loading and unloading food, iron, war
booty, and oil; giant cranes lifting and swinging heavy materiel
from one pile to another, huffing trains and puffing switch engines
created a discordant arena of activity.

Midst all this confusion, a pitiful sight caught my eye. A gang
of Korean coolies were carrying sacks of cement on their backs
from one of the merchant ships. Like docile beasts of burden, they
staggered under the weight of two 100-pound sacks balanced on
their shoulders, while teetering on sagging wooden ramps leading

from the dirty deck to the jammed dock. They moved silently under the watchful eye of a bulldog-like overseer, barking orders. These pitiful creatures were prisoners as well as slaves. I wondered how many thousands of lives Japan had already ruined in its crazy war of destiny and what lay ahead for its future victims.

Before disembarking, we were separated by age into two groups. The older internees, fifty and over, were sent to a different camp-site. Max Brodofsky and Al Hammelef, our oldest PanAm buddies, waved a sad good-bye as they boarded the bus. The remaining seventy-four of us walked slowly to the Seaman's Mission, five blocks from the waterfront. This was to be our home away from home for the next ten months.

On the way we passed hundreds of impassive civilians, rushing to work. Streams of bicyclists filled streets. Executives, in leather shoes and business suits, seemed intent and aloof. Dock workers, in slouchy caps and cotton pants, were unsmiling, but no less resolute. Secretaries, in kimonos and straw sandals (zoris), tripped along, too intent to notice this cluster of ragged humanity, walking in the opposite direction.

CHAPTER 17

Seaman's Mission

With growing anxiety, we turned into Ito-Machi Street a narrow, barren, nondescript side street lined on both sides with "go-downs" (warehouses) and small, colorless storehouses. The Seamen's Mission (or Institute) at 109 Ito-Machi, was a two storied unpainted structure squeezed between two enormous "go-downs". There was a noticeable lack of color on all the buildings nothing but drab, depressing, unpainted, weathered wood. A silly thought passed my mind; Sherwin-Williams Paint Company would have gone broke in Japan.

The Mission was not an architect's dream. Dull, gray walls, dreary gables, small barred windows, cracked tile roof, and no sidewalk setback made the place look lonesome for companionship. Despite its looks, the room arrangements were functional and practical. Best of all, it had inside plumbing, beds, and a potbellied stove, rare and luxurious necessities. A living-dining room, with shelves of books, tables, chairs, the stove and a battered piano, greeted us as we entered. A small kitchen was hidden in the rear. Various sleeping rooms, *benjos*, hallways and alcoves were scattered throughout each floor. Mr. and Mrs. Allen, an English couple and managers of the place, occupied a small, isolated apartment near the kitchen. Why all this luxurious space and equipment?

Throughout the Orient, Seamen's Missions were owned and operated by the British government for the benefit of their merchant mariners—a sailor's refuge away from home. Equipped with beds, kitchens and libraries, these establishments were enclaves of tranquillity in foreign lands. This particular mission was intended to accommodate about twenty persons in relative comfort, not a crowd of seventy-four homesick derelicts, bone tired and mentally paralyzed. The guards and managers were comfortably ensconced in the choicest quarters. We prisoners were stuffed into the remaining spaces. Psychiatrists would have wondered how we avoided claustrophobic nightmares. We didn't have the luxury of self pity so we bit the proverbial bullet and thought of food, home and freedom.

**First Meal at the Seaman's Mission.
Second Meal Was Fish Heads and Rice.**

Except for overcrowding, the Mission had several advantages. Hidden in a warehouse district with a minimum of pedestrian traffic, we had beds, benjos, laundry facilities, heat, and a good library. To the Japs, this place was a "tailor-made" internment camp. To us it was still a miserable mess of makeshift misery.

The usual hubbub of moving in was made easier by a loose organizational plan. From the classification report made on the civilians at Zentsuji a few days before, the guards knew this group was a cross-section of different ages, backgrounds, and professions. A few self-appointed leaders helped define the sub-groups.

We found names attached to the beds. Out of deference to their profession, the priests were given a room to themselves. In hopes of compatibility, the rest of us were subdivided into age groups. Sometimes, a few location trades were made. Three late comers, victims of overflow from other rooms, shared two beds among them. A benjo with shower and sink at the far end, was the most popular part of the setup.

The main dormitory upstairs held twenty cots lined along the two main walls, with a foot of space between beds. I ended up here between Jack Taylor's cot and the aisle leading to the entry door. Mine was a good-news-bad-news location. It was a long walk to the bathroom at night, but I was not disturbed by passers by staggering around in the dark. Granted, everyone passed my bunk as they entered or left the room, but I had an open side to my bunk where I could dress and undress comfortably. I stashed my belongings in my hammock under the bed.

We found ourselves under the jurisdiction of the Kobe "Kencho", the local police department. Izumeda-san was the chief of police in Kobe. Matsuda-san was the camp commandant, an unlikable bastard with a negative I.Q. who must have inherited his job through tenure instead of talents or skill. His cadaverous look earned him the nickname "The Skull" . His six underlings, three on a shift, were more humane and understanding. A few spoke broken "schoolbook" English, enough to bridge the communication gap. We were amateur internees and they were unskilled in internee control. So both parties inched their way along the learning curve. Obviously, the situation was tilted in their favor. They had power and permission to use it, we had nothing but hope and diminishing self reliance. We developed a numbed acquiescence, a pragmatic combination of "Wait and see" and "What else can we do?"

Bob Vaughn asked, "What do you think of our spacious quarters?"

Pondering the question for a split second, I replied, "This is no fancy Ritz-Carlton Hotel but this jam-packed arrangement is better than the tropical jungle and the mosquitoes, the Guam church, the hold of the Argentina Maru, or the Zentsuji barracks. We're coming up in the world. In time we may be sleeping in Emperor Hirohito's palace."

"When we get into his palace, I'll kick his royal ass into the stable with his white horse." Bob vowed. I was glad that was settled.

The most annoying things of our tranquil domesticity were the noises of the night. Human beings in slumber are not the quietest or most sedate animals on earth. A herd of hungry elephants or mating sea lions can't match the male homo-sapiens in rumbles, grunts, snores, and gaseous releases. If one didn't fall asleep quickly, he might be kept awake for hours by this symphony in B flat major. Mice and cockroaches skittered to safety and stray dogs detoured three blocks away.

At night, with the windows nailed shut and the doors closed, air circulation was cut off. Within an hour, the room smelled like a hibernating bears den after a long winter. In the morning, my mouth tasted like the inside of a dirty sock. Fresh air shocked us back to reality.

Obviously, the police had not been fully prepared for our arrival. Our first meals were catered by a nearby restaurant with china, tablecloths, napkins, condiments, and cutlery and we were served by neatly dressed waiters. The food, a labored imitation of American cooking, was delicious after six weeks of garbage. During the luxury of this salubrious cuisine, two cameramen snapped pictures of our bountiful table. Cameras we recognized as an ominous sign of worse things to come.

As expected, a few days later the fancy food and setups disappeared and we were back to fish heads, rice, seaweed, seaslugs, whale blubber, rotten meat, and stale tea. In far smaller portions. Hirohito and his culinary experts must have worked overtime on these concoctions. Often, we were driven from the dining room by the stink of rotten meat ladled from a metal tub delivered on a three wheeled, charcoal-powered motorcycle. The fancy catering system was, alas, gone for the duration. I often thought of the times I had refused to eat certain dishes as a child. I remembered my dear mother entreating my to finish my meal with the statement, "Some day you'll think of this food when you're hungry and alone on the road between here and Downey." (A little town twenty miles north of Malad). I recalled those words as I bit into a piece of decaying whale blubber.

Lack of space in the dining room forced us to eat in shifts. Some of us carried the food to our rooms and ate on our bunks. Finished, we'd wash our dishes in the benjos and stash them under our beds till the next meal. Sometimes, eating was a matter of sheer survival, and we gagged as we gulped down a small ration of putrefied sea slugs with rice gruel and hardtack. I often wished I was on that lonely road to Downey.

On January 31, we were told we could send personal messages via short wave to the States. Hopefully, mother would finally hear from me. Names and addresses of recipients, together with our short, telegraph-like letters were hurriedly prepared. Strict rules applied. We were not to mention our specific location, negative details of our treatment, or anything that might be revealing to America. The messages were heavily censored. I composed the following:

> To Mrs. Rhoda Thomas, Malad, Idaho, USA.
>
> Dearest Mother, I am safe in Japan. Am in good health and spirits. Am treated well. Don't worry. Tell my friends and don't forget to tell it to Sweeney.
>
> Love, Jim Thomas.

That last phrase had a double meaning. In Malad we declared our disbelief of anyone's statement by saying "Tell it to Sweeney" The message went through uncensored. Although later I regretted that my cleverness may have caused my mother more worry rather than less. It was a relief to have contacted her at last.

A few weeks later the Japs introduced a new drink that enlarged our vocabulary and tested our resolve. Its main ingredients were parched soybeans and burnt wheat chaff, with several scorched unrecognizable botanical additives. This concoction was stewed and served as a substitute for American coffee.

On one miserably cold morning, after a nauseating breakfast, we were treated to a cup of this Oriental version of Chase and Sanborn's Columbian grind. Larry Neass, a dour fellow, tasted this lukewarm cup of sludge, arose, threw the contents in the garbage can and stomped out shouting, "This is nothin' but stinkin' Kobe trash." The name stuck, eventually, shortened to just "trash." As unboiled water could promote a case of Hirohito's revenge, we laced our hot, sterilized liquid with stale, bitter tea. When tea leaf sweepings from the floors of warehouses were unavailable, we settled for "trash". With courage born of despair, we joked about this exotic blend but drank it nearly every day. We were beginning to be good prisoners, too intimidated to be anything else.

We were introduced to new footwear—straw zoris' and wooden clogs. A zori was a rice straw sandal with cloth straps that fit between the big toe and its minor partner. The local term for them was "Go Aheads" because that was the only direction one could walk. Padded cotton socks with a sheath for the big toe were part of the getup. Zoris were comfortable and practical. Clogs were made from softwood with two parallel wooden strips nailed across the bottom an inch forward of the heel. This allowed the wearer to walk comfortably by tilting forward with each step. A cotton strap over the instep kept them on. They were very practical in the shower. These Oriental Florsheims saved wear on our precious shoes.

Like a shackled giant, time lumbered on to slowly engulf our days and nights. Too tired to rebel and benumbed by the futility of our situation we sometimes succumbed to despair. Feeble attempts at humor to keep up our spirits were the most we could muster. Regrets for my mistakes of getting myself into this mess, haunted me as I lay in bed fighting sleeplessness. Sometimes these crazy thoughts invaded my dreams and I'd wake up in a cold sweat, relieved.

CHAPTER 18

Life at the Mission

The Seamen's Mission changed our nomadic lives. Like circus animals, we had been pushed and hauled from one miserable place to another for six weeks. Unheated barn-like quarters, repulsive guards, abrasive rules, and stinking food were constant reminders of our caged existence. No wonder we were anesthetized into a near-catatonic state. Now we had a place where we could settle down and try to live again. It was time to bring a modicum of order out of our unhappy lives. We had to protect ourselves from boredom and stagnation. These two culprits lurked in the shadows ready to destroy our health and sanity. We needed both physical and mental stimulation–classes, hobbies, amusements and exercise.

Overcrowding was one of the most aggravating and irritating conditions we had to endure. We milled about like a herd of restless livestock penned in a tight corral. We waited in line to eat, to bathe, and to use the john. We had to forge ahead or get trampled and forgotten.

Izumeda, head policeman of the local prefecture (political area) visited the camp once a week. He was educated and businesslike. Matsuda-san, the miserable camp commander under Izumeda, lived on the premises. His assistant was friendly Mabuchi-san. Another was Sakamoto-san, a fine educated gentlemen, acting as interpreter. Taura-san and others drifted in and out. Guards were constantly among us or spying from hidden points. With long swords strapped to their waists, they displayed authority and subtle arrogance as well as their gold teeth.

We needed organization and democratic rule. Since there were no servicemen to call to fix the plumbing, we needed maintenance men to keep the place shipshape. Work parties had to stoke and clean the stove, wash windows, repair plumbing, schedule shower baths and laundry chores. Exercise sessions required supervision and games needed refereeing. A president and a corps of assistants had to run the show to keep us from pandemonium or mayhem.

When we first arrived in the Mission, Chuck Gregg of PanAm, arbitrarily stepped forward and assumed leadership of the group. This makeshift arrangement lasted about two weeks when grumbling arose midst the contractors. They resented Gregg's presumptiveness of acting as camp leader and complained about his supercilious personality and arbitrary attitude. They rightfully demanded an election. Carl West, a popular engineer with the contractors, the largest group in camp, was elected leader by a voice vote. Gregg, with injured pride, stepped aside but remained head of the PanAm group and thus a committeeman.

New rules and regulations were hashed out and passed by all members in a general meeting. By-laws were written, debated and rewritten. A bulletin board displayed notices and group meetings were called for special announcements Stealing and goldbricking were strictly forbidden. Everyone had to do his duty. The leaders could pass judgment on misdeeds and punish the guilty. Extra duties for minor offenses or American style police action for major ones. (Thankfully, this last one was never put into practice at the Mission.) Disagreements and complaints would be arbitrated. We were a little, chaotic, noisy America behind enemy lines.

The guards sanctioned this arrangement wholeheartedly, for they insisted on talking only to the official leaders. Every suggestion or request had to go through channels. Only straight-line communication would be tolerated. Things were beginning to make sense.

Soon, we were allowed to walk the block long length of Ito-Machi under the watchful eyes of police guards stationed at each end. We appreciated this luxury of fresh air and exercise. But kindness and understanding was not the guard's main motive. Busy captives make peaceful captives like the proverbial idleness in the devil's workshop.

Life in camp settled into a workable routine. American money that had been smuggled in the prisoner's clothing and shoes was exchanged for yen on a one to one basis, a rip-off. Weekly shopping trips, under guard, to downtown Kobe broke the monotony. Eight to ten internees, chosen by lot, were able to buy toothbrushes, dentifrice, soap, razors, eyeglasses, and writing supplies, as ordered by their inmates.

The streets were bustling with kimono clad ladies with zoris on their feet and flowered umbrellas over their heads, giggling uniformed school kids, somber business men in black suits, and robe covered matriarchs and patriarchs mincing through the mass of humanity. The civilians paid little attention to us. There seemed to be ample supplies in the stores. Since the war was young and our navy crippled, rationing had not yet started.

Luckily, some secondary school English textbooks were found in the Mission's closet drawers. Classes in Spanish, Japanese, English, shorthand, algebra, and mathematics were started. Everyone taught what they could. I studied shorthand and taught elementary English composition. Ev Penning talked on algebra and accounting, Grant Wells gave a briefing on variable-pitch airplane propellers, Mr. Brunton demonstrated how the Chamorrans fished with nets and later described the heavens in a short astronomy class.

Charley Moneyhun, a multi-talented contractor, taught shorthand, tap dancing and freehand drawing. Carl West, a skilled engineer, gave an intensive course in bridge design and engineering. With all this talent, we could have produced a movie or built a pyramid.

Books saved our sanity. Subjects covering history, art, science, and religion filled the shelves. Classic fiction and non-fiction novels peeked out of the racks, inviting us to enter their secret worlds. A set of Encyclopedia Britannica settled many arguments. Oxford and Webster dictionaries broadened our vocabularies. Plato,

Shakespeare, Milton, Shaw, Spengler, Hemingway, Steinbeck and scores of other notables graced the list of authors. These literary gems became my best and most trusted companions.

However, not everyone read books. Tractor operators and roustabouts, although intelligent, were not necessarily bookworms. Many would rather talk shop, sleep, or stare at the stove. A windup Edison phonograph with a supply of worn 78 r.p.m. records ground away in a side room. Thankfully, we found playing cards and games in storage cabinets. Poker, cribbage, solitaire, checkers, chess and bridge filled lonely days between morning and evening tenkos and lights out.

Tenkos became an integral part of our lives. Every morning before breakfast and every night after chow we stood at attention at the foot of our bunks and shouted our number on a countdown as the guards passed by. Sometimes unscheduled tenkos were called to prevent anyone from going AWOL. We often had three to four tenkos a day. "Ichi, ni, san, shi" became routine but most of us couldn't count above ten in Japanese.

Lights out were scheduled an hour after evening tenko. This gave us time to visit the benjo and settle into bed. Friendly chatter and earthy humor often put us in a good mood to sleep. Morning tenko followed the wake-up bell. There was always a scramble for the benjo. Sometimes a sleepy goldbricker would feign sickness to sack in an extra hour. One absence from muster was allowed but twice in succession was not. If repeated, the guards would bring out a thermometer and take the malinger's temperature. If normal, the pretender would clean the guards's quarters for a week.

After breakfast, we made beds, swept up, did laundry, shaved, and showered according to the printed schedule. In cold weather many went back to bed to keep warm. Others played games or read books. Thus,, night followed day and day followed night and the weeks ticked away. The humdrum of confinement permeated every pore and the only escape was a mental jump out of the barren walls and into a make-believe world of books, games, and daydreams.

Some talked of escape so we held a meeting to discuss the matter. Most of us knew escape was impossible and besides we were deterred by thoughts of punishment. Once out of the camp, where would we go? Japan was a series of islands several hundred miles from the coast of China. There was no way to get to China except by boat and there was no way to get one. Roskowyck, a pile driver operator noted for his wisdom and tortured syntax, said it best. "They'd know we wasn't Japs by our vocabulary." The meeting broke up in a fit of laughter and the subject was dropped.

There were interesting people within this diverse group. Once faceless men became new friends. Roy Henning, of cable station fame, was still insightful, intelligent, uplifting. Bill Young, the legal eagle from Parma, Idaho gave elongated opinions on morals, food, and love. Jim O'Leary, the dry wit from the state of Washington who could read French. Andy White, the North Dakota farm boy who entertained us with country yarns too raunchy to repeat in a stag party. Jack Taylor, another Berkeley grad who loved a spicy story of illicit love. Nick Encerti a friendly Italian who made his rounds to pick up the latest news and circulated the latest gossip. Red Rupert, a cat-skinner from Muncie, Pennsylvania, who grew up in Amish country where he made "plummies" and apple cider. Eventually, I recognized everyone in camp, including the ugly guards.

"Shooting the breeze" became one of the main pastimes. Tall stories on every subject were spun and re-spun. Subjects, no matter how ridiculous or vulgar, were listened to with interest, the bawdier the better. Childhood reminiscences were recited and embellished. Past love affairs, real and imagined, lost or entwined, were attention grabbers. The farmer's voluptuous daughter had always succumbed. Every man there had been a Lothario and every girl friend a nymphomaniac. Hardened scriptwriters would have blushed at their exploits.

We heard personal adventures, family holidays, bodily injuries, medical operations, athletic exploits–anything to fill time. Construction stiffs had moved dirt and built bridges. Farm boys had castrated livestock or ploughed fields. Everyone had walked to school in snowstorms—sometimes uphill both ways. We heard spellbinding descriptions of gang fights by city boys. When a monologist turned one glassy-eyed, he'd seek another listener. Each telling added new dimensions to tired tales.

Not everyone was a storyteller. Some preferred solitude and confided in no one. Others talked only to intimate friends on serious subjects. Some killed time in other ways: books, poker, cribbage or daydreaming alone.

One rainy day, Roy and I were chatting our way through several subjects.

"I feel sorry for my folks." I mused. "I know they're worried about me and how I'm being treated. I know I'm all right but they don't. That's the worst thing about this crazy situation. Nobody knows what's going on anywhere. We don't know what's going to happen tomorrow. What's happening in the States. How is the war affecting my folks, my friends or Pan American Airways."

"I've often thought of that," he replied. "I imagine they think about beatings, starvation and firing squads. You can't blame them. They've heard a lot about the cruelty of the Germans and the Japs."

"They'd be relieved to know we're still alive." I continued. "The two worst things about this miserable situation are the confinement and the unpredictability of anything. We're worse than convicts on Alcatraz. At least, they know the length of their term. We don't know ours."

Roy pondered for a moment. "We've been fondled by the fickle finger of fate." We sat silently for several minutes, then picked up our books and entered a pleasant world of make-believe.

CHAPTER 19

Spring of '42

Our rations continued to race up and down the scale of edibility. Menus swung from palatable to nauseating. Several inmates were sent to the nearby hospital because of food poisoning. But many changes crept into our lonely lives. The Japs held air-raid practice with sirens whining and people running. Blackout curtains were installed with curt instructions to use them. Singapore fell and celebratory whistles tooted. The police held frequent, unscheduled tenkos to check for missing persons, search for phantom weapons and illicit literature, to find some new way to aggravate us. If one of us was found guilty of any infringement, the whole camp was punished so we policed ourselves.

The police chief told us that Switzerland, a neutral country, was representing American and British interests in Japan. Carl West and Gregg were taken to visit the local consular offices. They returned with good news. The Swiss were going to arrange for us to receive Japanese yen and they would also inform the States of our situation.

Mr. Champeaux (pronounced Shampoo), the Swiss consul, was a dignified and concerned gentleman. Sometime in March he visited the camp with blockbuster news. An exchange of prisoners had been arranged between America and Japan and we might be included along with Consular officials and lesser nationals in June 1942! This news sent us into delirious spasms of ecstasy. The thin prospect of going home dominated our talk by day and our dreams by night. The suspense was almost unbearable. To be going home!

What was home, where was America, was the world still turning? My old home in Idaho had never seemed more beautiful or more appealing.

Mr. Champeaux arranged for us to receive two daily English-language newspapers, the *Tokyo Nichi-Nichi* and the *Osaka Mainichi*. Biased as they were, they were our first contact with the outside. We read every word—propaganda, want ads and the limping stock exchange. We followed the decline of "Kobe Silk" on the stock reports until it finally petered out.

Newspapers were our life rafts in this sea of disaster. Besides international news, they gave us insights into the Japanese minds—their character, their culture, and their methods of waging war. Despite stilted, schoolbook English, the printed words reflected the thoughts of a tough, dedicated people. It was going to be a long war.

We followed, hoping they were wrong, the Japanese version of battle lines in the papers: Pearl Harbor, Guadalcanal, the fall of Singapore, the Philippines, and the battle of the Coral Sea. If nothing else, this war was becoming a good lesson in geography. We looked up the strange names in the Britannica and were hardly surprised to find that they were all Japanese victories. In every case, American losses were heavy and Japanese losses negligible. Claims of devastating damage to our navy from "near hits and near misses" of their deadly artillery were very disturbing. We didn't want to believe them but we had no proof to the contrary. These papers reported hundreds of our planes downed and scores of our ships sunk, while their navy went unscathed. We read between the lines and surmised that America had recovered from the disaster of Pearl Harbor and able to fight a two front war.

We read the propaganda about race riots and breadlines in America, people starving, food shortages, and labor strikes. Crime was rampant and society in disarray. America's armed services were untrained and cowardly, her people confused and longing for peace. Japanese submarines were shelling the West Coast at will while California cowered in fear of invasion. Japanese naval bombard-

ment had crippled the Panama Canal. Japan was on the verge of
victory and would soon accept America's surrender. We told ourselves otherwise, but the constant reiteration of these so-called facts
undermined our confidence and raised small, niggling doubts.

At this point, Japan found a hero with divine qualities to shore
up the war effort and give pride to the homefront. His name was
Kato who had shot down over 100 American planes in the South
Pacific and had never suffered a minor scratch in all these battles.
He was a super hero and his noble face and bemedaled chest was
proudly displayed on the front pages along with the declaration
"There was no Kato before Kato and there will be no Kato after Kato."
He eventually died a noble death for the Emperor in a dogfight
with the slovenly Americans when he was outnumber fifty to one.
But his memory was fostered on the front pages till the end of the
war.

When America interned the West Coast Japanese, Roosevelt
and his henchmen became devils incarnate. Tokyo screamed revenge. Our rations and privileges were cut. For two months we
lived on intimidation and bluster. Finally the crisis blew over and
our lives returned to normal—rotten fish, sea slugs and Kobe Trash.

The winter cold was subsiding. A volleyball setup appeared
from somewhere in the camp. We stretched the net across the
street near the camp's entrance, formed teams and organized. Volleyball filled our lives whenever weather permitted. Whooping and
hollering accompanied every point and personalities came alive.

As the weather warmed, the guards permitted us to walk in
the nearby Kobe Athletic and Racquet Club park. This quiet little
place was a haven of comfort. A baseball diamond with modest
bleachers was a popular part of the field. The Japanese, lovers of
baseball, worshiped Babe Ruth, or "Babu Luthu" as they pronounced it. We were told about the Babe on his tour of Japan in
1934, when he belted a home run over the fence into the surrounding houses 450 feet from home plate. His fans had placed a
marker on the street corner where the ball landed.

Semi-pro baseball players sometimes used the park for league games. If we happened to be there, we were allowed to watch. The players were skilled and the games lively. The few spectators were the very old and the very young—those unable to work or fight. They ignored us as part of the scenery.

Once again the fairy godmother of sports smiled and gave us a softball, a bat, and three mitts. Makeshift teams yelled and chattered but any resemblance to professionalism ended there. More time was spent chasing the ball than throwing it. The umpires were blind and the batters should have swung white canes instead of a bat. But the stumbling and fumbling loosened the joints, tightened the muscles, and tickled the funnybones.

On bright days of the fading winter, we'd circle the track or sit on the benches to soak up sunshine. From the top of the bleachers we could see a busy street, a few hundred yards away, lined with people, stores and commercial signs. Bouncing on the cobblestones, charcoal-burning motorcycles and trucks darted between swaying rickshaws and horse-drawn carts.

One sign in particular made us laugh. In bold letters it read, "BOOZE PARLOR – SMALL PROFITS AND QUICK RE-TURNS." This was my first encounter with Japanese Oxford English. Shortly afterward, we were exposed to more twisted linguistics. For instance, scarcity of fresh water prompted the guards to issue a directive tacked to the bulletin board, "Timely supplement of water 6-7 AM. Very speedy for them." Another ordered drivers to, "Tootle horn before crashing". This directive alone turned auto traffic into a bedlam.

CHAPTER 20

Doolittle's Raid

Winter surrendered its chilling blasts to spring's warm breezes and singing birds. Sunshine and flowers invited us to join them in the park. It was nice to know that mother earth still moved in her seasonal rhythms.

As the guards covered the entrance gates, Dick and I circled the track on a pleasant April afternoon. Little white clouds played tag in the blue sky. Cherry blossoms glistened in the sunlight and nesting robins hopped about looking for worms. We talked about our chances of going home, a sensitive subject requiring caution for fear our very thoughts might hex the operation.

I don't want to sound pessimistic but I'm following the old adage of 'hoping for the best, expecting the worst, and taking what comes'" I told him. "I have always said we wouldn't see America until the war was over and I've not changed my mind. We'll never be exchanged. The Japs want us for bargaining power when the chips are down. Besides, I don't trust the little bastards."

"I hope you're wrong but I'm afraid you're right." Dick replied. "The Swiss Consul isn't too encouraging. He seems vague and full of double-talk."

"I'm bracing myself for bad news," I continued, " I don't want to be too disappointed when it comes. To be exchanged, we need a strong dose of good luck, and our good luck ran out in Sumay, Guam last December. Some of the guys are so sure of getting on the boat, they may collapse if they miss it."

We'd decided to take another turn around the track when an

unexpected sound of an airplane caught our attention. Scanning the skies, we spotted a twin-engined bomber coming in from the northeast at a low altitude. We stopped to watch its approach. It didn't sound nor look like a Nip plane. Was it a fantasy? It was headed for the waterfront on a course directly over our heads. Then we spotted the insignia, a circle with a star in the center. My heart jumped into my throat. My God, it was an American plane, so low we saw the pilot in the cockpit. Our delirious waves and shouts were futile. The plane swung low over the warehouses, dropped a few bombs near the waterfront then dipped out of sight. It was apparently heading for China, probably at wave-top level to escape gunfire. (We later learned the assault was conducted by Lt. Col. "Jimmy" Doolittle.) In one blazing, exhilarating moment, 2:40 P.M. on April 18, 1942, the Doolittle raid on Kobe had happened. The attack had lasted less than ten seconds, but its effect on Japan was staggering.

As the plane disappeared, pandemonium broke loose. Every siren in Kobe whined into action. But too late. Frightened, every one ran for safety, sometimes in circles. Police whistles filled the air. Mystified about the plane's launching point and whether more bombers were coming, officials sustained the alert for several hours. Zero fighters took to the skies only to find disinterested birds and puffy clouds.

The people had been told that Japan was impregnable but suddenly the credibility of the authorities was shaken. Next day, the papers screamed revenge for the callous bombing of innocent civilians without warning. They never mentioned Japan's own sneak attacks on innocent civilians at Pearl Harbor, Guam or the Philippines. Nor in the rape of Nanking seven years earlier.

We were proud that America was, at last, on the attack. Doolittle and his brave crews had revived our hope. Optimism salted our conversation for weeks, while the guards remained sullen and silent. Later, the papers trumpeted that Tokyo, Yokohama, Nagoya and others had been hit—by sixteen B-25 bombers in all. Reports proudly claimed nine planes downed by superb gunfire

and brave fighter pilots, with the captured crews justifiably beheaded. (I subsequently learned that none had been shot down
and seventy-two of the eighty airmen had been recovered in China).
Roosevelt was quoted as saying the planes had come from Shangri-
La. This poppycock bugged the Japanese. Where in hell was Shangri-
La? Typically, the newspapers twisted this humiliating attack into
a Japanese victory.

Things were never the same after Doolittle's visit. It had scared the
bejabbers out of the high command, who had lost face because the
raiders had brought the war to the homeland. Their cockiness following Japan's reported victories during the first months of the
war was smashed beyond repair. Though the myth of Japan's in-
vulnerability had been shattered, its resolve was undiminished,
even strengthened, and the leaders snarled revenge. It would be
three long years before we would see another American plane in
the skies over Japan.

Our rations deteriorated after the raid. Delivered in open pots,
the food sometimes stank so badly we could smell it coming a mile
away, upwind. We held our noses before throwing up or throwing
it out. Diarrhea spread through the camp and morale sank to a
new low as victims begged for hospitalization. Confinement and
slow starvation worked their insidious damage. Quarreling and
fighting broke out amongst old friends and the camp leaders were
criticized for imagined deficiencies. The guards screamed for more
cooperation and respect. Exercise privileges were canceled. Air raid
practices and blackouts became routine. Confined to quarters, we
viewed the skies by peeking through curtained window panes.

Eventually, feelings simmered down, new events interceded,
and the raid became history. Normalcy returned –rotten food,
boring chores, walking in circles, and stupid bull sessions.

One day as Bob and I circled the track, we began discussing a
sensitive subject. Sex! We had already covered some of our past
exploits for the fourth time and now we centered on the situation
in camp.

"Do you ever wonder if there's any hanky-panky going on in camp?" I asked.

"I'm not sure, but I hear rumors that there are four queer contractors having a helluva good time. They're the only ones with smiles on their faces." Bob replied.

"We're so crowded—how can they do anything without being caught?"

"Beats me. Maybe in the benjo after lights-out. Maybe under the blankets. Who cares?" Bob snickered.

"I know of one homo who is not a contractor. He approached me on Guam. I'll never tell his name. I think he's the latent type." I muttered.

"The rest of us are too hungry to think about such things. Sex is the first thing a hungry man forgets and the first he remembers after a good meal." Bob philosophized.

"The way the guys brag about their horny past, they must be feeling better. According to your theory," I added, "if they ate a good American meal, it wouldn't be safe in the dark around here."

"Naw" said Bob. "What you hear is a bunch of harmless, frustrated guys working off steam by bragging a bit. We just got through doing the same thing. Frankly though, a beautiful girl is a beautiful thought. But right now, I wouldn't trade two nights with Dorothy Lamour and Lana Turner together for a T-Bone steak.

The guard's whistle jarred us back to reality and Dorothy and Lana were left to suffer alone.

Camp life had settled into a monotonous routine of day and night, tenkos, rules, meetings, discussions, debates, quarrels, fights, and endless arguments over trivial things like the number of rings on a ring-tailed cat. Needing a dream, we waited fretfully for the Swiss Consul to bring good news of the coming prisoner exchange.

Each time he arrived, we'd surround him like hungry kids jostling the candy man, begging for hope, straining for expectation. He'd field our questions skillfully, promising good news next time. He advised us to take care of ourselves and not give up, then leave. Disappointed, we'd silently shuffle to our bunks and lie down, sometimes wiping away a tear. Our morale sank to a new low.

One sunny day, I spotted Henning sitting alone in the stands. He beckoned me to sit beside him. He was in a mood to talk and listen. We discussed the weather, food, plumbing and latest gossip.

"Tell me about your younger days," he said idly.

I looked intently at his face. Was he ready for the story of my life? Would he make fun of the poor boy from Idaho? What the hell, we had to kill time some way. I figured I'd start the story and if his eyes glazed over I'd stop.

He really seemed interested, and probed again. "You told me once you were from somewhere in the Rocky Mountain region. Was life pleasant high in the mountains?

Like in the story of *Alice in Wonderland* I thought I'd start at the beginning, go to the end, then stop.

"I was born on a family farm in Malad Valley in southeastern Idaho in 1917. That makes me 25 years old. We fed and nursed pigs, chickens, horses, cows, dogs, cats, and sheep. My four brothers and I fought and played recklessly. We had an aunt and a doting grandmother to grumble about, and a brave mother to manage everything. Mother, the real heroine of this saga, was a battered woman. She kicked my drunken dad out when I was seven and decided to go it alone with five kids to raise and poverty staring her in the face."

"The lady had guts," Roy said. His admiration seemed genuine, so I warmed to the subject.

"We had to grow up fast. At five, I was doing daily chores; at ten I worked for wages at ten cents a day for a twelve-hour day on neighborhood farms to help pay the bills. Later, I got twenty-five cents a day. One summer, I earned $8.75, enough to pay for the car license, my school supplies, a pair of jeans, and one dollar for Christmas. I milked cows, shoveled manure, thinned beets, hoed weeds, pitched hay, and bucked wheat, just for starters. I delivered calves, castrated pigs and broke horses. I rode the range, dehorned bulls and butchered steers. I learned to swim in an irrigation ditch. I knew the facts of life at six and discovered girls at twelve."

I stopped for a breath, my mind on that faraway world and a long-ago time. Roy waited without a word, so I continued.

"Our house was a log cabin with no plumbing or electricity. We made a run for the two-holer out back even in the dead of winter. I was thirteen before I heard a toilet flush. We studied around a coal-oil lamp. We rode horseback two miles to grammar school and four miles to high school in rain, shine or blizzards. Our total income was less than two hundred dollars a year. We raised our own meat, eggs, fruits and vegetables and had ten cents to spend on a picture show once a month."

"You were near a town, then? If you had a high school and a movie house?" Roy was still listening, apparently.

"Yeah, the town of Malad, population 2,000. With no luxuries and the minimum of necessities at home, Malad was a thrilling adventure, the best and biggest city in the world. That Spartan life was good training for this stupid internment camp, rather like boot-camp in the Marine Corps. At least, this place has indoor plumbing and electricity. But we had freedom on the farm and good food, not this pig slop. So, I'm ready for the duration if my guts hold out. It's this goddamn confinement and uncertainty that grinds me."

" Me too. But you've adjusted to this life better than a lot of city kids could."

"Yeah, I realize that. I'm not asking for pity, just talking. And we weren't completely isolated. We had friends. My first playmate was a four-year-old Japanese girl by the name of Rhoda Sato. I was five at the time. Her folks rented a farm a mile from our place. My mother often acted as midwife, many pioneer women did, and she had helped deliver Rhoda Sato. She was named after my mother. I spent many happy moments playing with Rhoda and drinking Mrs. Sato's warm milk or apple juice before walking home. We played every day at her place or mine. They had lots of pet rabbits and they gave me some to keep. The rabbits multiplied so fast they nearly swamped us. A few years later, the Satoes moved away and disappeared into the big world outside our valley. I haven't seen them since, but I love them still. Now, here I am in their homeland as an enemy alien. I wonder if they're being treated as enemy aliens too. What a crazy, mixed up world."

"I can't imagine that kind of life. How did you get from there to Guam?"

"I left Malad in 1935 and ended up in Glendale, California to seek my fortune. It was like jumping from the nineteenth century into the twentieth. I got an Associate of Arts degree from Glendale Junior College and a B.S. degree from the University of California at Berkeley in the middle of the Great Depression, scheming, working a dozen jobs and all the angles I could find. But I managed to have a helluva time en route. I took a job with PanAm while waiting for my draft number to come up. They sent me to Guam with a bunch of other guys to help deliver planes to the Dutch East Indies. Yeah, it was quite a trip from Malad to Guam. Internment is a stinking reward for all my hard work."

We studied the free drifting clouds before returning to camp.

On May 10, 1942, the other zori dropped from our callused feet. A grim-looking Swiss consul arrived at the camp. We braced ourselves for the shock. He spoke slowly and deliberately.

"Because you were captured on an island that was being fortified, the Japanese government has classified you as Military Civilians and therefore ineligible for exchange." The bottom dropped out of our rice-bowl of hope. Stunned, many stared blindly into a blank wall of nothingness.

He continued, "You are requested to write letters home which will accompany the Asama Maru which is scheduled to leave Tokyo on June 10. The Swedish ship, Gripsholm, will bring the Japanese internees from America. The exchange will take place at Laurenço Marques, Portuguese East Africa. The agreement includes exchange of personal mail and supplies to prisoners still held in each country. Hopefully, the returning Asama Maru bring letters and gifts from your loved ones. There will be further exchanges and I hope you'll be on one soon. Good luck."

It would take time to digest his message. He left quietly, turning his back on our despair to not disturb our thoughts.

We wrote letters home without shielding our disappointment. But we didn't let the bad news cripple our will to stick it out. In fact, it was a relief to finally hear our fate. Now we could focus on something besides hopeless dreams. Snatching at American humor, Walt Pleitner, the contractor's cook, wrote on the blackboard in bold letters, SHAMPOO SAYS NO SOAP. It broke the tension.

CHAPTER 21

Battle of Midway

June brought many changes. Camp life slouched along. I'd read a half dozen books since my arrival six months ago. *The Way of a Transgressor, The Road to Endor, How Perry Opened Japan, The Good Earth* by Pearl Buck, *Lost Horizon* and *Thoreau* had given me many pleasant hours. With Charley Moneyhun as my teacher, I had reached 120 words a minute in Gregg shorthand. Through the newspapers, we got a biased look at the outside world and the Emperor's schedules, even his "daily ablutions" were printed. His pronouncements started with "We, the Emperor of Japan." The royal 'We' showed him to be greater than a single individual.

Japan's victories had, so far, amazed themselves.

Until June 4, 1942. This was the date of the Battle of Midway, the greatest and perhaps the most crucial sea battle in the war of the Pacific or, some say, in the annals of sea power, considering the number and firepower of the ships involved. Its effect on history equaled the battle of Trafalgar and the defeat of the Spanish Armada.

The bulk of each country's fleet clashed in the open sea with the fate of Midway and the Hawaiian Islands at stake. The course of the war hinged on its outcome. America had not fully recovered from the tragedy at Pearl Harbor and had been roughed up in the battle of the Coral Sea a few weeks earlier. The Coral Sea was a draw as to damage, though a strategic victory for America in the defense of Australia. Thinking America's air power had been mangled beyond repair, Japan was looking for the knockout punch.

They planned to lure America's crippled navy into a trap and destroy it. Miraculously, America was ready. The carrier *Yorktown*, damaged in the Battle of the Coral Sea, had been refitted in forty-five hours instead of the anticipated two weeks. More importantly, unknown to the Japanese, America had broken the Japanese code and knew Japan's battle plan.

Midway was an American victory. Our Navy sank the four main Japanese carriers, the heart of their task force. When the mother ships sank, their planes went down with them. The remainder of the fleet fled in disarray, never to recover. The tide had turned in America's favor. Midway spelled the eventual defeat of Japan. Yet, it would take three and a half years of hard fighting on land and sea before American troops walked down the streets of Tokyo.

As the news of Midway leaked out, a hush fell over the country. Our guards admitted it was a very big battle with an uncertain outcome. But their worried look made us think they had picked up the real news on short-wave radio. As usual, the papers shouted a triumph. To paraphrase their editorials: "After sinking half of America's fleet, the High Command had wisely chosen a strategic withdrawal to continue its domination in the Pacific and a march to eventual victory."

The Japanese capture of the islands of Kiska and Attu in the Aleutians was a diversionary tactic timed to coincide with the Midway operation. The tactic didn't work. The papers, nonetheless, boasted about Japan's capture of " a part of the United States", another "humiliating defeat" for America.

On June 10 the planned departure of the *Asama Maru* was delayed—no reasons given. June 16 became one of our saddest days of the war. Despite showers, every member of the camp rushed into the street to watch the repatriates passing two blocks away, skipping and dancing toward the train station on their way to Yokohama and the exchange ship. We noted, thankfully, that Guam's nurses and Mrs. Hellmers and her baby were in the group. We stood mute under the downpour as they gleefully threw their coats, hats, and umbrellas in the air. The raindrops seemed to wash away all hope of rescue. As the happy group skipped out of sight, we shuffled back into the dark, dismal, world of captivity. Many prisoners cried openly. Silence enveloped the camp for days.

The ship left Yokohama on June 25 with our letters and disappointments aboard.

The summer tedium set in, boring routine broken by occasional letters from the states. The *Asama Maru* had not yet returned from Lorenço Marques. The Red Cross had somehow delivered mail through a most circuitous and dangerous route. Was it by the Trans-Siberian railroad to Vladivostok? Through Switzerland and Germany? Through the south Pacific on marked freighters dodging torpedoes? Or were the letters from Heaven as the recipients claimed? Anyway, the letters came and we rejoiced in knowing that our folks were trying to reach us.

With dreams of rescue shattered, hopelessness replaced hope and camp politics reared its ugly head. I was still the leader of the PanAm group, and tried my best to keep peace. The exchange of prisoners at Laurenço Marques took place on July 24, a day of great bitterness for us, and the *Asama Maru* returned to Tokyo on August 20.

Talk of another exchange, with a departure date of September 20, began immediately and kindling faint hopes once again. Then negotiations broke down. The Guam group was the point of issue. The Japs had again refused to let us go and the September exchange, too, was canceled. I had good reason not to trust the little bastards.

CHAPTER 22

Transfer to Canadian Academy

Meanwhile, across the street, workmen were renovating a warehouse into a new prison camp. On October 1, 1942 the *Lisbon Maru*, carrying British prisoners of Hong Kong was sunk by an American submarine off Shanghai. The survivors were brought to Japan on the 6th to be housed in the new quarters. On the 9th, before they moved in, we were told to get ready to move. The next day we packed our duds and all the good books we could carry. Our luggage and contents were not cruise-line quality cardboard boxes or blanket rolls wrapped around soup cans, knives, forks, spoons, zoris, and clogs. My overcoat with *Huckleberry Finn* and *Works of Shakespeare* were shoved in a pillow case and wrapped in my hammock. With the usual Japanese inefficiency, we boarded open charcoal powered trucks that rumbled and backfired toward the north end of the city.

It was late evening when we chugged to a halt at our new location—known as the Marx house. Refusing to listen to our pleas, the screaming guards tried fitting seventy-four of us into a five bedroom house. They insisted we set up our bunks. We couldn't move—tables, chairs, beds and baggage were piled high on the floors and spilled into the yard. Convinced it wouldn't work, they huddled for a conference. Then they called the kencho office. After much "*mushi, mushi*" (hello-hello) and arm-waving, they ordered twenty-four of us to go to the Canadian Academy, on the northeast side of town. Luckily, we nine PanAm men, the Capuchin monks, and a few civil service men were selected. We wished our buddies "good luck" as we climbed into the trucks. Totally spent, we arrived at our new camp about nine that evening. Greeted by the courteous camp leaders and given the best meal since capture, we were led to our rooms in the attic where we flopped into bed at midnight.

CHAPTER 23

Canadian Academy

The Canadian Academy was the most fortuitous move so far in our internee career. A popular high school for non-Japanese nationals, its three storied, unpainted, time-worn wooden building sat on a rectangular acre of gently sloping land. A non-threatening wood and wire fence surrounded the complex. In front, a flowered rock garden greeted us. In the rear a modest recreation yard invited us to play games and exercise.

We were met by thirty-five friendly internees concerned about whether we were their new companions in misery or intruders into their exclusive lodgings. Well dressed, educated, mannerly, they represented a mixture of American, European and Japanese cultures. As foreign nationals whose countries were at war with Japan, they were potential enemies and therefore imprisoned.

After a warm breakfast of toast, oatmeal and real coffee, we were taken on a tour of our new camp. We found the building functional and sturdy in spite of having hosted thousands of teenagers over the years. A stone staircase led into an entry porch. To the left was a large dining room-assembly hall adjoining a fully equipped kitchen. From the guard's room one could watch the front yard, the entryway, and inside foot traffic. Dormitories on the second floor were filled by the local internees. A full sized bathroom with a tub, showers and a couple of commodes was located off the central hall. The two attic-like rooms comprising the third floor were assigned to us—the Catholic fathers in one and we PanAmers in the other. If we tried to stand upright, we banged our heads on the rafters. We had to manage the stairs in the dark to get to the second floor bathroom. A partial basement held a sanctuary and an organ for religious services.

Our new cellmates were a mixed blend of Dutch, Belgians, French, Guatemalan, and English nationals, with several Eurasians of British and American citizenry. Some were married to Japanese women and others were bachelors with concubines. Except for a few missionaries, priests, and teachers, all were former business-men engaged in import-export activities. They spoke English and Japanese fluently. Most seemed financially secure. All had refused to return on the first exchange ship. Their homes and families were in Japan. In some cases, their loyalties, were ambivalent. We were aware of possible spies amongst them. These sleazy characters were ready to pass on information to the guards for cheap personal favors. The smallest gossip or even our innocuous personal opin-ions were reported. We quickly learned to watch our tongues.

Clifford Wilkinson-Price (Cliff), a British subject and co-leader of the camp. He was a rich, handsome, dynamic bachelor, the Eurasian son of the owner and founder of the Tansan Bottling Works (one of the most popular drinks in the Orient) in the city of nearby Takuradsuka. Reggie Price: Cliff's younger brother, equally dynamic and personable.

Harold Mason: co-leader of the camp. An American-Eurasian business man with an upper eyelid problem that forced him to tilt his head as if he were a bit of a snob. Dignified, helpful, intelli-gent, he was impeccably honest and forthright.

David Hatter: a warm and trustworthy American-Eurasian with a Japanese wife and family, his blind son living at home was his main concern.

Stan Pardon: an Englishman schoolteacher with a Japanese wife. He was one of the funniest most likable men in camp. He had a secret source of sake, probable his wife. Two drinks on holi-days would set him off. He had the best repertoire of bawdy songs and jokes I have ever heard. They'd make your hair curl even as you rocked with laughter.

Alan Kawasjee: a nineteen year old British subject and a Parsee-Indian-Eurasian student with broad shoulders and a friendly grin became a pal. One night, to everyone's bewilderment, he disappeared from camp: After the war he told me that his freedom was achieved through the efforts of his mother who had friends in high places. His benefactor was a Japanese general, that had bounced infant Alan on his knees years before. This general and his army was now occupying the Philippines. He pulled rank and heeded her pleas for Alan's freedom.

Father Spae: a Belgian priest and linguist, could speak eighteen languages; he read the Japanese papers to us every day translating from Japanese to French to English.

Reverend Johnson: a down to earth, Canadian missionary previously stationed in China.

Mr. Brand: a Dutch businessman.

Jimmy Ambrose: a Brit in charge of the bath room and a reciter of dirty limericks. I learned to appreciate them all but I found a Mr. Blyth the most intriguing man in Japan.

R.H. Blyth: an Englishman, Zen Buddhist, scholar and teacher was one of the most influential and charismatic persons I've ever met. His keen intellect, winning personality, easy manner, humility, humor and tolerance of human frailties over-whelmed me. He seemed content and at peace with himself and the world. I listened for hours as he talked about Buddha, Mohammed and Christ. He was a handsome man, with a shock of wavy hair, piercing blue eyes and a disarming smile. Dressed in a black wool sweater and a pair of ragged cotton shorts. As he walked, his straw zoris flapping on his bare feet, he'd patiently answer my guileless questions. Most of the time, he'd squat, Buddha-like, on his bunk surrounded by open books, pen in hand, working on his latest book, *Zen in English Literature*. When it was published, he honored me with an autographed copy which disappeared during the frantic time of my rescue. One of life's ironies, the valuable stuff gets lost and the trash can't be given away.

The Canadian Academy's standard of living was unexpectedly

comfortable, almost like a cloistered country club. The inmates had connections in the community, friends in the local kencho and in social clubs. Japan was their adopted country. Their families were still free and could pull strings. Their wives and sweethearts had weekly visiting privileges when they brought cakes, cookies, and goodies for Elevensies (a morning snack before lunch) or for afternoon Menkeis (tea times). Many were members of the Kobe Athletic and Racquet Club where we internees had exercised while at the Seamen's Mission.

We wallowed in our new-found luxury. Our food was now prepared by a camp cook, served three times a day by kitchen help in a typically British fashion–tablecloths, napkins, cutlery and teacups. We went on hikes, played softball and volleyball, learned bridge and chess, and read choice books from the school library. We joined classes in Spanish, French, Dutch, and Japanese languages and English literature.

Buddy Durham, a former navy corpsman, assembled a portable medical kit which he carried around like a gentleman country doctor administering eye drops, painting mercurochrome, and spreading good cheer to the sick and needy. He was our Florence Nightingale in baggy pants.

November brought two pieces of good news. American troops had landed in North Africa to help Britain fight Rommel and his Africa Korps. At last we had taken the offensive in Europe. Closer to our immediate needs, we learned of a shipment of Red Cross supplies waiting to be delivered.

These supplies arrived on the 30th. The ecstasy of opening a kit of American food was beyond description. Corned beef, Spam, chocolate bars, soap, powdered milk, and cigarettes reminded us of home. Christmas, 1942, was like a gigantic Mardi Gras. We had a party with extra chow, sake, beer, and speeches. Believe me, a slug of warm sake can make the horizon spin and the world glisten.

American cigarettes were a special treat. We had been smoking Japan's equivalent of Lucky Strikes which seemed to be made from fermented horse manure and seasoned bat droppings. With a tar content like creosote, two cigarettes could transform a filter into a dripping mess. We blissfully smoked our new Luckies and stashed the butts for emergencies.

A week later, we were measured for a desperately needed suit of clothes to replace our pants and shirts held together with patches, mismatched cotton threads, and safety pins. The tailor made suits were delivered three weeks later. Made from sufu material, all were coal black, single breasted, cuffless, and ill-fitting. They provided little or no warmth. Moreover, the staple fiber had no resiliency: when we sat down the pant legs reshaped and never hung straight again. When we stood up our knees appeared bent and we all looked as if they were about to jump. Several months later, these "jumpsuits" began falling apart and were eventually consigned to the garbage sack.

The temperature hovered around zero from December till March. A late spring limped into view. The robins were subdued and the flowers smiled wanly.

Our daily existence was brightened, if not exactly enriched by *Saddlebags* our prize rat. Every night this huge varmint would gallop across our floor in search of food; a thumping ghost on a mission of aggravation. We had no rat trap so we designed our own. Our resident genius, Ev Penning, found a tin box about fifteen inches high and eight inches wide. He strung electric wires in the bottom sufficient to electrocute the marauder. He attached a tin paddle resembling a fly swatter to the upper lip of the box. This platform, baited with cheese, balanced horizontally over the pitfall. Ev then built a ramp for the rat to get to the top. The idea was that the nosy rascal would crawl out on the paddle which would bend under his weight, and he would fall into the box and be electrocuted.

About midnight, the spooky pest appeared. He shuffled towards the box in the middle of the room and everyone waited for the trap to spring. Nothing happened. The stupid rodent was not interested in cheese. The Japanese never ate dairy products so *Saddle-*

bags had not acquired a taste for the stuff. Figuring he might go for rice, we put a small rice ball on the paddle.

The next night *Saddlebags* loped towards his execution chamber. He scrambled up the ramp. Again we waited. Kerwham!! He fell in and started a wild commotion to escape. When he hit the hot wires, he snarled and tore them apart before jumping to safety. We never saw him again. Relieved to have him gone, we nevertheless admired his spunk.

In March, the local papers screamed about atrocities on the Japanese prisoners at Tule Lake, California. They printed stories about American guards stealing hundred-pound sacks of sugar from the camp canteen. Ironically, thievery by the Japanese guards was commonplace in our camps and we hadn't tasted sugar in twelve months. In another report, a Jap at Tule Lake was forced to sweep out the camp's movie theater. My, what cruelty! What was a movie theater anyway? Finally, the papers threatened that if the Tule Lake cruelties didn't stop, all the internees and prisoners of war in Japan would be shot. That thought disturbed our sleep. But we only had our exercise privileges cut and a few new restrictions issued.

Visits by the families of the local internees were cut from weekly to twice a month. Air raid precautions were increased with nightly blackouts. The possibility of air attacks became a topic of debate. We got permission to build an air raid shelter in the back yard. Plans called for a trench forty feet long, ten feet wide and six feet deep. With spades and picks, we began digging. The roof was covered with rotten one inch boards and a foot of dirt. By May air raid squads were organized and practices held, to everyone's discomfort. Sometimes the alarm would sound at 2 A.M. We'd pile out of bed, dress, and stagger into the shelter with our few belongings dangling from our backs. Every Japanese inspection party thereafter was shown the shelter by the proud camp commandant who pretended the whole thing was his idea and that he had supervised its construction.

About this time, through default and an urge to do something new, I became the camp barber. For ¥10 (yen), Dave Hatter got me a set of barber tools, a hand mirror, and a storage box. I had never cut a head of hair in my life. I bluffed my way through the first dozen clients as if I knew what I was doing. Good thing they weren't fussy and had no place to go. An added benefit was for me to get to know everyone in camp.

My first victim was George Conklin. He had a black, shaggy mane hanging over his ears. Perched on a stool and draped with my cloth, he looked like an executive getting ready for a board meeting. Like a pro, I asked him if he wanted a medium trim or a touch-up. He nodded at both choices so I had unlimited freedom. The clippers came first, gingerly up the back and over the ears. So far so good. Checking the sideburn level from the front, I noticed the left side higher than the right. So I trimmed right side higher to even things out. Woops, too much. So I trimmed up the left side. Too high! His cut finally ended up in the middle of his skull with a "Mohawk." He screamed into the mirror so I suggested a "butch." Pacified, he controlled his vanity, realizing his hair would grow out in a few weeks. Actually, he was so pleased with the "butch" he wore that style for the duration.

My questionable reputation spread and soon an exclusive clientele lined up for my services. (ok, ok, so I had a monopoly.) At first, I sheared on call but soon this arrangement became too haphazard so I set up a schedule of twice a week at half a yen per cut. When inflation set in, I raised my price to one yen. With my vast earnings, I bought soap and talcum powder.

About this time, the Japanese army adopted a new weapon that was to strike terror into the hearts of Americans—armed balloons to bomb the cities of the West Coast. Launched from the Japanese mainland, these floating missiles were designed to ride the jet-stream to America and drop their deadly cargo on Seattle, Portland, and San Francisco. Terrified, America would sue for peace.

Monday, 8th March 1943, The Canadian Academy, Kobe

Monday, 8th March 1943, The Canadian Academy, Kobe
Backrow:
L-R: Umeda-San, W.L. Vaughan, T.G.O. Crane, Felde Britta, Fr. Alex, Fr. Felix, W.J. Toms, G.W. Gabaretta, E.J. Kitson, J.R. Price,, Fr. Ferdinand, H. Arab, W.R. Hughes, Br. Gabriel, Fr. Alvin, T.O López, C.M. Attatoon, Fr. Spae, Rev. J. Stevenson, C.W. Brand.
Middle Row:
Fr. Xavier, C. Rolandus, R.N. Huston, H.J. Turner, P. Gasille, R. Smith, E.C. Koop, A.C.v.d.Kieboom, J.O. Thomas, T. Nakamishi, A.R. Kawasjee, T. Matsuda, R.T. Conger, M. Muranaka, R. Arvidson, H. Sumida, C.F. Gregg, T. Maeda, G.I. Blackett, H. Moritani, H.K. Ramsden, S.A. Pardon, W.H. Hickman, E.H. Penning,, G.M. Conklin, P.G. Walker, Fr. Theophane, H.C.W. Price
Front Row:
Tilde H. Moore, D. Hatter, Rev. H.K. Johnston, H.J. Ambrose, A.W. Peacock, W.E. Durham, A. Tada, Fr. Arnold, Fr. Pauliot, F.E. Down, F.B. Oppenborn, H.K. Brinkerhoff, H.J. Griffiths, R.H. Blyth, Fr. Marcian, R.J. Vaughn, G.S. Wells, R. Down, G.E. Brown, H.J. Mason
Inset: Akabane, B.T. Jones

14218-THOM

CHAPTER 24

Yamamoto's Death

To fight the boredom, I started reading *The Decline of the West* by Oswald Spengler, a profound tome by an extraordinary man. It was slow going, about three pages a day. I had to read each paragraph two or three times to absorb its meaning. His theory of the rise and fall of civilizations and the inevitable emergence of Caesar-like dictators aggravated Hitler so much that Spengler fled Germany to stay alive.

In April 1943 we heard Admiral Yamamoto, Japanese super hero and planner of the attack on Pearl Harbor, was killed somewhere in the South Pacific. Unknown to the Japanese, America had broken their code before the war and had learned of Yamamoto's planned flight to Guadalcanal. The American squadron of P-38s ambushed his plane and shot him down. His death was a fracturing blow to the High Command and the nation. Pearl Harbor had been partially avenged.

On May 24 the British citizens marched up and down the hallways with a slug of sake in their hands celebrating Queen Victoria's birthday. They insisted we have a snort and salute their favorite Queen. We gladly accepted. The sake put its customary spin on the horizon and fostered an intimate comradery. The Queen's birthday became a pleasant tradition to anticipate. It meant a free drink and a rendition of Stan Pardon's alehouse songs. We Americans reciprocated on the Fourth of July, but the Brits furnished the drinks.

Looking around for a project to satisfy an urge to create something with my hands, I spotted a seasoned cherry tree trunk along side the building. With permission to use the wood, I borrowed a saw from Mr. Peacock, a personable Australian with a full set of jealously guarded tools. I sawed out a slab of unblemished heartwood and let it season for three months to see if any cracks appeared. None did, so I cut the board into two equal pieces that could be hinged and folded together. A piece of broken glass served as a smoothing plane. A small, two bladed pocketknife helped shape the boards. Patiently, I scraped and polished the wood to a shiny glow.

A bent limb and a stray leather thong may have looked like a fiddle bow, but became a part of a wooden drill. Drawing on Boy Scout lore, I made a drill bit by flattening a nailhead and driving the pointed end into a shortened broom handle. Looping the leather thong around the broom handle and sawing back and forth, I managed to drill the 120 holes needed for two players. This procedure alone took three months. With the pocketknife I gouged out slots for the cards and pegs. Discarded window hinges connected the two pieces; when folded, the sides matched perfectly. Whittled bits of toothbrush handles made good pegs. For an extra touch, I carved a set of fraternity letters and a PanAm insignia on each half. I was pleased with the results. That cribbage board, a priceless memento of my time in Japan, now commands an honored spot on my library shelf.

The hot, muggy summer brought mosquitoes, flies, bugs, sweat and irritability. Father Pouliot, a kind, Canadian Jesuit Priest, was struck and knocked down by an irate Japanese guard for some minor infraction. Internees intervened to stop the altercation but tense feelings resulted on both sides. The *kencho* promised to investigate the matter. Nothing ever came of it.

I kept attacking *The Decline of the West* as if it were an adversary, a challenge that taxed my mentality and tenacity. I practiced shorthand, cut hair, played bridge and took up chess to pass the time. These diversions saved my sanity.

On one of his shopping trips, Fred bought a cheap violin with the intention of becoming a new Paganini. He'd saw away on "Old Black Joe" till his arm ached and everyone had been driven from the room. Finally, we gave an ultimatum—either practice in the yard, sell the damn thing, or better still, smash it to pieces. He finally gave up and hid it under his bed.

We whiled away many cheerful hours circling the playground and talking. We'd wave to youngsters passing by on their way to school a block past our camp. At first, the kids were curious but polite to us peculiar looking Americans. They'd stop their sauntering gait and call back to us. I enjoyed their youthful enthusiasm. Suddenly, one day they shocked us by torturing a kitten to death. They literally pulled it apart in front of our eyes, giggling all the while.

A few days later, their friendliness changed to hatred —perhaps anti-American propaganda had tarnished their innocence. They threw rocks and shouted insults at us. A nearby guard dashed after them as they fled towards the school. He grabbed the ringleader and slapped him before dragging him into the principal's office. A few minutes later, the guard and the principal dragged the frightened kid back to the camp. We stood thunderstruck as the principal slapped the kid violently and forced the crying youngster to apologize for his actions then marched him back to the schoolhouse. The children were models of decorum after that. The episode revealed the complex character of the Japanese—the paradox of the military's cruel, ruthless, sadistic arrogance and the friendly, courteous concern of shopkeepers, neighbors, and the ladies who had given us tea in Todatsu.

"Slim" Huston, a tall, lanky Standard Oil employee from Guam who had attached himself to the PanAm group, was a whiz on the sewing machine we had acquired through the help of Cliff Price and Harold Mason. Deprived of playmates as a child by a domineering mother, Slim had learned to sew. He ripped, patched, hemmed, and tailored shirts, shorts, pants and jackets out of cotton sacks, worn pants and window curtains. He was a professional scrounger, hemstitcher, and bull-shitter. When I asked him how come he was so clever, he dead-panned, "I've been a long way around the pisspot looking for the handle." In a philosophical mood, he observed "Science and skill don't have a chance against ignorance and superstition." It was amazing to find such hidden talent, ingenuity, and wisdom within this assorted group.

Fred Oppenborn ("I'm a bastard and proud of it."), surly and mysterious, always plotting against the Japs and imaginary enemies, vowed not to shave or smoke his hidden cigar until rescue. His beard was two inches of motley-colored tufts. He's the only person I've ever seen who could look busy standing still. He'd stare silently into space with the stance of a Socrates on Mt. Olympus and thoughtfully stroke his scraggly beard. Finally, after a dignified time, he'd nod his head as if a powerful decision had been made and then stride off alone. Everyone felt cheated at not being privy to his contemplative thoughts.

Somehow, as a result of his pondering, Fred accomplished the near impossible. Through guile and bribery, he acquired two laying hens. He built a small coop of netting wire, in the corner of the front yard and added a nest of straw. The hens ate table scraps and dandelion greens as he coddled and coaxed them into action. His first egg was fried over a hibachi. We nearly died of envy.

The kencho built a seven foot wooden fence around the camp as a barricade against mobs. For a few weeks, our entire world revolved within its fragile walls. Then, thankfully, a high wind from a passing typhoon blew it down and it was never rebuilt. Anyway, the remaining wire-netting fence seemed sufficient.

Dick Arvidson earned the reputation of "Elmo, the Mighty" in a softball game played on a sunny afternoon. He hit successfully and made it to second. The next batter popped a safe fly and made it to first. The third batter drove a hit directly at second base. Dick caught the ball putting himself and the batter out. Then he threw to first and put out the helpless teammate who was caught off base, and retired his own side. Only an extraordinary player can be on both teams in the same inning.

After months of waiting, I got my first letter from home in

July 1943 and learned that all was well and that mother had heard I was alive. Her handwriting brought tears to my eyes. The dog-eared message was one year old. I harbored the letter for the duration.

The war was now beginning to take its toll on the Japanese home front. Food was getting scarcer as black market prices sky-rocketed. Eggs were selling for ¥14 apiece, up from ¥5 a month before. Sweet potatoes, formerly three for a yen, jumped to one yen each. An overcoat would go for ¥1600, and shoes were ¥100-150, if you could get them. My wooden clogs and straw zoris matched my ragged shorts and patched shirts. As the temperature and rations dropped, our swollen fingers showed signs of beriberi. Our fingers and toes itched from chilblains. My eyesight weakened from lack of vitamin A. Morale sank and the fellows drew inside themselves. The locals continued their *menkei* (afternoon snacks) and the priests enjoyed their feast days from food given by devout Catholics. Those of us with no outside connections sat to one side and watched them eat.

July 19 was *Imperial Rescript* day with flags, overflights and parades. The rescript was printed in every paper and posted on every building to renew resolve and boost morale. Children danced and waved banners. In the distance, we heard a military band "oompahing" down a street proudly playing *The Stars and Stripes Forever*—a weird choice of music for the occasion, we thought.

One short pleasant episode happened to me in a surreptitious way. I've kept it as a secret memory all these years. Even the camp members never knew about it. It involved a beautiful Japanese-Eurasian girl. She was the niece of Mr. Moore, a reputed turncoat and far from the most popular guy in camp. For some reason he took a liking to me. One day, he beckoned me to follow him into the guard's office. I was nonplused and fearful the guards wanted some kind of a confession from me. Instead, I was introduced to and invited to sit next to a gorgeously beautiful girl tastefully coiffured and neatly dressed in western clothes. She had an aristocratic bearing—intelligent, educated and charming. Her name was

Miyoku. Having been educated abroad, she spoke perfect English. She had the beauty and charm of a Madame Butterfly. The caress of her hand on mine sent tingles up my spine. I nearly fainted from the thrill of touching such a delicate angel. She tactfully asked me about my happiness and well being. After all these months of confinement, I was infatuated by this beautiful creature. I stammered an answer. After a few golden moments, the guards ordered me to leave and our precious interlude was over. She squeezed my hand in farewell and promised to come back. I never saw her again. Shortly thereafter, I received a sweet but sad note telling me the *kencho* prevented her from visiting the camp. The note was signed, Sayonara, Miyoku. I answered through Mr. Moore, thanking her for the joy she had given me and wished her well. I kept her note for many months and her memory to this day.

I shall always be grateful for that thrilling moment. It was impossible, of course, to think a permanent relationship could exist against such overwhelming odds. But my feelings of ecstasy, though brief, was nevertheless sincere. I suffered in silence. Fortunately, time passed and distractions intervened. I've often wondered whatever happened to this angel that touched my hand and heart in my darkest hour.

As August 1943 came and went, there was talk of another prisoner exchange. Our passport photos were taken as the scuttlebutt increased. Finally, the consul said we were still classified as "military civilians" and would not go. Only three of us: Oscar Lopes (son of a Guatemalan diplomat) Reverend Johnson (a Canadian missionary), and Mr. Conger, (a repulsive American businessman), all noncontroversial individuals in the eyes of the Japanese, were notified they were qualified to leave on the boat.

The Reverend Johnson agreed to get a message to my mother and tell her about our situation. We worked out a secret code to get word back to me. For the word "grasshoppers" I would read Jap planes, for the "lower forty" the South Pacific, "crops" food, and "babies" victories. He'd write to me as soon as possible.

On September 9, 1943, Italy surrendered. That night Mr.

Sakamoto asked us to be calm and dignified in our natural joy over the news. He added that it was a blow to Japan and her allies but for our own welfare we should subdue our feelings and not mock the concerned citizens. It was a sensible request but a hard one to comply with. Back in our rooms, we stomped and screamed with delight.

The papers announced an attack in the South Pacific on a hospital ship, the Argentina Maru, the very ship that brought us to Japan from Guam a long time ago.

On September 12, the three men being exchanged left for Yokohama to board the Teia Maru for Goa, India, where they would board the Gripsholm for America. We sang "For he's a jolly good fellow" as they passed down the street. Some of those left behind had moist eyes and quivering lips. I blinked a few times in silence. The ship sailed on September 14 without us. Again we were doomed to stay behind.

To fill the vacancies created by the departure of the lucky re- patriates, three men from the Butterfield house were transferred to our camp. Art Smith, a likable contractor, Al Hammelef, PanAm's hotel manager, and Max Brodofsky, PanAm's chief mechanic, were reunited with our group. They had tall tales to tell about their camp life at Butterfields. The older group had their differences and friction was rampant.

Max immediately made himself at home. Somewhere in the place, he found the remnants of an old forge. Being a man of ac- tion, he stoked the fire pit with coal dust and charcoal. With the fan driven bellows feeding the flame, he made metal parts for trunks, broken beds, door hinges and stoves. He was a whirling dervish with the flame, tongs, hammer, and anvil.

Max, with his flaming forge and Mr. Peacock with his carpen- try tools made quite a pair. Midst sawdust and showering sparks, they'd chatter and gab, hammer iron and saw wood under the rear overhang by the hour. Mr. Peacock made me a footlocker for my private stuff and Max added an extension to my short bed so I could sleep more comfortably. Max persuaded Father Xavier to turn the blower by offering to fix the padre's broken bedstead. I've never seen Max happier during his stay in Japan.

With a large needle from Mrs. Hatter, I converted my hammock into a duffel bag. A sturdy canvas strap allowed me to carry the loaded bag over my shoulder. I was now mobile in case of an emergency. I still have it as a memento.

Earthquakes were common averaging about one a month. One day we felt a sharp jolt of a quake, about four on the Richter scale. In addition, a typhoon swept through the southern Japan islands, leaving flattened houses in its wake. Except for our fence and a few flying roofs, Kobe suffered little damage.

We Americans were asked if we'd care to go to a South Pacific island to assist the Japanese in establishing improved technical services. We were offered special food and accommodations plus other enticements if we volunteered. We shuddered at the thought and quickly but firmly declined. We reported this offer to the Swiss consul. The Japs made no further effort to recruit us.

I was reelected to the camp committee as leader of the Guam group. There was much to be done. Air raid squads were reorganized and practices held. Work parties for cleanup, furnace tending, and general maintenance groups were arranged.

Jimmy Ambrose, of limerick fame, was again in charge of the bath and shower schedules. He'd stoke the fire to heat the water on bath days and yell out for the next guy up. He even entertained us with his stories comparing the endowment of various guys.

Bob Vaughn confided in me that he'd like to piss in the Skull's bath some day. I agreed to cooperate in the plot. We sauntered into the bathroom when Jimmy was drawing the Skull's bath. Jimmy suddenly said he had an errand to finish and walked out, leaving Bob and me alone.

Bob whispered, "Now's my chance to piss in the bastard's bath. You watch the door."

He ran to the steaming tub and proceeded to let go. The golden stream arched like a rainbow and splattered into the hot water.

"Here's a present from Hirohito with love." he laughed. Finished, he proudly buttoned up and strode triumphantly away. "Take that you bastard. I hope you get the crawlin' crud," Bob said gleefully.

Jimmy returned and wondered what we were laughing at. He never found out and, thankfully, neither did the Skull. But every time we passed the Skull in the hallway Bob would whisper, "You know, that bastard smells funny, kinda like a pisspot."

Bob was prouder of that act than anything else he did during internment. After fifty-five years, he still brags about it.

By late summer, all our heating stoves had been confiscated for the war effort. We refused to haul the stoves to the collection point claiming our right to resist the Japanese war effort. The guards screamed and threatened, but we stuck to our principles. The kencho took little notice and hushed it up.

On November 5, the British crowd warwhooped with glee.

"What's going on?" I asked.

"It's Guy Fawkes Day fellah" answered Stan Pardon

"Who in hell is Guy Fawkes?"

"He's the brave fellow who tried to blow up Parliament way back when. We think that was a good idea, so he's one of our heroes. Blowing up Parliament should be an annual affair. Have a drink of sake. In fact, have two." He hiccuped.

We found the local papers accurate on international news and on the war in Europe. But their reporting of the war in the Pacific was grossly distorted. In the battle of Bougainville on November 10, for instance, the Japs gave our losses as four battleships, one aircraft carrier, and four heavy cruisers, one light cruiser, four destroyers, four medium transports, and one small transport for a total of twenty-four warcraft and transports. On the second battle of Bougainville, November 18, we reportedly lost three more aircraft carriers, and three cruisers while Japan's losses were only five planes yet to return.

On December 7 the papers carried a box score for eleven air battles over Bougainville and the Gilberts from October 27 to December 3. Our losses were twenty-two aircraft carriers sunk and eleven damaged, four battleships sunk and three damaged, twenty-seven cruisers sunk and twenty eight damaged, ten destroyers sunk and five damaged, thirteen transports sunk and eleven damaged, and eight hundred twenty-six planes shot down. Their losses, in small print, were two destroyers lost, two cruisers damaged and one hundred sixty-five planes yet to return.

The approach of Christmas 1943, was accompanied by rumors of Red Cross supplies coming to Kobe from the exchange ships. On December 23 the supplies arrived—bundles of real woolen clothes, shoes, overcoats, shirts and fatigue uniforms topped off with one food kit apiece. The distribution was made that night. We donned everything including the overcoats and paraded around with an American cigarette in one hand and a chocolate bar in the other. The next day, we received a telegram from the Red Cross and one from General George C. Marshall wishing us well. Extra chow and spam was the best meal we had from then until our rescue.

CHAPTER 25

Winter of 1943-1944

The cold winds of January 1944 ushered in the worst winter Japan had experienced in decades. Our rations hit bottom along with the temperatures. With the stoves gone, we had no heat. Our diet was ten ounces of bread and two spoonfuls of rice a day. Fish, that staple of the Japanese diet, became ever scarcer as American submarines kept vessels from venturing out to the fishing grounds. With temperatures below freezing, some men lay in bed and shivered themselves to sleep. Others bitched about the goddamn "slopeheads". From the window near my bunk I watched the cold rain splattering off the tile roofs outside the compound. My view swept further to the military airfield filled with fighter planes looking like grounded ducks with ice water dripping from their feathers. At a greater distance, beneath the scudding clouds, lay the waterfront and the lapping shores of the Inland Sea. Sometimes I'd stare quietly at this depressing scene, seeing nothing, feeling nothing. Like Neil Campbell, long ago on the deck of the Argentina Maru, I began to think of other things and the change of focus brought a perverse form of happiness.

As luck would have it, I was felled by a violent case of food poisoning. I heaved till my guts ached and the diarrhea sapped my strength. I shivered in the dank, frigid room and stumbled down the stairs to the benjo. With no medicines, I fought this curse for two miserable weeks, losing ten valuable pounds during the siege. Finally I began taking nourishment and the world seemed slightly brighter again.

Renewed, I went through the motions of normalcy. With a sigh of relief and a touch of pride, I finished the *Decline of the West* and waded into Tolstoy's *War and Peace*. I played bridge in my overcoat and hoped to be dummy so I could stand up and beat my arms to stay warm. The locals, as members of the pre-war leisured class, had perfected their bridge game and were willing teachers. We played every day, sometimes eight hours at a stretch. Ely Culbertson, my enfeebled brain, and the worn decks got a salutary workout.

One day, I dealt thirteen hearts to my partner, George Conklin. It was puzzling to see his reaction when he unfolded his hand. A cautious player, he counted and recounted his cards to make sure he had a full hand of hearts without a diamond hidden amongst them. As in case like this, a cinch hand, we bid in stages so our opponents would double so we could redouble. He played the hand—a grand slam bid of seven hearts, double-redoubled, and vulnerable. We were shocked when we saw George's hand. Having witnessed the shuffle and the cut, we knew things were on the up-and-up. They say the odds on such a hand are in the area of eighty-seven million to one. If we had done this in a legitimate tournament, Culbertson would have given us a $500.00 prize. As it was, we never received even a lousy yen.

In the course of this winter, Father Spa—a bright, effusive Belgian padre—singled me out as a possible convert to Catholicism, a prime soul worth saving. As we walked around the yard, he carefully spun his web by tactfully asking questions about God, the universe, and humanity. I was curious to learn what Catholicism was all about although not seeking to replace the confused faith I already had. He invited me to his room for an intense converting session on his all-consuming subject, Catholicism. It was interesting to see him defending his dogma. He was well prepared, a professional. But every time I asked him a controversial question, he'd refer to the importance of "faith." After several weeks of give and take, I thanked him for his concerns over my soul's welfare but politely declined his invitations to join his journey to heaven. He was a good sport and dropped the subject. To his credit we remained friends.

While this was going on, Slim Huston, Carl West, George Blackett and Max were busy modifying the stovepipe of the bath stove to entrap the heat going up the chimney. They had come up with the idea of inserting tin baffles in alternate positions in the smokestack to force the heated air to curl around these obstructions. Since the stovepipe rose from the basement through the third floor to the roof enough heat could be collected en route to warm every floor a little—enough, at least to temper the chill. With pliers, tin snips, hammers, and elbow grease, they labored like soot-covered beavers for a week to finish the job. The hot stovepipe was a success—we had one of the warmest abodes in Kobe.

A few letters from home lightened the misery of that wretched winter. The folks were fine and all was well in Idaho. The very sight of my mother's handwriting moved me. I read her letters daily and hid them under my pillow. The Japs were good about mail deliver—they took only twelve months to deliver the letters from Tokyo.

One of my letters was from Reverend Johnson. "The grasshoppers in the lower forty are leaving fast," he wrote. Soon there will be none left. It should be a good summer and next year will be even better. Lots of new babies are being born and the family is happy. Your mother is fine. Don't worry. Signed: Your Uncle Johnson." Good news, indeed, from a nice guy.

The papers stated that America was trying to get food to us through Vladivostok but the Nips refused to accept it because of the Tule Lake incidents and the bombing of the Argentina Maru. The miserable little bastards.

The agony of that winter finally passed and spring reluctantly allowed the birds to sing and the flowers bloom. But we paid a price for that winter. Three internees in the Butterfield house died from old age and broken hearts. Mr. Hickman, a frail seventy-year-old local, passed on. Mr. Griffiths, age sixty-two, died of a heart attack. Mr. Wickman, a thirty-year-old contractor at Marks, died from a gall bladder operation. Their food supplies were raffled off – a ghoulish procedure but a practical necessity.

The best news was that Matsuda-san, the "Skull," was drafted into military service. We waved a tearless farewell to the miserable bastard with the hope he'd get his ass shot off by an American sniper.

Our favorite guard, Sakamoto-san, was a real gentleman, kind and understanding. He prided himself in his knowledge of American history proudly brought us a long, rolled parchment containing his version of the life of his hero, Abraham Lincoln. The entire scroll was a work of art. He could recite the Gettysburg address in almost perfect English. When he was drafted, we bade him a sad farewell. They say familiarity breeds contempt but it can also eliminate prejudice and hatred. The "Skull" exemplified one and Sakamoto the other.

In May, we jumped for joy to read that America would be allowed to send one thousand tons of food, clothing, and letters to Japan via Vladivostok. With their own people suffering from hunger, would the Japs allow this food to reach us?

Cliff Price, a considerate, intelligent guy, fell in alongside me as I circled the yard. A thoughtful and pleasant conversationalist, he was theorizing about the war in the Pacific. He surmised that status of independence that Japan was giving to conquered countries formerly under the yolk of Great Britain and America (like the Philippines, Singapore, Hong Kong and Guam) would have a lasting effect on the future of East Asia.

"These people will have tasted the joy of independence," he predicted, "phony as it is under the circumstances, and will yearn for it after the war—with the help of firebrands yelling slogans, communists stirring the pot, and nationalists wanting their place in the sun. I think colonialism is dead. Even India will be affected. We can laugh all we want about these fake figureheads and Japanese puppets that now parade in full dress before captive audiences but the seeds they plant will sprout revolutions."

"So the Greater East Asia Co-Prosperity Sphere will come about after all," I mused. "And Japan, even though defeated, will have made its mark? But Japan's aim is simply to kill European colonialism and replace it with a colonialism of its own."

"Yes, in a way, but Japan's role will be diminished, I hope, because Japan is not a good ruler or leader and therefore not qualified to inherit the earth."

I've often thought of his prophecies since that day and how right he was in those predictions.

On another day, I caught up with Blyth on his walk around the yard. I wanted to talk to him about a matter of great importance to me.

"Over the past year," I admitted to him, "a subtle change has taken place in my thinking. I feel as if the past has diminished like an object viewed through the wrong end of a telescope."

"That's only to be expected," Blyth replied. "The same thing has happened to me, to everyone who has allowed this situation to work its wonders. If we dwell only on the past or pine endlessly for the future, we are going to miss the present, the best part of living." Blyth replied.

I continued my train of thought. "Then it's best to live in the present, make short range plans that can be filled and controlled by immediate attention."

"Exactly! You, of all the people in camp, are on the right track. You can't do anything about the past, so why dwell on it at the expense of the present? The best thing you can do about the future is to prepare for it by studying, making friends, protecting your health, developing skills, and keeping your sense of humor. In fact, a sense of humor may be the one thing that will pull us through. If we can see the nonsensical actions of the guards instead of their reckless stupidity, we can cope with the ridiculous without growing ulcers."

I agreed wholeheartedly. "I have already started on that road, I assured him. "I vowed long ago to make this a learning experience. I hope to come out of this a better man than I was when I came in."

"Now you're talking. Thinking in this fashion is a natural transition. It has nothing to do with loyalty, patriotism, weakness or vacillation. On the contrary, it shows maturity, strength and a proper sense of values. Besides, whose business is it but yours? You've got the right and obligation to be at peace with yourself and live with a peace of mind."

Blyth was a cooling towel to a fevered brow. He was a saint disguised in a black sweater with straw zoris flapping on his feet. I asked him to tell me more about the Buddhist precepts. His reply, as usual, was clear and simple.

"It is the aim of Buddhists to make themselves as small and inconspicuous as possible. This can be accomplished only by controlling the ego and all its frailties: selfishness, domination, arrogance, conceit, and pomposity. The concept calls for humility, gentleness, mildness, balance, self control and love."

"And this helps you deal with confinement?" I asked him.

"I take one day at a time. I concentrate on the present. I never think of food nor do I envy those who have more than I. I don't hate our jailer, for they are just as confined as we. I try to make the most of every minute by concentration and writing my book. I'm oblivious to my environment."

The strength and sincerity of his faith were evident but I was not yet ready to completely convert to Zen.

Our endless appeals to the Swiss Consul to have us moved to a safer place out of the city, finally paid off. In May 1944 we were told to pack our stuff. Our efforts were bearing fruit. We were leaving the city for the countryside. This move saved our lives.

CHAPTER 26

Move to Futatabi

On May 13,1944, we were preparing for the big move to a new camp somewhere outside of Kobe. I filled my footlocker with a Red Cross food kit, my sufu "jumpsuit", ragged pants, and overcoat. My duffel held my shirt, shorts, zoris, clogs, barber kit, knife, fork, mug, toothbrush and razor. Then that classic military maneuver, hurry up and wait.

Five days later, we learned our destination was a former school for wayward children in a canyon at the foot of Mt. Futatabi, five miles north of town. The disorderly kids had to move out before we could move in—thus the delay. The Japs were consolidating the three civilian camps in Kobe, about 225 internees, into this campus in the mountains. We were happy to be reuniting with our old Guamanian cohorts. Now all civilian internees, especially our friends, would be together and relatively safe in the mountains. After all, Kobe was a prime military target, and bombed civilians might be revengeful toward us.

The new camp was three miles as the crow flies but five miles by road from our present site beyond the outskirts of the city. Coordination between the Kobe camps was necessary. Two men from each camp formed a committee to design a layout of the new camp and make room assignments to avoid arguments and keep compatible groups together. All the work of readying the camp, moving personal belongings, repairing bridges, and clearing the road rested in the hands of the internees. The Japs could furnish only sputtering trucks and churlish screaming guards.

On May 23, 1944, we began the move to Futatabi. A light, intermittent rain cast an annoying pall on the whole operation. Three trucks arrived early, accompanied by thirty guards. Every able-bodied man began emptying the rooms and stacking the tagged contents near the exits. The youngest and strongest loaded the trucks. The older men fussed around and took frequent rest breaks.

The new camp was accessible only by a mountain trail leading from the road over a steep ridge into the campsite a half mile beyond. This meant unloading the trucks at the trailhead and carrying beds, boxes, suitcases, and bundles over the trail to the camp. Forty of the strongest internees with sturdy backs were stationed at the unloading spot to act as pack mules. Grunting, laughing, and cursing, these two-legged beasts of burden staggered back and forth over that narrow trail for three days with teetering loads, until every item from all three camps was piled ceiling high in a hopeless clutter in the preassigned rooms. The overflow was heaped in the front yard for later pickup by the owners. After a bowl of cold rice soup and a stale biscuit at nightfall, the packers collapsed and slept in the hallways and corridors of the new buildings.

My job was to coordinate the loading of the trucks at the Canadian Academy. It took ten trips to empty our camp alone. We loaded our bunks last so we had a place to sleep every night during the move. We were given a bowl of rice gruel and a biscuit twice a day, more than we expected. Fred Oppenborn sat on top of the last truckload with his two hens safe inside the wire cage on his lap and a satisfied look on his hairy face.

We slept in the halls and doorways the first night and took stock of the situation the next morning. The belongings scattered on the yard had to be sorted and moved into the buildings and then to the 8 ft. x 14 ft. rooms, six men to a room. Thankfully, the advanced assignments prevented mayhem between parties fighting for position and space. Tired guys, yelling for right-of-way, staggered down hallways with arm loads of paraphernalia spilling on the floor from ripped sacks and overstuffed pillowcases. The scene resembled a rocky beach with a bunch of sea lions roaring and scrambling for mating space.

East end of Futatabi Camp. My room is 2nd floor between the trees. Photo by Jack Taylor upon liberation, 1945.

On the positive side we were meeting and greeting old friends from the Marx house and Butterfields, our noisy recognition's adding to the general hubbub. Eventually, we sorted ourselves out and took a good look at Camp Futatabi, our new home-away-from-home.

Three large semi-attached, tile roofed buildings of unpainted wood snaked through a narrow canyon. The biggest, easternmost structure was a large two storied dormitory with small rooms leading off a hallway; at the farthest end were two huge barracks-like rooms holding twenty two men each. The middle building housed a dining room and a small kitchen. The building on the western end was a dormitory with a series of small sleeping rooms connected to a central hall; the older Butterfields crowd was domiciled here. A few smaller detached structures completed our new layout. Somehow, we all shoe-horned ourselves into this sparse encampment that was to be our home for the rest of the war.

In general, we were pleased with the set up. At least we were out of the ugly city and into the safety of the mountains. Surrounded by forested hills, the location offered the novelty of fresh air, quiet, privacy and even beauty. Crowded but relatively comfortable, we had beds, showers, a benjo in each building. We had the amenities of a porch, a loud-speaker system, a piano in the dining room. We also had six surly guards constantly on duty.

My room was on the second floor on the south side of the main building. Eight foot ceilings separated the room from a pitched roof attic. Wood and paper sliding doors controlled air circulation and gave a modicum of privacy. All but one of my roommates were part of the PanAm group. Fred Oppenborn took the bunk, on the inside corner along the wall stroked his beard and announced sagely, "The more I see of gentlemen, the better I like my dog." Ev Penning, Dick Arvidson, Grant Wells and I, squeezed ourselves into available space. Hal Brinkerhoff, a stocky federal employee, shoved his bunk into a wide closet.

Our main irritation was the proximity of the benjo across the hall. This classy oriental latrine attached at right angles to the building was ten by twenty feet in area and two stories high.. Slots in the upper floor allowed the squatting user to aim for the giant pots below. The urinal trough along the wall emptied into these same pots, resulting in a huge volatile liquefying reaction giving off quantities of methane gas. A coolie with his honeybucket emptied the pots twice a week. Sometimes, the odor was blinding. The stench permeated the building, especially our end. Only an occasional breeze cleared the air.

A chronic water shortage plagued the camp. Shallow wells and a dinky lake supplied a minimum amount of this precious liquid and polluted sources required the drinking water be boiled. Between rainstorms, we rationed the supply. Sometimes one shower a week was allowed. At other times two a month was a luxury.

My room in Futatabi. My bed in the foreground

On exploration, we discovered a tunnel through the nearest ridge to the southwest leading to a narrow canyon terraced for garden crops. Within this handy plottage, we were encouraged to grow our own vegetables! As a side benefit, we used the tunnel as a bomb shelter.

From our canyon, a well worn trail led to the city about three miles to the south. This trail, soon became a clandestine route for black marketers, a select bunch of gutsy entrepreneurs from the Marx house who had made their contacts earlier by bribing their guards in Kobe. Once they got the lay of the land, these "feathermerchants" did a brisk and profitable business after dark.

The bumpy, winding road running at a slightly different angle, was two miles longer than the trail and passable by carts and small vehicles. We soon learned the kencho could not deliver food to the camp, as their charcoal-burning, three-wheeled motorcycles and small trucks couldn't navigate the steep, rocky hill. We'd had to find a way to deliver it ourselves or go without.

"Bread Trips" became a scheduled daily routine. Twelve-man teams guided a two-wheeled cart down the five mile road to the food center at the outskirts of Kobe then hauled the supplies— bread, rice, seaweed, whale blubber, seaslugs, rotten fish and a few vegetables—back up to the camp. Two long ropes, one on each side, were tied to the front of the cart. Four men on each rope pulled while four men pushed. The ten mile round trip took all day. Each man got an extra biscuit for his efforts. If the weather was good these trips were actually enjoyable. Besides the camaraderie, we were able to see a bit of big city activity, pick up gossip, and look at pretty girls.

Girls! They had become a foreign species in our isolated lives, a pleasant memory from a distant past, a romantic dream of bygone years. Our normal sexual urges had been sublimated through lack of contact, starvation, and the constant effort to survive. So "girl watching," though a scant benefit, was better than nothing. What a pity, spending the most highly-charged years of my life in a Japanese prison camp with a bunch of ugly guys only dreaming of freedom instead of practicing romance. However, things could be worse. The guys could be uglier.

CHAPTER 27

Japanese Propaganda

We were still getting Japanese and English language newspapers. We read them avidly. Though a few days late, they were our only contact with the outside world. Having been lifted from various wire services, we eventually found the European news surprisingly accurate.

Japanese versions of the Pacific theater were fictional and highly distorted. Battle locations gave us a geographical picture of the course of the war by divulging Japan's defeats, retreats and strategic withdrawals. High flown praises were endlessly repeated, every soldier was valiant, every battle a victory. Fantastic cases of heroism would appear, such as "a soldier gnashing his teeth in anger, bringing down a P-38 with a rice ball." Another time, "the spirit of the dead pilot flew the plane 250 miles back to the base." They sank our entire navy at least seven times and shot down 90,000 American planes. Ten battleships were sunk in a single battle by the numerically inferior Nippon units. When the American navy appeared after a defeat, credit for the renewed attack was given to American production. Whenever the U.S. captured an island the Japs "died valiantly, welded together into an iron ball of determination against 100-1 odds." They called on their people to "heighten their indignation", "renew their determination", to "smite the foe to the finish", and "kill the beastly Americans."

Whenever a Nip soldier died during an important mission, he was made into a "warrior-God" and posthumously decorated. "So and so, Sakamoto-san at so base on so day tore the belly-plates off of a North Carolina class battleship with a stick of dynamite between his teeth", etc. The paper was full of warrior-Gods. The greatest warrior-God of all was still a guy by the name of Kato, who had destroyed a hundred enemy planes over the South Pacific.

For Nippon's brilliant victories, it was reported that the Prime Minister was given a basket of fish by his Majesty, the Emperor. The Japs never spoke the name of the Emperor, to have done so would have been sacrilege. He was "His Majesty" at all times. "His Majesty was concerned about this or "His Majesty was pleased about that", or "His Majesty deigned to give permission for the diet to convene and discuss certain subjects."

Pictures of bustling factories, "somewhere in the co-prosperity sphere" would appear in the paper, also "a flight of bombers on their way to strike terror into the enemy" made the news daily. "The Japanese sacrificed armor, armament, speed, and maneuverability in their planes for fighting power."

When Tojo called upon his scientists to invent some method of repelling enemy attacks, some of the brainier suggestions were: to build giant air-pockets around Japan to swallow the planes; to cover the cities with transparent domes of glass; to build invisible noiseless airplanes with which to pounce on the enemy.

To show the superiority of Japanese science, one article told of a certain Jap who had spent twenty years experimenting with different types of sand throughout the world and had come to the startling conclusion that an engine will wear out faster with sand in the crankcase than it will without sand in the crankcase. It was a Jap who invented the airplane.

In this spring of 1944, the papers divulged the war in Europe had turned in favor of the Allies. Germany, its reputation of invincibility smashed, was retreating on all fronts. In the five years of fighting, the Allies had figured out how to take a page from Germany's military book and to master the art of modern warfare. Now, over-extended in the east and bled white by Russian winters and the Stalingrad debacle, Germany was retreating like Napoleon had a 132 years earlier. A rearmed America was fighting briskly on two fronts while simultaneously rearming their allies despite the German blockade. A second front in Europe was expected momentarily and a massive military force was rumored to be poised in England ready to cross the channel.

By following the battle places in the papers, Japan, too, was on the retreat. Apparently, American forces were island-hopping from Guadalcanal up the South Pacific archipelagoes, leaving thousands of stranded Jap troops to starve and rot in the jungles. After Midway and other battles, the Japanese navy was badly crippled. Its airforce was outnumbered, outgunned and plane production slow for want of raw materials. Our pilots were better trained and as brave as the *kamikazes*.

Certain signs of impending defeat did reach us. Food and supplies were short. Stores were empty, clothing patched, medicines low, weeds and grasses supplementing vegetables in depleting rice bowls. More subtly a portentous mood filled the air. To boost morale, local papers shouted about phony victories, lauded heroes and blessed the Emperor. The government screamed, "We will defend our homeland unto death!"

This Nipponese bravado did not fall on deaf ears. It worried the hell out of us. We could only guess how the end would be played out. If invaded, would Japan commit suicide and kill us in the process? Would we be killed by an errant bomb? Would an angered populace storm our camp with scythes and machetes? The subject was constantly debated among us with no conclusions.

We had wasted little time in electing camp leaders. Art Woodruff and Bill Falvey shared the leadership with skill. I was elected one of the three committeemen to assist them and to represent a faction including the PanAm group. We spent many hours organizing work parties, negotiating with the commandant, pleading with the Swiss Consul, and dispensing information to the internees.

Our immediate situation was relatively safe. We were hidden in a canyon, out of target range of aerial attack. We were a minute cell of harmless, helpless, and forgotten by-products of a raging war that seemed a million miles away. Maybe our unobtrusiveness would be our salvation. Our guards were minor cops doing their duty. We did not fear them despite the long swords dangling from their belts—they were part of the landscape. Our world had shrunk to fit within these canyon walls. Food, shelter and safety were our main concerns.

Within these narrow parameters, our lives continued, with as much variety we could find or invent. A table in the dining room was constantly filled with crafty poker players, eyeing each other suspiciously. Another two tables were taken with bridge players engrossed in overbid hands. In the corner, a slow chess game was in progress, with cobwebs forming on the pieces between moves. The exercise yard was always busy. Getting their daily constitutionals were many pairs of amiable friends engrossed in serious talk; others spun tired yarns to wearied listeners; some lone individuals remained lost in their own thoughts.

Barbering satisfied my need for diversion. I had cut over 1500 heads by now, all custom-styled. I turned out everything from Hollywood trims to second-front bobs. Two other guys, one from the Marx house and one from Butterfields, had taken up this tedious but honorable trade. We each had our own clientele. We traded hair cuts; they cut my hair when I began looking like a cave-man. I tried growing a beard until my reflection scared me half to death.

The Marx gang had, early on, mastered the art of elevating beds. By stilting them on four foot bamboo poles lashed to the bed legs, the men could live in the newly created space underneath. The idea spread through camp and put a premium on bamboo which had to be purchased on bread trips.

Bamboo, in fact, became one of the most useful items in camp. Pollution required all drinking water to be boiled, and fuel was scarce. Whoever said "Necessity is the mother of invention" must have been an internee.

So a couple of ingenious guys invented a hot water heater. They cut a four-inch piece off the end of a bamboo pole. A wire coil was made by curling a stripped copper wire (stolen from the attic or a dead outlet) around a pencil-thin stick. This coil was then wrapped around the piece of bamboo and connected to an electrical outlet. Completely immersed in a pot of water and plugged in, this gizmo could bring a small pot of water to a boil in two minutes. Thus, was the "Stinger" conceived and born. Hidden from the Japs, stingers became standard equipment in every building. Pots of tea and Kobe trash bubbled in every room and diarrhea virtually disappeared.

Hot plates were made by using wet plaster of Paris poured into a round shallow container to harden. As the mixture set up, circular grooves were carved in the plaster base to resemble a hot plate. Again, a coil of purloined copper wire was laid in the grooves and attached to an electric lead. A metal frame steadied the fixture. Voila! A hot plate to fry eggs, boil rice, make stew. Some clever owners cut holes in the wall and hid their stoves between the studs. Some stoves were hinged to the cutout and could be quickly hidden if guards approached. Thanks to a system of lookouts, the naive Nips never detected a single appliance but often wondered why the smell of food and "trash" filled the air.

I was on a bread trip on June 7, 1944, a memorable day in WWII. We suspected something wrong by the averted eyes of people we passed. We'd picked up our load and two newspapers, one English and one Japanese. As we grunted up the hill, nothing much was said. At the rest stop, I glanced at the paper and let out a scream. "My God, the Allies have landed in France! The second front is on!" Everyone froze for a second before going wild.

As we trudged on, I read the article aloud to the happy crew. Atop the trail, we yelled the news in unison. Delirium hit the camp as the word spread. The guards, sullen and quiet, knew this was another nail in the Japanese coffin.

CHAPTER 28

Secret Radio

Through the papers, we followed the daily progress of Ike and his troops on the Second Front in Europe. It was a geography lesson to read such names as Caen, Brittany, Southhampton, St. Lo. I regretted being so far from the action in this momentous point in history. This war was passing me by as I sat on the sidelines helpless and frustrated, in the enemy camp. All I could do was root for America's victory and weaken the enemy's strength by eating all the food I could get and thus weaken the Japanese economy. I say this with "tongue in cheek," of course.

On the surface, the camp was peaceful and benign—an ideal cover for Fred Oppenborn, a summa cum loude graduate of the International School of Scroungers. A rare faculty inherent in only a few gifted men, scrounging requires large quantities of nerve, cunning and resourcefulness. A good scrounger needs the daring of a wolverine and the stealth of a leopard. A touch of kleptomania helps. His senses are sharpened to smell an opportunity any ordinary observer would overlook. The riskier the operation the bigger the challenge. The bigger the prize the bigger the thrill. We had a lot of good American scroungers in camp but Fred was one of the best.

Fred cased the storage building for days. Peeking through the dirty windows, he saw the place filled with exotic treasures. He salivated like a hungry dog in a meat house. Being noble and unselfish, he wanted his hands on the choicest valuables before some wanton, pilfering, no-good pirate beat him to them. He had learned long ago, it's best to shop early. It became his obsession to break in and garner his rightful share. He examined the locks, tested the hinges, and sniffed the air. And chose the night he'd make his move.

It was one of the greatest scrounging coups in "the history of the civilized globe" to quote Dick Arvidson. After midnight, Fred jimmied the lock with a crude iron bar and crept inside. With the eyes of a cat on a midnight prowl, he rummaged through the hoard. He was amazed at the tools, school supplies, tatami mats, stoves—all neatly stacked in place. His eyes fell on the most unexpected treasure of them all—a broken-down radio. He quickly snatched the dust-covered receiver, complete with tubes, earphones, dial, and wires. Quietly placing them in a sack and sealing the door, he crept back to his room. Stashing the loot under his bed, he crawled in and went happily to sleep. He'd been gone less than thirty minutes.

Being suspicious and cautious by nature, he waited before venturing to the next step. Now that he had acquired the essential components, he had time to cogitate, stroke his beard, and pick the brains of Dick Arvidson, our radio technician.

Secrecy in camp was paramount and secrecy was adrenaline to Fred's soul. He needed technical assistance from someone in his room he could trust. Dick was tailor-made for the job. They were the perfect pair—the scrounger and the technician. Their first problem was a tricky one: where could they repair the receiver and operate it in total secrecy—out of sight of the Japs and the known spies from the Canadian Academy slithering around in camp? Fred and Dick called a meeting of their roommates. We huddled in the corner like robbers planing a heist as Fred and Dick explained their dilemma. We decided, first of all, to keep knowledge of the receiver within the confines of our room, and shook hands to seal our vow of silence. Fred loved the furtiveness and conspiracy of this plot. But the time wasn't ripe; they needed more equipment.

Meanwhile, like busy little beavers ambitious artisans with makeshift tools and lots of ambition were stumbling over each other renovating the camp into a food factory and semi-retirement home. Doors and windows were repaired, plumbing fixed, showers built, water pumps refitted and electrical wiring pirated to fit outlets for stoves and stingers.

Slim Huston's legs were weary from pedaling the sewing machine. His teeth were sore from nipping thread. He was still producing shirts, jackets, and shorts from tattered clothing or moldy piece-goods from downtown. He kept his whistle wet and hands busy by having his borrowing cup filled with "Kobe trash." This prize mug could hold a half-quart—enough to last Slim an hour.

Max Brodofsky, without his forge, paced the floor like a caged lion. I cut hair, walked the yard and read the *Encyclopedia Britannica* for a pastime. I'd read twenty seven other books by this time. The older folks sat on their bunks or napped between laundry duties, benjo trips or gnawing on hard biscuits. Time and torment were taking their toll. Mr. Kopp, an American transplant in Kobe, died from a heart attack and the carbon-monoxide fumes of his hibachi.

Garden plots on the other end of the tunnel were allotted to those with farming instincts and green thumbs. A tiny spring furnished irrigation water. I only grew tomatoes and corn because of sanitation problems from night soil scattered by the guy with the honey bucket. These vegetables tasted like blessed fruits from the Garden of Eden.

July 21, 1944, was a big day in our pinched lives. We learned from the English paper that American forces had landed on Guam. We wondered if our Chamorran friends were still alive to celebrate that longed for invasion. Was our little bungalow standing in place on the hill and was the diesel engine still humming in the PanAm compound?

General Tojo, the pugnacious Prime Minister, resigned on the same day. Good riddance! This rapacious, predatory bastard had started the war. He'd failed to bring victory but still wanted to fight to the death. Calmer voices intervened. Voices of reason and peace, we hoped.

Saipan was invaded on June 15 and surrendered on July 9.

Nearby Tinian was attacked on July 24 and secured on July 31. Japan was now within range of large American bombers. Guam was secured on August 8 and Japan was suddenly a prime target for destruction. We rejoiced at the recapture of the Marianas and prayed for our Chamorran friends.

Coincidentally, the camp was blessed with an additional occupant the day Saipan fell. A light brown bundle of joy entered our lives in the form of a Dachshund puppy. We named him "Saipan." "Saipy" for short. Since everybody fed him scraps and scratched his ears, he belonged to the entire camp. His wagging tail wiggled into our hearts.

That same month, a siege of conjunctivitis (*pinkeye*) swept through the camp—highly contagious, through the use of common water faucets. I was blinded for a week. God bless Buddy Durham and his medical kit. He administered eyedrops and solace daily to all the victims. Finally, the scourge disappeared and we could see again.

The quantity and quality of food was declining rapidly. Small portions of rotten whale blubber, sea slugs, spoiled shrimp, rice gruel, kelp, benjo-burgers, fish heads, and boiled daikons (a type of radish) assaulted our nostrils and challenged our guts. A typical meal was two tablespoons of boiled onions and a small, inedible, rotten eel. Protests to the police fell on deaf ears. Even the Swiss Consul was helpless, so the black market business went into high gear.

Because no fence surrounded the camp, crafty packers with makeshift backpacks slipped out after evening tenko and hoofed it down the trail to rendezvous points on the outskirts of Kobe for pickups. All transactions were cash on the barrel head. Money for food was collected in advance by the capitalist who'd arranged the exchange. He'd place his orders and prepay for the next pickup. Suppliers charged extra for the risks involved and the entrepreneur would up his price for the same reason. The hungry customer took this double markup as a matter of course. Packers were paid in food so everyone got something, including payola to some of the guards.

Three or four of these illicit businessmen controlled the entire operation. Competition kept prices in line. Many yen came from the Swiss consul. Extra yen came from bartering clothing at the pickup point. An overcoat brought ¥1500 one week but inflation might increase its worth to ¥1800 a week later. Shoes ran from ¥500 to ¥800 depending on size and condition. IOUs were taken under strict usury agreements.

As questionable as it may seem, black marketing kept the camp alive. I bought rice occasionally and supplemented my diet from Red Cross items. Nevertheless, my belly shrank and my weight dropped to 130 pounds. I rattled when I walked.

Friction arose between the locals, whose wives brought food on weekly visits, and the Guamanians, who watched this procedure in helpless hunger. I realized it was hard for the locals to share their food fairly. I received an occasional gift of salted fish from Blyth, who was a vegetarian. When the next shipment of Red Cross packages arrived, the locals' share was reduced because of what their families had brought. Hot arguments ensued but the Guamanians held fast. My sympathies were with the locals, because their families had sacrificed their own meager rations to bring food to the camp. It would have been nice for the husbands in turn to share their packages with their families. Hunger can destroy good manners.

All the while, Fred and Dick were anxious to get going on their radio. Their plan was practical and sneaky. They intended making a sound proof room in the attic and needed our cooperation as lookouts. Fred scrounged some thick bamboo poles lying in the weeds. Cutting them in five foot lengths, he lashed them to the legs of his bed, stilt-like, and raised his bunk to within three feet of the ceiling—higher than other elevated beds. A cloth curtain, torn from a blanket, was tacked to the ceiling and hung around his bed for privacy. Since his bunk was in the corner his actions were easier to hide. An added benefit of this arrangement was the additional free space under his bedstead. He arranged his stuff within this tiny area where he could pursue his pastimes and hide his accumulated crap. He used a movable stool to get into his elevated bunk for a bamboo ladder permanently strapped to the bed might have alerted snoopy guards. As it was, he waited a week for the stupid guards to get used to the curtained bed. Knowing Fred was an eccentric, the Japs never commented on the drapery. We were ready for the next step.

Fred went back to the storage building and found a small Japanese pruning saw that cut only on the pulling motion. With the help of a knife he'd found in the storeroom, he sliced a hole in the ceiling behind his curtain big enough to insert the saw blade. With lookouts in strategic spots talking in loud voices to smother the sounds, Fred began sawing a hole large enough to slide a three-by-six-foot tatami mat into the attic. The cut-out slab could be slid back into place between broadcasts to hide any evidence of alteration.

Again he raided the storage place, now his private hardware store, for more mats. The additional mats made a light and sound-proof room in the attic. Pirating a ten-foot length of electrical cord and a bulb from a kitchen lamp, he tapped the line in the attic and lit up his studio. Except for the radio, he was in business.

With pliers, a knife, and ingenuity, Dick climbed into the attic studio, his so-called workshop, and began the tedious job of building a short-wave radio. With the skill of an artisan, he wrapped short-wave coils and twisted together electric connections to convert the standard receiver into a short-wave radio. Three weeks later, on October 14, 1944, Dick came down from the attic with a smile on his face. Finished, the receiver was a jumble of twisted wires resembling a tangled fishnet on a Portuguese trawler, but it worked.

Fred was the chief radio operator. After all, it was his bunk, his studio, and mostly his baby. Besides, this exclusive link to the outside gave him a feeling of importance. And believe it or not, that crude, bastardized electronic gadget with cheap, ill-fitting earphones could pick up Tokyo, Moscow, Berlin, London, New York and dear old San Francisco. It brought a world we had almost forgotten into our measly, stinking room and changed our miserable lives for the duration.

Fred's first scoop was the landing on Leyte, Philippine Islands on October 23, 1944. He soon learned broadcast schedules, eliminating the need for constant monitoring of the airways. The flood of news overwhelmed us. To get American battle reports from the front lines gave us a feeling of involvement in the war. London's and San Francisco's version differed markedly from Berlin's and Tokyo's. The Allies' renditions were more accurate and believable. Morale inside the room rose from the bottom of the pool to the ten meter springboard level. Keeping the secret from our other PanAm buddies troubled me. Since they were two of my special friends, I especially wanted Bob Vaughn and George Conklin to know. But a vow is a vow is a vow, as Gertrude Stein would say.

CHAPTER 29

Life at Futatabi

Time, internment, and isolation had altered our attitude since the church and Seaman's Mission. Then, at the beginning of internment, we were naive, innocent, amateurish, and scared. Now we were professionals at conniving, deception, scrounging, and stealing. We had learned to roll with this Kobe "Trash" living without self-pity. The guards and barbed wire were only part of the enemy. More insidious were boredom, monotony, rancor, and hunger. Our defensive arsenal consisted of hobbies, friends, projects, books, studies, and—perhaps the biggest weapon of all—a sense of humor. We learned to focus on the immediate, the imminent, the necessary. Memories of home, though never forgotten, were categorized and filed away for future reference. Self-analysis had a chance to bloom.

This change was good for me. Somewhat to my dismay, I got better acquainted with myself. I had learned something about my limitations, strengths, weaknesses, and tolerances. In three and a half years, I had grown from a wide-eyed kid into a groping adult. Internment, so far, had been a post-graduate course in psychology, adaptability, and survival. If I were a better man for the experience, then this stinking place was not a waste of time after all but an opportunity to say hello to myself and my future.

My teachers were hard-nosed and unforgiving: confinement, the Japs, hunger, pain, and 284 fellow inmates representing a cross section of humanity. Ages of these cohorts ranged from twenty seven to eighty. In addition to a few British and American Eurasians, there were a scattering of Canadians, French, English, Australian, Belgian, Dutch, Anzacs and Britons from Nagasaki, and over two hundred of my fellow countrymen. The Americans ranged from grammar school drop-outs to college graduates with master's degrees. I was stimulated by discussions with Christians, Jews, Buddhists, Shintoists, and atheists. Ancestries and cultures covered the map. Hitler would have regurgitated over the racial mixture.

Considering the diversity of the group, they got along surprisingly well. The one vital common element that permeated the camp was our communal predicament—imprisonment by the same enemy. An occasional fracas over some minor irritation was soon quelled. Many adopted a fatalistic attitude—a shrug of the shoulder towards the situation. *Shigataganai* as the Japanese would say. Everyone complied with the rules for it was a part of our new life.

The younger Americans were the most rambunctious. On the whole, I tip my hat to my fellow countrymen. They could be aggravating, irritating, arrogant, selfish, and downright miserable. They were also energetic, inventive, cooperative, amusing, individualistic and boisterous.

Sometimes their innocent meandering backfired. Take Ken Fraser for instance. A frantic call to nature started it all. Ken rushed to the benjo near our room, unbuttoning his pants on the way. He quickly squatted over the middle slot and settled down to do his business, lighted cigarette in hand. After a couple of draws on his smoke, he tossed it down the slot. When the glowing butt hit the explosive methane gas in the pot below, a muffled explosion shook the building. Since the huge pot was only half full, the exploding gas blew upward, geyser-like, taking the liquefied contents with it. Ken was completely drenched by this fountain of flowing excrement squirting through the slot. Caught with his pants down, as the saying goes. Confused, saturated from head to foot, he staggered into the hall, his dripping pants at half mast. We led him outside and turned the hose on him full-force. He kept asking, "What the hell happened?" It took two clothes washes and a long shower to make him socially acceptable. We posted a sign "No Smoking in the Benjo," closing the gate after the horse had left the barn, so to speak.

We had fun playing cat and mouse with the guards. Successful little tricks went a long way toward conquering boredom and achieving a bit of sly revenge. Black marketing was the most daring and beneficial conspiracy of all. Boiling water and cooking secretly was also satisfying. Our hidden radio was the ultimate deception of all. But not all plots had to be fruitful. One night, Dick and I pulled an innocent and pointless prank.

Dick had the habit of studying Spanish in bed before lights out. One night I got this brilliant idea. At least, I thought it was brilliant.

"Dick, I remember an old movie with Slim Sommerville. He went to the barbershop for a shave and fell asleep in the chair. His buddies, with the help of the barber, painted his glasses black and closed the side gaps with dark paper so he would be completely in the dark. When he awakened, he thought the sun had gone down. They gave him a flashlight and sent him home."

"Sounds like Slim Sommerville all right." Dick answered.

"Well, I've got an idea. Tonight when the guard comes for his usual bed check, pretend you are reading a book in the dark. When he turns on the light and sees you with a book in your hand he'll assume he's interrupting your reading, maybe. How's about it?"

Being a good sport, Dick agreed to try it for laughs. The rest of the guys thought it was a jolly good idea, which just shows the level of our morale.

When we heard the guard shuffling down the hall checking beds, I told Dick to get ready.

Switching on the light, the guard spotted Dick concentrating on his book. Dick turned to the guard with a look that said, "Turn out the light, stupid, so I can read."

Taken aback, the guard said "Oh, so sorry." and switched off the light. We sniggered ourselves to sleep.

Charley Craver, of the contractor gang, was an ex-showman

who had traveled the entertainment circuit in his younger days. He played a mean fiddle, sang country songs, told corny jokes, and danced funny little jigs. He was the best entertainer in camp.

He heard Fred Oppenborn futilely playing his fiddle and sweet-talked Fred into lending it to him for a hoe-down session. At full throttle, Charley was in his element, arm swinging, feet stomping, and fingers flying over the strings. *The Wabash Cannonball* and the *Virginia Reel* never sounded better. We'd stomp, war-whoop and clap in rhythm. Charley would go on for an hour reenacting his memories.

Until the night Charley made the mistake of playing *Marching through Georgia*. Fred blew his stack. Fred was an unreconstructed Southerner and no goddamyankee was going to play that tune on his fiddle. Seething, he yanked it from Charley and stomped away. It took three weeks of apologies and a can of Spam to get Fred to forgive him. After that Fred censored all the tunes that Charley played.

Jack Taylor, always busy at something, had been involved with the inventions of the stinger and the hot plate, and was a natural for the black market. He'd arranged a contact in Kobe through a local prisoner and was sneaking out after bed check twice a week. He'd arrange his bed with pillows and stuff to resemble a sleeping body, then leave for his rendezvous.

All went well until a wary guard caught on to his trick. Before Jack returned, the guard crawled into Jack's bed and lay still. About midnight Jack came in, unloaded his loot in the dark, undressed and climbed into bed. Yoiks! The sleeping guard let out a scream and Jack catapulted three feet into the air. Other guards, in on the plot, rushed in, flashlights in hand and swords at the ready. They had Jack red-handed. After a tongue lashing, he was off to the hoosegow in Kobe.

Twenty-nine days later, a subdued, flea-bitten Jack came limping back into camp, under guard. We greeted him as a hero but wouldn't let him in the building without a bath. We filled a tub on the lawn and added a disinfectant found in the storage shed.

He stripped naked and scrubbed down, smiling despite his grue-
some experience. Jack was a gutsy guy. He had to toss in his clothes
and scrub out the fleas. We were taking no chances.

He'd shared a crowded cell with ten dirty, ragged, stinking
convicts. For lack of space, the cellmates had to sleep on the floor
in shifts. Two rice balls and a radish, with a cup of water for dessert, completed the day's dining festivities. One clogged slot in
the floor served as a benjo. He was not allowed to stand up or talk
to anyone. He sat silently, Buddha-like, on the floor. He spoke
once and was clouted on the head with a kendo stick. Coming
back to camp, he nearly had to learn to walk again for his legs had
suffered partial paralysis from the constant squatting position. San
Quentin was a Riviera spa by comparison.

He learned the Jap's system of justice was to sentence a convict
to twenty-nine days in jail. If he were uncooperative, he'd be transferred to another jail for an additional twenty-nine days, then another, and so on, until he changed his attitude. Evidently, Jack
had quickly acquired the right perspective for he served only one
term.

It was fun to see Neil Campbell again. He was still expound-
ing on any subject relative or not. He'd capture a few innocent
victims and proceed to tell them about bootlegging during prohi-
bition, the Pendergast machine in Kansas City or gangster Al
Capone in Chicago.

Some guys were professional "sack artists". Enoch "Horse thief"
Lowe was the champion. He'd earned his moniker "Horse thief"
for being the veterinarian who took care of the Governor's horse on
Guam. Horse thief suffered from "Bunk Fatigue" by spending up
to twenty hours a day in bed especially in the winter time. As
Campbell said "Horse thief sleeps all right in the morning but
rolls and tosses in the afternoon." Lowe had a unique quality of
never getting mad at any unflattering remark. He was always happy
and smiling like Alfred E. Newman of "Me Worry?" fame.

CHAPTER 30

Mr. Higasa

On October 23, 1944, I heard my first American broadcast from the secret radio in the attic. With Dick and Penning as lookouts, Fred and I slid through the opening into the attic studio. There sat the jumbled receiver, our lifeline to the outside world. Fred checked me out on the technique of operating this precious instrument. With trembling hands, I clamped on the earphones and slowly spun the dial as I had the safe's dial in the airport office in Guam, years before during the bombing attack. The first voice I heard was that of Doris Day singing *A Sentimental Journey*. I nearly died with the thrill of hearing America singing. I fell in love with Doris that day. Lying on my stomach in a vermin infested attic in the middle of Japan, in the midst of the war, after three years of captivity, hearing that melodious voice from America singing was one of the most exhilarating moments in my life. Today, even after fifty-four years, I fall in love again when I hear sweet Doris sing that song.

I turned to a newscast, from San Francisco and was enlightened by America's version of the war. Her propaganda was subtle and convincing. America, the victor, could afford the truth. Japan, the loser, had to rely on pretense and ballyhoo. Japan' mind set was strange and unconvincing. America's slick and professional versions proved to be more accurate.

We six roommates had to be on the alert to keep ourselves from divulging the source of our news. An idle detail on a battle might raise an eyebrow of suspicion. Often, I classified the tip as an off-the-cuff opinion and quickly changed the subject. These faux pas taught us self-control as life in camp went on.

Internee Ed Maxim, the biggest black-market honcho of them all, was caught outside camp again—his fifth arrest. He explained to the police that he was going to town to see his girl friend. The police didn't buy his story so they threw him in jail. A month later, he returned in rough shape. Emaciated and filthy, he babbled nonsense and cackled idiotically. He had forgotten where he was and where he lived. Eventually, he recovered and continued his clandestine enterprise.

In November, Mr. Higasa became our new commandant. His arrival was one of the most auspicious events in our Kobe calamity. Educated in the University of Tokyo and a prominent member of the home police force, he was civilized, compassionate, understanding and fair-minded—a credit to his race and profession. He not only maintained the dignity of his office but was genuinely likable. He listened to our complaints and tried to solve our problems. He proved the fallacy of generalizing about races, creeds, or cultures. He earned the respect of everyone, and I shall always have a soft spot in my heart for Mr. Higasa.

He took inventory of equipment and supplies. One of his main concerns was heat. Three heating stoves and six hibachis—small, moveable, open-grilled, iron, fireboxes, commonly used in Japan for heating and cooking, were found in the storehouse.

Mr. Higasa asked for volunteers to set up one stove and two hibachis in each major building. We were short on stovepipe so he encouraged the mechanically talented to make additional pipe from cans and odd pieces of tin. Even though some felt it to be the captor's duty to furnish us with these niceties, most of us jumped at the chance to help ourselves.

He gave us permission to gather firewood for the coming winter. We went into the mountains, under guard, with saws, axes, and ropes, prepared to be our own Paul Bunyuns and carry the forest into the camp.

The wood trips were an exercise in exercise. We felled trees, trimmed branches, and sawed trunks into convenient lengths for two men to hoist on their shoulders and carry back to camp. Rewards for the volunteers were a hot bath and an extra ounce of bread. It was a mystery how we mustered the strength to do it, but we struggled into the mountains three times a week for three months.

Between trips, men proficient with carpenter saws, cut the logs into burnable lengths. Handy men with axes split the logs for the stoves.

Concurrently, Mr. Higasa let us make charcoal for the hibachis. Charcoal production was one of the highlights of our miserable winter. An elderly Japanese charcoal maker showed us how to make a kiln. First we dug a four-by-six-foot hole two feet deep abutting a clay bank. The excavation was bordered by a clay-mud wall three feet high and capped by an arched roof with four air vents. A large opening in the end allowed us to enter. The finished product resembled an igloo.

Intermittent rain never hindered our project. Following instructions, we cut, trimmed, and sectioned selected trees. Four-foot logs, about five inches in diameter were closely stacked on end till the kiln was full. The front opening was reduced in size to act as an air funnel. Burning branches were placed next to this small opening. The kiln, acting like a drafting stovepipe, sucked the flames inside, through the pilings, and out the ceiling vents. The heated sap turned into steam that hissed out the vents like a volcano. We'd spell each three-man team every four hours. The front fire was kept roaring until the wood was emptied of its moisture and resins. About forty hours later, as conditions dictated, the logs themselves ignited with a blast. The front entrance was quickly sealed and the roof vents adjusted to dampen the flames. At the proper time, depending on the height of the glow, the vents were closed, cutting off the oxygen supply to kill combustion. Only then, could the teams relax and get some sleep.

Twenty four hours later the kiln would have cooled enough that we could unseal the opening. The charcoal logs were hauled to camp in large woven baskets hanging on poles carried on the shoulders of two men. There, the logs were broken into small pieces for the hibachis and distributed by the camp committee. We made three batches of charcoal and cut four cords of wood that winter. Families of the locals brought extra hibachis which were distributed to the old and sick. Besides warmth, these little charcoal burning furnaces boiled gallons of Kobe Trash and countless cans of rice that winter. Finally, we had heat and hot water. And, thank God, just in time, for the temperatures soon dropped to zero.

Meanwhile, there was a first-class war going on and we were becoming involved. Air raid alarms became commonplace. The shout *Keikai Keiho Hattsurei* (enemy airplanes from the sea) signaled an alarm. Sirens punctuated the air with mournful wails; people dashed for cover and we watched the skies. Occasionally, we'd see single contrails at 30,000 feet; sometimes three or four crossing each other like a tic-tac-toe diagram. The radio told us they were B-29's from Guam flying overhead. We were amazed how the Americans had made the Marianas combat ready in such a short time.

Finally, we'd hear *Keikai Keiho Kaijo* (air raid over), and everyone returned to their business. Poker players upped the ante, bridge players reviewed the bidding, and "sack artists" went back to sleep.

A load of Red Cross kits and clothing came in from Vladivostok. The food was literally a life saver for the coming winter and we were happy to get underwear and socks from John L. Lewis, President of the CIO labor union. Pope Pius XII also contributed clothing on behalf of the Catholic church.

Christmas 1944 was welcomed with mixed emotions. There were no celebrations and little to eat. On the plus side, local air raid alarms gave us hope. Our radio gave disheartening news about the Battle of the Bulge. Germany was retreating on all fronts except in Belgium where they were pushing America back into France.

Food supplies dwindled. More men sought solace and warmth by retreating to their bunks after morning tenko. My farm-boy habits prevented me from returning to my bed. I stayed up and hovered near the closest hibachi between daily walks in the yard.

To enhance our diet, we decided to trap the sparrows that flitted around looking for food. Constructing a trap from a cardboard box and a figure-four Boy Scout tripping mechanism, we enticed the birds under the leaning box with rice and bread crumbs. A quick jerk on the trip cord resulted in a supply of fluttery feathered fowl. Dressed and fried, there was little to chew on but one good bite of bills, body and feet. A dozen of these little birdies made a fair addition to a biscuit and a spoonful of rice.

Some ravenous dolts began eyeing Saipy, our friendly Dachshund, with ulterior intentions and salivating jaws. But word went out that Saippy was off limits and if that dictum were ignored the culprits themselves would be turned on a spit like a roasted pig. Saipy survived for he was everyone's special friend.

Saipy was safe but two stray cats weren't so lucky. They had ventured into camp in search of mice which we had a plentiful supply. One cold day the cats mysteriously disappeared. Afterward, a couple of guys were seen picking their teeth and belching with satisfaction. Rumor had it that cooked cat was tough and stringy but satisfying.

Oppenborn protected his two chickens like a hovering hawk. He posted a sign warning "Death to Thieves". The code of honor not to steal from a fellow prisoner was firm and the chickens survived.

New Years day 1945 broke cold and wet. A bunch of us went around camp on a mission of spreading good cheer. Mr. De Angelo, a crusty, stocky Guamanian of sixty-five, was leaning against the barracks, hands in pockets and a sad look on his face.

He yelled, "Happy New Year, De Angelo."

He grumbled, "A Happy New Year, a kissa my ass." So much for good cheer.

To us, there were two distinct wars in the Pacific. The first one started on December 8, 1941 with the bombing of Guam and our capture two days later. There followed a three year lull wherein we slouched behind the silent walls, isolated, forgotten, hungry, and bewildered. Now, at last, in the spring of 1945, the second war was about to begin and it would envelope us in its monstrous fury.

Iwo Jima, after a fierce battle, was captured on February 23. Our forces were getting closer to Japan. Manila was occupied on March 3. General MacArthur had returned. Okinawa was next. These islands were stepping stones to victory in the Pacific. On March 17, 330 B-29's from the Marianas hit Kobe a devastating blow. And we had ringside seats.

CHAPTER 31

Kobe Bombing

"*Keikai Keiho Hattsurei! Keikai Keiho Hattsurei!*"

The air-raid warden's screams, which warned of enemy planes from the sea, cut through the chilly night air. Off to the south, behind the canyon's edge, a lone air-raid siren crescendoed from a groan into a wavering, high-pitched whine. Like a pack of wolves, other sirens joined in and began to howl. Their mournful wails intensified, echoing off the nearby mountains before bouncing back adding to the chorus. Searchlights waved back and forth in a crazy dance through the night sky over Kobe. The date was March 17, 1945, St. Patrick's Day. It was 2:20 a.m.—a helluva time to hold an air raid.

Nearly three years earlier our prison camp had witnessed an American attack when a Doolittle raider swept low over our former camp near the Kobe waterfront on April 18, 1942. The sight of an American warplane had brought a fleeting sense of elation, and we watched as the B-25 swooped in seemingly from out of nowhere. The attack lasted only 10 seconds. The closest any action had come to us since then was the small raid a month ago.

After nearly three years, Allied planes returned on February 4, confining their target to the waterfront and sparing the city itself. We knew from our hidden radio that twenty miles to the east, Osaka, an industrial city about the size of Chicago, had been pounded several times. Most of Tokyo was flattened, and Yokohama lay in ashes. We began placing bets on the due date for Kobe, watching the skies and waiting. Now the waiting was over, and it suddenly didn't matter who won the bet.

"Here we go again," I muttered to no one in particular as I groped in the dark for my socks. Outside, the cool air and heavy cloud cover forecast a coming storm. This alert was the second of the night. A lone B-29 scout plane ducking under the overcast, flew the length of the city, and disappeared untouched. The sirens died, and everyone went back to sleep. Two hours later, another lone bomber, approaching from the east, dropped a trail of parachute flares that seemed to hang from the clouds like a string of suspended light bulbs. Suddenly, the sleeping city became a massive, glowing arena—a waiting, exposed target.

"This could be it," said Dick, "Hold on to your hats." The night air was filled with the sleepy grunts of other inmates who were now milling about the barracks in the dark. We waited for the roll call. Apparently the guards had fled. From a balcony we watched as the flares and searchlights, their light show an accompaniment to the sad wails of the sirens. The seconds dragged by.

Then, through the din, came a barely audible rumble, increasing to the roar of a wild Kansas tornado pounding across the prairie. We looked skyward, straining to catch the first glimpse of this ghostly, winged armada.

"There's one, far to the left, just under the cloud cover. Gad, what a monster!" Dick yelled as the searchlights flickered off the sleek fuselage of the lead plane.

"They must be coming in over the Kii peninsula and banking to the right over the Inland Sea to cut across the narrow part of town," I said, calculating their course like a tactician. "They couldn't fly over Shikoku Island and take all that flak."

"Let's go up on the ridge for a better view," Grant, suggested. "The guards aren't watching, and it's only a hundred yards away. We can get back in time if there's a roll call."

The three of us bounded up the trail toward the ridge. From our new vantage point, we had a panoramic view of the blacked out city below and the unfolding drama.

As the first planes lumbered into view, the Japanese opened up with every gun they had. Undaunted, the Super Fortresses flew in staggered groups at different altitudes and in different formations. Confused ground gunners pumped streams of lead and colored tracers into the sky. The planes opened their bellies, each one pouring out five tons of incendiaries. The cargo tumbled slowly, stringing out behind the mother plane then exploding on the roofs below. Houses and factories in Kobe flared like match-sticks. Red, green, and yellow tracers, missing their targets, streaked in long arcs over the city.

Flames leapt more than 300 feet in the hot air. Exploding gas tanks blew houses apart, and the burning debris created firestorms. Firefighters were powerless. Light from this glowing furnace turned the sky into a quivering fireball, and the underbellies of the B-29s reflected the brilliant orange hue from below.

Zeros darted in and out like angry blackbirds chasing pesky hawks. The tiny Japanese fighter planes were gutsy but outgunned. The belly and tail gunners of the Super Forts sprayed heavy artillery into their reckless, desperate attackers, and many Zeros exploded from taking a direct hit. Others, wounded and sick, would tailspin out of control. Ground gunners aimed technicolor tracers and pom-poms from scores of spewing pillboxes.

But the bombers kept coming. Wave after wave. Those brave airmen who held their course through that lethal fusillade were impressive. It was a fight to the death, and we had ringside seats. The glow from below bounced off the Super Fortresses, creating optical illusions. The props, which were spinning at about 1,800 revolutions per minute, resembled slow-turning, three-bladed windmills. Tracers, missing the planes, seemed to curl around the fuselages and continue their upward trajectories.

Even in their deadliness, the B-29s were big, sleek, and beautiful. Huge four-bladed propellers powered by four 2,200-horsepower engines pulled those 70-ton monsters each with eleven crewmen, through the flak at 200 mph. Their fuselages carried three 50-caliber turret guns, a 20 mm cannon in the tail, and 10,000 pounds of bombs that could wreak havoc from 30,000 feet. These planes had earned the name Super Fortresses.

Not all the Super Forts escaped unscathed. Two peeled out of formation and tumbled into the holocaust. It was devastating to see a proud bomber in its death throes, spiraling slowly downward like a wounded bird with a smoke plume trailing behind. A few parachutes blossomed and floated to earth, silhouetted against the glowing sky.

"My God, I wonder what's going to happen to those poor guys if they survive the jump?" Dick muttered when the first plane spun out of control.

"The Japs say they'll execute all captives," Grant replied. "Maybe it would be better to die first."

But we had no time to dwell on aftermaths. Adrenaline was flowing unchecked: in the veins of the airmen as they dove through that deluge of gunfire; in the veins of the Japanese civilians as they clawed to escape their blazing houses; in the veins of my fellow prisoners as we watched the horrible yet fascinating spectacle.

For years, we had listened to our Japanese captors as they chortled about their victory at Pearl Harbor. We had been imprisoned in this hellhole for three and a half of the best years of our lives. Now we were ecstatic, relishing the sweetness of revenge. We were overjoyed to see those magnificent machines glistening above the bonfires of Kobe, Japan. But at the same time, it was agonizing to know that civilians, especially innocent women and children, were suffering and dying in the flaming streets below.

The planes were almost overhead as they finished their run and headed back home to Saipan and Guam, 1,800 miles to the south. Black smoke was melting into the overcast sky, obscuring our visibility. Hot air currents swept flaming debris more than 2,000 feet in the air. Ashes and scorched paper paneling floated into the canyon. Thousands of refugees sought shelter in the foothills: some straggled into our camp only to be pushed back by the guards who had suddenly reappeared. Kobe was burning out of control, and the fire hoses were empty.

After two hours of unrelenting bombardment, the bombers were now completing their run directly over our camp. All at once, as if lighted by a flaming meteor, the entire sky exploded above our heads. A kamikaze had rammed his plane into the middle of a 70-ton B-29. Four thousand gallons of high-octane gas detonated in a colossal thunderclap that nearly tore the roof off our barracks. Every tree on the mountain range quivered, and the camp shook to its foundations.

We covered our heads and crouched on our knees awaiting the crash. Parts of the two exploded planes scattered over 200 acres of hillside. Flaming wreckage cartwheeled in the air and slammed into the ridge 300 feet above the camp and about 400 yards from where we were standing. The rear end of the B-29's fuselage and tail section blazed across the canyon and smashed into the mountaintop. One of the radial engines crashed into a slope near the main building and disintegrated. The other four engines bounced and rolled, tearing up swaths of underbrush. One massive wing, with flaming gas tanks inside, slowly circled like a spent and twisted boomerang. Finally, it plummeted into the undergrowth and lay smoldering.

Crewmen's bodies, some still strapped in their seats, were scattered amongst the twisted metal. Other crew members were blown to bits. The camp, whether by freak or by design, remained untouched except for an unexploded incendiary, a dud, which landed on the roof directly above my bunk.

And still the bombers kept coming with a roar like 100 Niagara's pounding together. The camp was in pandemonium. Guards were helpless as some of the inmates fled to the surrounding hills for safety. The whole world seemed to have gone crazy.

Then suddenly there was silence. The raid was over. The clouds continued to glow, reflecting the light of the burning city. With no electric power, the searchlights dimmed, and the sirens slept. By 5:30 a light snow began to fall. Everything was so quiet that I could hear the tiny flakes land on my coat sleeves. Our surroundings turned white and peaceful, like a scene on a Christmas card. Slowly, we walked back to camp.

"That was one helluva show," I said, trying to lighten the mood. "Now, what are they going to do for an encore?" No one answered. There was nothing to say. We sat on our bunks and waited for sunup as the soft, quiet snowfall continued to cover and conceal the charred landscape.

The morning sun, pacifying and reassuring, finally peeked over the mountains. The guards called muster and took a body count. We greeted each other with nods and tentative smiles. Some related their experiences to anyone who would listen. Others walked alone. There was no breakfast gong that morning. Our camp leader held a committee meeting to take stock of the situation. To our relief, we found everyone alive and well, though somewhat shaken. There was no food or electricity—the intercom was serviced by a generator.

Major Fitzgerald with co-pilot, Lt. Copeland.
Photo courtesy of William Copeland

At midmorning a small group of police entered our camp with a captured airman. He was young, handsome, uniformed, and well-fed. He was also covered with dirt and blood. We peeked through the door of the guards' room as they interrogated him. He gave us a thumbs up and a friendly smile. An hour later, a dozen soldiers took him away. We lined up to see him go. He signaled another OK and waved good-bye. We cheered him on as he disappeared over the hill. He was beheaded the next day. His name was Robert Nelson.

After the raid, the camp's routine was irrevocably changed. Although we were confined to our quarters for a week, the raid had broken the monotony, lifted our spirits, and spiced our conversations. However, our food supply had been cut off, and we didn't eat for three days. With no lights, we went to bed at sundown, trying to submerge our hunger in sleep.

Finally, word came that our food depot had been restored, and, under the watchful eyes of the guards, we resumed our routine hauling of rations to camp. Four days after the raid, I went down to Kobe on the first bread trip. I was shocked by the extent of the devastation. Brick chimneys stood like stark tombstones over mounds of ashes and smoking rubble. The stench of death permeated the air. Police wandered uselessly among the sad, silent survivors. Homeless, destitute, dirty, and hungry, bedraggled groups were poking stoically in the smoldering debris for bricks, stones, or sheets of tin to make temporary shelters. My heart went out to them in their suffering. But nobody gave us a passing glance.

From the attic radio we learned that 330 planes had taken part in the raid. The Japanese claimed to have destroyed 100 enemy planes. The Americans admitted three planes missing. Thirty percent of Kobe was destroyed, and at least 250,000 people had been burned out, wounded, or killed. The docks and rail yards were heavily damaged, and military production was beyond recovery. Yet Tokyo's propagandists declared a Japanese victory and swore to fight on until the enemy was driven out.

With the guard's permission, we scrounged the hills for salvageable parts from the two planes that had crashed near our camp. Everything movable was smuggled into camp and stashed out of sight under beds or beneath floorboards or above rafters. At least a ton of material was carried down from the mountains. With limited tools, a few ingenious fellows turned oxygen tanks into pressure cookers, cotton curtains into shirts, leather strips into half-soles, electric wire into hot plates, and armor plates into griddles.

Days earlier, we had requested permission to search for the bodies of our fallen comrades. After our camp electricians had restored electric service to the camp, as a reward, we were allowed this search mission. Eight crew members, bloated and mutilated, were buried and given a grave marker and a prayer. Their dog tags, along with crude maps showing the locations of their graves, were given to the U.S. Army after our rescue. Two crew members were never found.

A few weeks later, the remains of an eleventh crew member, the pilot, were discovered. He was still strapped in his seat. His dog tag identified him as Major B.J. Fitzgerald. We rescued his papers and personal items before burying him, then added the location of his grave to the map showing the other sites. We kept his .45-caliber pistol just in case it might come in handy. Later, his belongings were mailed to his wife in the Midwest.

To Allied High Command and the flight crews, the raid on Kobe was just another episode of the war. But to those of us who witnessed the raid that night, the memory lives forever. For the rest of my life whenever I hear the wail of sirens or feel the caress of snowflakes on my coat sleeves, I shall think of the night the Americans bombed Kobe.

A few weeks later, the Tokyo Nichi-Nichi had an article on the Kobe raid:

"It was announced yesterday that Sgt. Ogata crashed into a B-29 over Futatabi Mt. On the 17th in the morning the lively Ogata did not show up at the base. After frantic searches by his platoon, the undercarriage, propeller and the complete hood of the engine of Ogata's plane were found in the fuselage of the B-29 whose remains are now strewn over Mt. Futatabi, after having used up all his ammunition, must have cried out: 'There you go! You rat of a B-29.' and then he carried out his charge, body crashing in the center of the plane. The charred remains of the 5 crew members of the B-29 were found in the wreckage, bespeaking the fear which the moment of body-crashing must have brought them.

"Ogata's left glove and his flying boots were found several thousand meters from the scene of action. His remains were reverently taken up by his companions not far from the spot where he bodycrashed.

"On the fuselage of the B-29 which crashed on Futatabi Mt., a woman's leg was painted. This picture of a high-heeled shoe of a Yankee girl shows the rotten atmosphere of the people behind the guns in the States. There is also another picture on the armoire showing Mickey Mouse firing a machine gun with his two legs. On the other side Mickey Mouse is wielding a sledge hammer. These pictures are proof of the wild hopes of the Americans to invade Japan."

A newspaper article showed how the Japs were coping with their desperation.

"The expected landings on China are also aiming indirectly at Japan. Therefore we should not lose time in making preparations for the enemy's invasion. Now that people talk so much about the special attack's spirits, no slackening of our war efforts is to be allowed. We should by all means, realizing that the worst may happen, avail ourselves of the time which is left to us. Our communications with the South have become precarious and the flow of our war materials is restricted to Japan, Manchuria and China. If the worst comes to the worst, the Japanese Mainland will have to become self-sufficient. We will have to overcome great difficulties but should maintain faith in final victory."

CHAPTER 32

Bombing Mounts

Life, even in camp, went on. Observing from the sidelines, I witnessed the conversion of a man to a new religious philosophy and a new way of life. Bob Aiken, a tall, thoughtful, intelligent chap connected with the contractors, and Roy Henning were walking in the exercise yard with R.H. Blyth, my Zen Buddhist friend. Bob and Roy were completely entranced as if in a state of hypnosis as Blyth explained some fine points of Zen. In Blyth, they had found a soulmate. Roy was quietly thoughtful, but Bob was captivated, converted and convinced he had found his Nirvana in Camp Futatabi in Kobe, Japan in the middle of a war. Teacher and students walked together nearly every day until our rescue. I was happy to see that Bob and Roy had found inner peace in the midst of this squalor and turmoil.

Now that Iwo Jima was available as an emergency landing field for crippled bombers returning to the Marianas Islands the pace and size of aerial attacks increased. Shikoku and Kyushu Islands were bombed daily. Tokyo was the main target on Honshu. Since November and March 9, 1945, more than 1432 B-29s had unloaded their high explosive bomb loads on the capitol—an equivalent of 7160 tons!

Firebombs were wiping out major cities like Tokyo, Nagoya, Osaka. Mined harbors bottled up the merchant fleet and fishing was confined to inland waters. Rice fields were burned and railroad yards blown up. Transportation by rail and ship was crippled. Japan was slowly being strangled to death. But, there were still

3,500,000 highly trained and well equipped soldiers guarding the mainland and ready to fight to the death if ordered to do so. Civilians, from children to aged adults, were being mustered for defense of the homeland. To increase hatred and harden resolve, the papers screamed defiance.

The propaganda mill kept grinding. In reference to enemy planes over Japan, they printed "after reconnoitering over Tokyo and Yokohama and dropping bombs on Nagoya and Hamamatsu for four hours, the planes were seen to flee southward." On another raid when 200 planes came over, "The brave garrison, on the spot, shot down 201." Another time, "the Diet arose as one man and, gnashing its teeth in anger, bombarded America with "thought waves."

Our food supply hovered between scarcity and nothing. Yet, we were surprised to be fed at all. Like us, the people were eating weeds, kelp, salted fish, and weevil-riddled rice.

Charley Craver was caught by the police and tossed in jail. Leon Harris, our camp leader at the time, and Mr. Higasa went down town to rescue him. Charley was confused and incoherent. He was fully dressed in all his clothes including his overcoat, two pairs of pants, two shirts and a knapsack. He insisted he was going home to see his family. They brought him back to camp. Slowly, he regained his composure and settled down.

A few weeks later, we learned Mr. Higasa had lost his house and all his worldly belongings in the fire raid on Kobe. His family had barely escaped with minor injuries. Yet, he never complained nor inflicted any retribution on us. One day on his walk back to the city, a small event took place that added to his stature in the eyes of the camp. A group of camp scavengers were busily dismantling a section of the downed B-29 fuselage near the trail. They froze into silence when they spotted Higasa approaching for they were off limits and were risking the hoosegow. To save face and diminish the situation, Mr. Higasa ducked his head to avert his gaze and walked by them without stopping. Dumbfounded, they mentally saluted him in passing. Understanding their urge and need to tinker harmlessly with an American airplane, he had very simply avoided an embarrassing confrontation. Furthermore, the next day he ordered his guards to form hiking parties to scavenge the scattered wreckage covering the hillsides. Mr. Higasa was a gentleman.

CHAPTER 33

President Franklin D. Roosevelt Dies

On the afternoon of April 13, 1945, Fred crawled out of the attic studio with an ashen face. With quivering lips he whispered to me that Roosevelt was dead.

Plopping on my bed in a state of shock, I tried to imagine the world without Franklin D. Roosevelt. The props had been knocked out of my adult life. I had been an ardent fan of this great man since high school. He was really the only president I had ever known. I wondered what had killed him but I didn't want to ask. As the shockwave passed, I suddenly felt an overwhelming sadness. A few minutes later the sorrowful announcement was made over the intercom.

The first question was who would succeed him? The second was what about the course of the war? Soon both questions were answered. Harry S. Truman from Missouri, the vice president whom we didn't know existed, was our new president. Pleitner, who had lived in Kansas City, told us Truman was a cog in the Pendergast machine—hardly a recommendation. Truman must have been a man of action, for he announced immediately that Roosevelt's war strategies would continue. The Allies sighed in relief and the Axis was put on notice that there would be no change of course.

Our radio told us of Roosevelt's last days and Truman's first days as President. The transition seemed smooth and professional. It was good to know that Truman was retaining Roosevelt's team and was making decisions. We felt relieved in our sadness. Mr. Higasa offered his condolences.

Bizarre events in the world were piling up and rolling over each other. Mussolini was executed by an Italian mob and strung up by his feet in Milan's Piazzale Loreto on April 30. The same day Hitler blew his brains out in his Berlin bunker while the Russian troops closed in on the heart of the city. The war in Europe was all but over and the Thousand Year Reich was already history.

It was a strange coincidence that Roosevelt and Hitler came to power in the same year, 1933, and they died with their boots on the during the same year, 1945. FDR's boots were bright and shiny, Hitler's were covered with blood.

We were shocked by the radio news about the German death camps. Millions of helpless, innocent Jews had been systematically slaughtered for the phony cause of racial purity. The Jap papers openly published these horrible detailed newscasts. Father Spae translated them from the Jap paper to a hushed audience. I expressed my dismay over this horrible news.

He blithely replied, "Hitler was justified in killing the Jews. They killed Jesus Christ."

Stunned, I slumped in the corner. I never expected such a cruel and hateful answer from a supposedly religious man, especially one I considered so wise. I'm sure millions of good Catholics all over the world would disagree with him.

With Germany vanquished the Allies could concentrate on Japan. Heretofore, the United States had been fighting in the Pacific with one arm tied behind its back. Now the bombing of Japan continued unabated. I had found a skilled reporter in the camp—my Polish friend, Roskowyck who'd give me a battle report every day. He'd come to my room after a raid and give me battle statistics in slurred English without gestures. He reported on items in the Jap papers, unsubstantiated rumors, or insightful observations from the vast knowledge gleaned while operating his piledriver in Guam.

On June 1, 509 super Fortresses hit Osaka in broad daylight. Sitting twenty miles away, we saw the whole ghastly spectacular operation. The raid went on for four hours and smoke blackened the skies.

After the raid, Rosky came in with his special report.

He stammered. "Geezchris, I never seen so many goddam planes in all my life. There wuz tousans and tousans, more dun dat—hunerts." I took his word for it. He didn't have to wait long to see an even bigger raid.

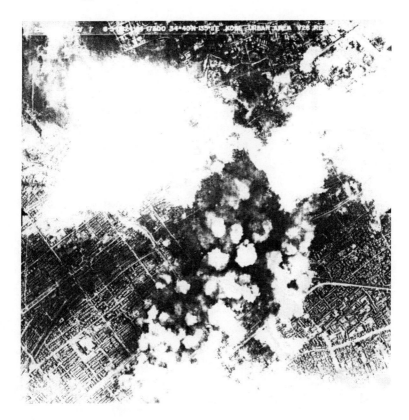

Bombs hit Kobe on 5 June 1945.
The white clouds partially obscures the target.

Four days later, on June 5, 530 Supper Fortresses burned and flattened what was left of Kobe. The sirens sounded at 7:20 A.M.

and the loud-speaker screamed the familiar *Keikai Keiho Hattsurei*. We tenkoed and hit for cover. Most of the camp ran for the tunnel. Some of us recklessly sat in the dining room for a better view. In the March 17 raid the west end of the city had taken the biggest hit. This raid was wiping out the east end and the remainder of downtown. The bombers came in at a high altitude, possibly fifteen to twenty thousand feet, in formations of twenty to forty planes. Each formation took a swath of the target, like harvesters in a grain field. Each aircraft was loaded with tons of incendiary bombs that dropped like tumbling bowling pins before exploding into a thousand flaming torches a few hundred feet above the ground. Flames reached three hundred feet into the air. Burning oil tanks blackened the sky so completely that sunlight disappeared and a false nighttime fell. Oppenborn's chickens went back to roost and we had to light candles to see. Saipy whimpered in fear. Shrapnel clattered on the roof of the camp as we instinctively hit the deck and covered our heads with our hands.

We saw six wounded planes, trailing smoke, leave the formations and drift slowly earthward. We may have missed others in the darkness.

Four and a half hours later the last bomber, with empty bomb racks, turned for the long flight home to the Marianas Islands, leaving an obliterated city of 1,500,000 shell-shocked people behind. Kobe's role in the war was finished.

Two days later, to ease the anxiety of the local internees, Mr. Higasa walked the entire city to check up on the fate of their homes and families. Every local's house was destroyed except three— Messrs. Hatter, Mason and Pardon. The families of the other internees had moved to the country weeks before.

Again, our electrical power was knocked out. A repair crew of camp electricians ventured out to fix the damage. They located an open circuit breaker on the edge of the city, a minor problem. Closing the breaker restored the power.

When I visited the city on a bread trip a few days later, I could see the suffering and despair of the people. Despite their plight, not one was seen crying or cowering. No one threatened or showed resentment toward us.

Bread trips now were almost useless. Our rations consisted of three and a half ounces of rice or soy beans daily. Biscuits were scarce. Our reserves of Red Cross food were diminishing. The black market and our garden supplies were all that kept us from starvation.

The worst of all, Mr. Higasa was transferred to another duty. We bid him a sad farewell. His successor, Mauritani-san, was an officious, unsympathetic nuthead.

CHAPTER 34

Misery Loves Company

Centipedes, lice, and bedbugs crawled out of cracks to pester us. The devil must have invented these critters to test our resolve or collect for our sins, maybe both. Counter-attacks against these pests were our private battles behind enemy lines.

Futatabi—1945. Packing for home and airing bedding to kill bedbugs. My room on top left.
Photo by Jack Taylor with borrowed camera

Centipedes appeared first to scout the territory. These multilegged crawly-creepers invaded our socks, pants, and bedding. Shaking them out of our clothes at night or before morning muster became routine. I sat on one in the dark and jumped half way across the room when he bit me on the you-know-what. We squashed them, slapped them and swept them out the door. Satisfied they had done their duty, they marched off with their multitudinous legs stepping in unison.

Lice came in as the centipedes went out. They crawled in our hair and clothing like Jap snipers in a tropical jungle. We scratched ourselves raw and countered with soap, water and prayer. God didn't answer and the devil laughed at our misery. So we washed our clothes and showered our tortured bodies between screaming sirens and bombing alerts. Soap and water finally won the day. They hadn't learned to swim.

Bedbugs, the main assault troops, then attacked. These parasitic creepers spread their attack through camp with the speed and persistency of a vicious rumor. We burned, drowned, poisoned and squashed them. Like bunker warfare at Stalingrad, the course of battle swung back and forth for weeks. Dislodging them was like storming a Russian blockhouse with a squirt gun.

They attacked at every angle, climbing up the bed legs, swarming through the clothing, and after finding their target by smell and dead reckoning, by dropping from the ceiling. These miserable, pimple-sized pests, were nearly transparent until filled with our blood which darkened them to visibility. It was disgusting when these bloodsuckers plopped on your head at midnight. If you slapped in self-defense, you smeared your face with blood. If you smashed them in your sleep, the bedclothes were stained with reddish plasma.

Our weak defenses proved futile. To stop their advance along the floor, we placed our bamboo bed legs in cans of water. Every morning, the cans were filled with drowned bugs. But this didn't stop their attack. The dead bodies merely served as pontoon bridges for hundreds of followers to advance like brainless battalions of army ants marching toward rotten carrion.

Their millions drove us out of the building. We moved our bedding into the yard away from this citadel of hell. To our delighted amazement, we found sunlight killed the blood-sucking beasties. We spread our clothing, bedding, and mattresses in the sunshine and slept under the stars. With nothing to suck on in the building and with sunlight cooking their bloody guts in the great outdoors, the bedbugs eventually disappeared. We moved back into our rooms, anemic but victorious.

CHAPTER 35

Okinawa

The invasion and seizure of Okinawa, 350 miles south of Japan, was one of the most vital and vicious battles of World War II. In two and a half months, both sides threw everything they had into the conflict. Japan was fighting a last ditch battle to defend its homeland. America needed Okinawa to invade Japan. With fanatical zeal, Jap troops fired their guns from caves and mounted suicidal *Banzai* charges directly into flame-throwers and blazing gunfire. Was this how Japan would defend its homeland against an invading army?

Many brave Americans died with valor in this bloody battle. But the Jap losses were heavier. Out-gunned and out-fought, Japan's ragged infantry and desperate kamikazes were no match for the U.S. Marines and naval air forces. Okinawa fell to the Americans on June 22, 1945. The island could now serve as a final staging area for an invasion of Japan. This invasion, we learned later, had already been scheduled for early November, 1945.

In Japan, food had virtually disappeared. There were no open markets. Farm production was hampered by fire bombs, drought, and labor shortage. Their merchant marine was at the bottom of the sea. All imports had stopped. Fishing vessels were confined to shorelines, harbors and the inland sea.

Our camp was nearly out of rations. On one food trip we managed to get fifteen pounds of rice for two hundred and fifty men, enough for two spoonfuls of rice soup per man. Black marketeers in camp fanned out in all directions: over the hills to the next prefecture, to the countryside, into farming villages. They bribed police, slinked in dark alleys, stole apples, and daikons from farmers, and paid exorbitant prices for rice from their contacts. Everyone was scrambling to survive but the internees scrambled harder and against heavier odds than anyone else, for they were in enemy territory. The guards were distracted and disinterested in our plight. Their minds, too, were on survival.

With Okinawa airfields only 350 miles away, P-51 Mustang fighters were escorting B-29s on bombing runs. Japanese Zeros were no match for the superior Mustangs and the aggressive, better-trained American pilots. Admiral Halsey's task force was shelling coastal cities unopposed and his carrier planes were attacking fishing fleets, merchant ships, and armament factories along the shore. American forces had complete domination of the air and sea but Japan's army still ruled the land. The government and the presses resolved to fight to the end.

Japan's populace was destitute but resolute. People stood in food lines for five hours at a time to get a weekly ration of a single cabbage head and a cup of rice. Black market operators flourished. As money lost its value, prices skyrocketed and bartering took over. Sugar was up to ¥400 a pound, rice ¥75 and soybeans ¥60, an increase of 500% to 2,000% over pre-war levels. The poorer class suffered most unless a rich relative or a friendly farmer could help them. Inflation was rampant. The black-market exchange rate of Yen for dollars rose daily and dramatically: From pre-war of ¥4 to one dollar, the rate climbed to ¥40,000 to one, then to ¥80,000 to one. At war's end it went as high as ¥4,000,000 to one.

Japan's war structure was crumbling and its social structure was in disarray. Leaders yelled about the threat of invasion, trying to inject adrenaline in an already moribund heart. The people stoically obeyed as they had been taught for centuries. Battalions of civilians, the very young and the very old, were armed to defend the homeland with wooden spears and pitchforks. If Japan decided to fight to the end, the battle could kill millions on both sides. Our short-wave warned against over-optimism.

Planes appeared every day out of range of the anti-aircraft guns. One day, several pamphlet bombs landed near the camp. Some carried copies of the *Hawaiian Times* showing pictures of Japanese Nisei troops in the American army, counteracting Japan's propaganda that this was a holy war between Orientals and Caucasians. In the dead of night, Halsey's shells whistled overhead and exploded in the city below. Mines in the harbor blew up heedless ships that sank before leaving the breakwater. We grew accustomed to weird and unidentified explosions. The war was reaching a climax and no one knew precisely how or when it would end.

CHAPTER 36

Hiroshima

We didn't have long to wait. On August 6, 1945, the city of Hiroshima was pulverized by one bomb dropped from a lone B-29. The Japanese newspaper on the 7th carried a vague story about a new fire bomb that was dropped by parachute. They told the people there was nothing to fear if everyone lay prone on the ground, wore extra garments and shielded their eyes.

Frankly, the Japs didn't know what had happened at Hiroshima. The city center was flattened and all access to it destroyed. Bridges, railroad tracks, telephones, and transportation facilities were knocked out. The devastated area was left completely isolated for days. No wonder the reports were vague and confusing.

On the night of the 7th, Oppenborn came out of the attic with the American report that an atomic bomb, with the explosive power of 20,000 tons of TNT, had been dropped on Hiroshima, wiping out eight-tenths of the city and an estimated 90,000 people. The report was incredible—a Buck Rogers nightmare. As rescuers entered the demolished city, reports of horror spread across the land.

American propaganda, through radio and leaflets, pounded the Japs twenty-four hours a day, revealing all the horrors of this new weapon. A leaflet fluttered into our camp reading, "*Get out of cities or die.*" America threatened to annihilate the entire country if it refused to surrender.

Three days after Hiroshima, Nagasaki was obliterated with a second atomic bomb, substantiating America's threat. To share the spoils, Russia joined the war and the camp went wild. Our radio scooped the Jap radio by only five minutes on that story.

On the 10th, the papers carried ghastly stories on the destruction of Hiroshima and Nagasaki. Was the government laying the groundwork for surrender? Rumors piled on rumors: Japan was ready to surrender; Japan was going to commit mass suicide; America was going to invade the island of Kyushu first; Kobe was next on the hit list with an atomic bomb. Our radio fed the rumor mill as we inadvertently slid in a piece of information from the short-wave. Like others, I packed my duffel with emergency supplies for a sudden dash to the hills. Since the atomic bombs had been dropped from single B-29s, a lone plane would make everyone rush for cover. It had now turned into a war of nerves.

On the night of the 10th we were sitting on the porch having an armchair session and analyzing rumors. A gentle breeze wafted the aroma of pine needles down the canyon as the moon peeked coyly through passing clouds. Looking over my shoulder, I noticed Fred Oppenborn sitting in his corner with an unusually happy look on his face and a cigar in his mouth. He had just come down from the attic with the latest news. His smile and his cigar seemed equally strange. I didn't immediately catch the significance of the cigar, even though years before he had told us he would smoke his stodgy if or when peace was declared. The conversation grew louder and more animated, he walked over to me, puffing away. I stood up to listen to what he had to say. He mumbled in my ear, "THE WAR IS OVER. JAPAN IS READY TO QUIT."

Thunderstruck, I slumped back into my chair, unable to move or speak. When I could stand again, he continued under his breath, "Susuki, the new Premier, has agreed to unconditional surrender providing the Allies don't compromise the prerogatives of the Emperor. If the Allies agree on that point, the war will be over. The radio says it would be best to have the Emperor stay in power and help with the peace process. It's going to take five more days before we'll know for sure. But it looks certain that Japan is ready to throw in the towel. We'll have to keep it quiet because of our radio, so don't say a word outside of this room." He took a victorious drag on his stale cigar. Its smoke suddenly smelled unbelievably fragrant.

The news was overwhelming. My thoughts tumbled in confusion. We were going home, home, home. This goddam nightmare was over and we were still alive. This madhouse was ending and we were free, victorious, and a little mad ourselves. We had beaten the arrogant bastards at their own game. Pearl Harbor was avenged.

I wanted to yell from the roof-top but I was stuck with the need for secrecy. It took all the strength I could muster to act as if nothing important had happened.

Fred walked back to his corner puffing his cigar. I followed to get more details.

He said, "I think the Allies will accept the condi-tions and we can start packing and get the hell out of this goddam country."

So I suppressed my enthusiasm for five days on the most sensational revelation in my life. This was the greatest effort of self control I have ever exerted.

CHAPTER 37

Japan's Surrender

U.S. General Curtis Lemay took advantage of Japan's jitters. Solitary bombers streaked back and forth across the sky at 35,000 feet, out of gun range. They flew unopposed, with no Zeroes to attack them. People were exhausted from lack of sleep and bruised from diving into shelters.

On the night of August 14, a single B-29 came directly over camp. When the shrapnel started falling, the men headed for the tunnel. Our radio warned us of Japanese treachery. We waited breathlessly. The local radio and press announced the Emperor was to speak to the people at noon the next day. Everyone in camp knew the speech was coming but only we six knew the contents of the message. There were no U.S. air raids that day so the people could listen without distraction.

The local papers temporarily subdued their vitriol. Were they preparing the country for surrender, even though there were factions within the government unwilling to quit? Militants, defying the Emperor, wanted the country to fight to the end and, unbeknownst to us at the time, were trying to sabotage the peace process. At noon on the 15th of August,1945 everyone in camp stood motionless and quiet. Some looked at the ground; others stared into space. Grim-faced and obedient, the guards in their office, stood silently at attention, facing Tokyo and the Emperor. They bowed their heads in supplication and respect. In somber tones, the announcer in the Imperial palace introduced the speaker. After a few minutes, the quavering voice of the Emperor, speaking in a strange, upper-class dialect, issued from the radio.

"To our good and loyal subjects"

"After pondering deeply the general trends of the world and the actual conditions in our Empire today, We have decided to effect a settlement of the present situation by resorting to an extraordinary measure.

"We have ordered our Government to communicate to the Governments of the United States, Great Britain, China, and the Soviet Union that our Empire accepts the provisions of their Joint Declaration.

"The sacrifice and sufferings to which our nation is to be subjected hereafter will be certainly great. We are keenly aware of the inmost feelings of all ye, our subjects. However, it is according to the dictates of time and fate that We have resolved to pave the way for a grand peace for all generations to come by enduring the unendurable and suffering what is insufferable.

"To strive for the common prosperity and happiness of all nations as well as the security and well-being of our subjects is the solemn obligation which has been handed down by our Imperial Ancestors, and which We hold close to heart. Indeed, We declared war on America and Britain out of our sincere desire to ensure Japan's self-preservation and stabilization of East Asia, it being far from our thought either to infringe upon the sovereignty of other nations or to embark upon territorial aggrandizement. But now the war has lasted for nearly four years. Despite the best that has been done by everyone—the gallant fighting of military and naval forces, the diligence and assiduity of our servants of the State, and the devoted service of our 100-million people, the war situation has developed not necessarily to Japan's advantage, while the general trends of the world have all turned against her interest. Moreover, the enemy has begun to employ a new and most cruel bomb, the power of which to do damage is indeed incalculable, taking the toll of many innocent lives. Should We continue to fight, it would not only result in an ultimate collapse and obliteration of the Japanese nation, but also it would lead to the total extinction of human civilization. Such being the case, how are we to save the millions of our subjects, or to atone ourselves before the hallowed spirits of our Imperial Ancestors? This is the reason why We have ordered the acceptance of the provisions of the Joint Declaration of the Powers.

"We cannot but express the deepest sense of regret to our allied nations of East Asia, who have consistently cooperated with the Empire toward the emancipation of East Asia. The thought of those officers and men as well as others who have fallen in the fields of battle, those who died at their post of duty, or those who met an untimely death and all their bereaved families, pains our heart night and day. The welfare of the wounded and the war sufferers, and of those who have lost their home and livelihood, are the objects of our profound nation continue as one family from generation to generation, ever firm in its faith of the imperishableness of its divine land, and mindful of its heavy burden of responsibilities, and the long road before it. Unite your total strength to be devoted to the construction for the future. Cultivate the ways of rectitude; foster nobility of the spirit; and work with resolution so it may enhance the innate glory of the Imperial State and keep pace with the progress of the world."

(Imperial Sign Manual)

CHAPTER 38

Aftermath of Surrender

The entire nation was stunned. Many people did not understand exactly what the Emperor had said, for this was the first time they had ever heard him speak. When the Emperor had finished, Harold Mason reached in his pocket, pulled out a cigarette, struck a match and took a long drag. Perspiration stood out on his forehead. He fingered his cigarette and said quietly "It's peace."

We, too, were stunned. Everyone, including the guards, stood transfixed. The import of that statement was just too great. We had waited too long; had yearned, hoped, and prayed too hard to absorb the significance of victory so suddenly. Then in a moment, with a sudden surge of emotion, everyone went stark raving mad with joy. We jumped, screamed an yahooed with ecstasy. Working off four years of frustration, the inmates smashed furniture, and threw it out the windows. Grown men began to cry. Everyone hugged everyone else. Screams of rapture filled the canyon. Even Saipy barked with happiness.

In those few moments, a flood of elation poured over me, filling my entire being. For the next few days, I tottered over a new realization of being alive and free.

While we wept for joy, the police, in despair, wept for a different reason. In an amazing show of good sportsmanship, two of them came up, shook our hands and congratulated us on winning the war. Perhaps they wanted us to compliment them so they would not be treated as war criminals. Until then we had planned to tear the police office apart but that grand gesture deflated us. The cops announced that there would be no more roll calls, but for our own welfare would we please show up in camp to sleep? Imagine that, they said "please."

That night the guards disappeared and were never seen again. We were in the habit of seeing them swagger around with swords dangling from their belts. In fact, I was hoping to acquire one of their swords as a souvenir but it was too late. Now we were on our own. To our surprise, it was disconcerting at first not to be directed to arise in the morning, not to stand in line for tenko, not to ask permission to lie in bed an extra five minutes in the morning. For the first time in four years, we could come and go as we pleased.

And come and go we did. We were victors in a defeated country and were now INVITED guests of the Emperor. We were no longer "military civilians" but "victorious American civilians" eligible to return to our country. Justice was gratifying.

The younger guys scattered over the landscape to find food and see the territory. The older ones basked in the sunlight.

Most of us paraded down the trail to Kobe and wandered undisturbed amongst the ruins. What we saw horrified us. Kobe, a city of more than a million people, was now a pile of rubble, ashes and burned tile. As far as we could see in any direction there was nothing but heaps of bricks and broken concrete. I walked from one end of the city to the other and, except for a very few areas, I estimated that 85% of the city was destroyed beyond restoration. Large buildings that looked intact from a distance had been gutted by fire. Some of the waterfront remained intact but badly scarred. The foreign residential section was untouched as if the bombardiers in those two mammoth air raids had purposely avoided the district. There were freakish cases of houses standing alone untouched while in the surrounding vicinity nothing remained but bent lamp posts and skeletons of twisted girders.

In the midst of this wreckage, people in rags were living in makeshift shelters. Huts of tin roofing with walls of burned tile housed eight or ten people. Water mains were leaking. Lack of plumbing added a stench to the despair. Not one shop or store was doing business. The people plodded and tripped along the broken streets, blanked-faced and silent. At night, when the full moon lighted the town with an eerie paleness and silhouetted the naked shrines and chimney stacks, the city resembled a graveyard of some ancient, lost civilization.

Back at the camp, the locals said good-bye and headed home. Blyth clutched my hand as he whispered, "Remember, Zen is in your smile and in your eyes. You have it. Keep it. Take good care of yourself." That was the finest compliment I have ever received. I waved as he went over the hill and disappeared from my life, but his singular goodness and influence are among my strongest memories.

Surprisingly, some of the guys shacked up with their female black-market contacts. In fact, four contractors decided to marry their newly found sweethearts and bring them home as war brides. It all seemed like a gigantic holiday. Every minute was filled with surprises. Fred shaved off his foot long beard. His white face looked strange but happy and, the biggest surprise of all, twenty years younger.

We learned that General Douglas MacArthur was to govern the occupation of Japan. A good choice. We figured he was imperial enough to match the Emperor.

The next day a few B-29s swooped low overhead and circled the city looking for prison camps. We received a directive from the American High Command, through the Swiss Consul, to paint "PW" in huge bright capitals on the roofs of our buildings in preparation for a air-drops of badly needed food and medical supplies. The Japanese furnished the paint and the painters. We happily supervised. Eager to please their conquerors, our munificent captors jumped into action. Soon the vivid lettering could be seen from ten thousand feet. Looking skyward, we waited for our celestial bonanza.

Within a few days, the action started. Scout planes, from somewhere out of paradise, circled above and wiggled their wings as a sign of friendly recognition. Soon thereafter came high-flying B-29's, laden with precious cargo. Only a week before, these same behemoths were blowing Japan to smithereens, but now they were on a mission of mercy. One could almost see halos above their wings.

The following description of the air-drops, under the title *Prisons, Parcels and Parachutes* was printed in the Los Altos Town Crier.

This unexpected assignment, however, evidently caught the U.S. military flat-footed. Their personnel, untrained for this assignment, had no special equipment on hand to do the job. They had to improvise and, like good Americans, they rose to the occasion. Unorthodox types of containers were pressed into service: netting, wooden crates, cardboard cartons, canvas tarps, 50-gallon drums, sometimes two drums welded together end-to-end–all to be dropped by parachutes. The only chutes available were those designed for paratroopers, adequate for 200-300 pounds, but nothing heavier. Some of these containers must have weighed 500-1000 pounds.

**B-29 dropping supplies on the camp after
the surrender. Photo by Jack Taylor**

Another important factor were the winds. On a calm day, the

colorful chutes and attached containers might float gently to earth near their targets. But in a swirling gale at ten thousand feet, the lighter loads could sail out of sight southward and splash into the Inland sea or ten miles east into the next prefecture. When two welded 50-gallon drums filled with goodies were dropped, things really went awry. Popping open after a long free-fall, the tiny chutes tended to rip off, leaving the drums to tumble like wild projectiles. Smashing to pieces upon impact, they destroyed themselves and everything else in their path.

After several unsuccessful drops, the pilots and bombardiers altered their strategy by coming in lower and slower. One day we watched a Super Fort roar up the canyon below ridge level. We could almost see the pilots in the cockpit. Whoever had packed these supplies and secured the chutes knew his business, for this time everything held together. Out of the drums spewed boxes of medicine, canned goods, magazines, sheet music, candy-bars, and cigarettes. We scurried after the packages like street urchins scrambling for coins tossed from a tourist bus. I stared at the Milky Way bar in my hand and realized the war was actually over.

Soon the Navy got into the act. Gull-winged, F4U fighters from an offshore carrier swooped and darted overhead like frisky swallows. They, too, had boxes of supplies garnered, no doubt, from the ship's galleys. With Navy fighters and Army bombers vying for air-space, it was like an aerial circus at the county fair. We had to duck and weave through this barrage of missiles of mercy.

I nearly became a war casualty—killed by a baked ham. As I was running for cover in the midst of a culinary bombardment, an F4U dove in with me in its gunsight. As it leveled off at 300 M.P.H., a 20-pound tin of baked ham tore from its chute and hurtled in my direction. I had a split second to step backwards and hit the dirt. The ham smashed into a clay bank barely ten feet from my head. When the tin exploded, bits of ham spewed like water from a sprinkler head, some landing on my quivering back. I smelled like a ham sandwich for a week afterward.

The next day, a five-hundred-pound wooden crate, sans para-

chute, tumbled from the belly of a B-29 and crashed into the side
of our main barracks, tearing a twenty-foot hole through the wall
of the second floor barely missing Max Brodofsky and a guard. But
the crate disintegrated upon contact, and the contents exploded
in all directions. We found candy bars, toothpaste, canned peaches,
cigarettes, crackers, canned milk, Spam, butter and coffee grounds
stuck to the ceiling, on the walls, under the bunks, and in the
bedding. The room was filled with the damndest mixture of gro-
ceries we'd ever seen. It looked as if half of a Safeway market had
been run through a giant mix-master and shot from a fire hose.

Max Brodofsky at busted window

Rescue teams of American troops showed up a few weeks later, and we were saved from further air-drops. The U.S. Army hand delivered our food, clothing, and medical supplies from then on. We had survived the war but were nearly killed in the rescue.

CHAPTER 39

Peace & Rescue

As days dragged into September, we became bolder in our ventures from camp. George, Dick and I took a free train ride to Osaka and back stopping off in Kobe. We were impressed with the smoothness and speed of the ride despite previous rail damage from heavy bombing. We mingled freely and confidently with the people. We explored every building left standing amidst the rubble. In Kobe, we found a military prison camp filled with Americans, Brits and Aussies. This was the camp being prepared when we were ordered to leave the Mission in 1942. They were disturbing to see, for their conditions were pitiful. They had been slave laborers on the waterfront and showed us their calluses, scars, and sore bones. Several of the inmates were obviously insane, lying on their backs and staring silently at the ceiling. Unable to take care of themselves, they required constant attention. A sad fate for such fine young men.

Part of the PanAm group at Futatabi after the war and before
rescue, 1945. My room is upper center. L-R-Dick Arvidson,
Grant Wells, Ev Penning, Jim Thomas, Fred Oppenborn,
George Conklin, George Blackett. (3 weeks of good food)

They told of six out of nine unmarked ships from the Philippines being sunk by American aircraft and submarines on their
way to Japan. These men had survived by stealing food from warehouses and ships on which they were working as stevedores. They
received no medical care and very few clothes. The air-drops had
torn up the street in front of their camp, but at least they now had
food.

**Site of former Canadian Academy after bombing of Kobe,
17 Mar 1945**

Saddened, we returned that evening to Futatabi, our home
and symbol of security.

Cliff Price, part owner of the San Miguel Brewery in the Philippines with a branch in nearby Takuradsuka, sent forty-four barrels of beer to the camp. It was the greatest beer-bust in history.
Lack of tolerance to alcohol caused some drinkers to heave after
every snort, but others quickly adapted and proceeded to get high
on a few glasses of foamy suds. The beer supply ran out in two
days.

4218-THOM

Futatabi, 1945. Packing for home.
Note part of the PW sign on roof.

The air-drops continued and we piled our new-found loot on the lawn. One day, some sheet music fluttered out of a parachute. Moneyhun grabbed some and ran to the piano. *I'll Be around after You've Gone*, a new tune to us, brought lumps to our throats. After a few bars, he'd hum the tune and do a fashionable tapdance to the clapping of his audience.

Mr. Brunton and Roy Henning built a short-wave receiver from parts furnished by the kencho. Now everyone could hear American broadcasts although we still kept our radio a secret to avoid resentment among our friends. Reports said mine-sweeping would be required before ships could enter Japanese harbors. We heard that United States occupation troops would soon be landing in Japan. We waited impatiently to welcome them. The three-ring-circus of rescue was about to start and we had free passes to ring side seats.

Kobe after firebombing. Remains of Marx House.
Photo by Jack Taylor

We sent an ultimatum to the kencho for food, any good food, to be delivered immediately to the camp. Suddenly, large quantities of rice, vegetables, and canned fruit appeared. Cooks came to prepare the meals. Evidently, hoarding by the officials had been commonplace. With the air-drops in full swing and good old American chow supplementing the rice supply, we gorged ourselves. Shrunken stomachs limited our appetites. But every day spent at the table added to our eating capacity, and the positive affects were remarkable. We gained strength and weight daily. I was now up to 160 pounds and gaining. "Tiny" Luke, a 300-pound dragline operator, had lost 120 pounds. Panels of skin hung like blacksmith aprons from his mighty frame. He managed to gain over 60 pounds before rescue. No longer needing the eggs, Fred, with a lump in his throat, gave his beloved chickens to Dave Hatter.

Some patriotic souls planted two flagpoles, for Old Glory and the Union Jack. Musty flags appeared from the bottoms of knapsacks and mattresses. After forty-six months of seeing the "flaming asshole", our hearts were lifted by the sight of these banners waving in the breeze. The Rising Sun had set.

I filled my footlocker with food from the air-drops. Dick, Grant and I carried it to Harold Mason's house as a gift. Another box was given to Dave Hatter. Luckily, their houses had escaped the fire bombs. Each family invited us to dinner with warm sake and sushi for appetizers. It was thrilling to dine in a home, laughing and talking together with beautiful wives and children. Having returned to a little corner of civilization, we had to recall our table-manners.

We roamed at will. Other prisoners drifted into our camp to swap stories. On September 6, Bill Young ran into fifty American soldiers and nurses that had arrived in Kobe the night before. Waldorf Morse, one of my high school classmates, was among them. He sent me his regards and congratulations. Bill was told that a rescue team from Tokyo was on its way to liberate our camp. Things were finally happening.

On September 7, Bob Vaughn and Stan McNulty were in a near fatal accident when the truck, in which they were riding, crashed into a tree. Bob catapulted into the tree and was nearly paralyzed. The British drivers who had pirated the truck ran away and left them screaming in agony. Found, by some Japanese, they were carried into a nearby house. They were hauled to camp on a stretcher. It would have been ironic to die in the midst of rescue after forty-six months in prison.

At long last, we learned that we were leaving Futatabi the next morning.

At 8:30 A.M. on September 8, 1945, a United States rescue team of eight soldiers, headed by a First Lieutenant, entered the camp. How strange they looked—friendly, efficient, well fed, neatly dressed. We wanted to ask them a thousand questions about America and the war that had passed us by, but they were too busy to talk. They assured us that everything would be all right and quickly got on with their job.

We gave the Lieutenant a list of the deserving locals and their addresses, with the request that they distribute the excess food on the lawn to these families

We were to be ready to leave the camp by 4 P.M. that day. Trucks would take us to the train station for a 5 P.M. departure for Yokohama. We were limited to a minimum amount of luggage. We'd never been rescued before, so we were amateurs at the routine. We stood in line to answer dozens of questions about our health, identities, and possible injuries that needed attention. We filled out citizenship forms. We were bathed and deloused with disinfectant spray. After all this, we were issued a large duffel bag, a G.I. uniform, shoes and socks, and a jaunty cap.

I returned to my room to pack. It was a solemn assignment, sorting out my belongings. The spoon, fork and mug that had carried me through the war were wrapped in my socks and gently placed in my pack. In my new duffel went my overcoat, an old patched jacket, a shirt, my home-made cribbage board, a rocker arm from the B-29 that had crashed over our camp, a hara-kiri knife, razor, toothbrush, a pair of zoris and my canvas bag. My pinup girl, Phyllis Thaxter, had been almost destroyed by admiring inspectors. So I folded her damaged picture respectfully and tossed it out the window and bid her "thanks and Sayonara." I had given my barber kit to Dave Hatter.

Filled with nostalgia, I inspected my room, the hall, and the benjo. I stared at the canyon, went through the tunnel to my garden plot and walked quietly and alone around the entire camp for a last look. My emotions were mixed. I felt a strange and unexpected affinity for the place. This had been my home and my world for nearly two years. I had agonized, laughed, starved, despaired and cursed the place a thousand times. But today I was like an adolescent leaving home to seek his fortune in the great unknown. At the same time, I wanted to leave Futatabi behind forever. Respectfully, I waved a friendly good bye to the place as I went over the hill for the last time.

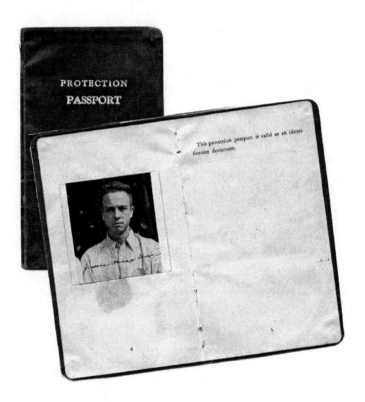

CHAPTER 40

Leaving Japan

Facing Osaka twenty miles to the east, the train was sighing patiently at the Kobe station. Following orders from the Lieutenant, we piled into the first three cars. As we stashed our baggage under the seats and on the floor, the train chugged out of the station headed for Yokohama 350 miles north.

We'd barely settled down when the train ground to a stop at Osaka. We had thirty minutes to stretch and look around. There on the platform was the most beautiful sight we'd seen in forty-six months—a chic, neatly uniformed, vivacious, blonde WAC exuding All-American charm. A welcome sight to our hungry eyes. I can only imagine her impression of us, the ugliest band of wolves ever assembled. Was she real? Mustering my nerve, I stepped forward.

"Are you a real American girl and can you speak English? May I touch you to see if I'm dreaming?"

She held out her hand, "Yes, I am real and you may touch me." The crowd roared. Every man began firing questions at her. How was America? Were there women in the B-29s? What were they going to do with us? Had America changed during wartime? Was Deanna Durbin dead? What was the latest song? The train's whistle told us our time was up. Climbing aboard, we settled down with the realization of what we had missed most in our cloistered lives. I wanted to tell her what a thrill she had given us that night.

We passed Nagoya—the entire city flattened. At each station, the Japs gave us a bucket of hot water to drink. But we had no

cups so it cooled as it sat unused. In tunnels, smoke poured through
the open windows. Coughing and groping in the dark, we slammed
the windows shut. Lice and fleas kept us busy, but we didn't mind
such trivial matters. We were going home.

Dusk settled in as the engine pounded and whistled through
the countryside. We passed small villages and farms relatively undisturbed by the war. Box lunches and tea were served for dinner,
plenty to satisfy our shrunken appetites. Night closed in and the
clacking wheels lulled us into a fitful sleep. We were headed north
to freedom.

At 9 o'clock on the morning of September 9, 1945 the
train pulled into the Yokohama station. We stumbled out of
the cars into a strange and unbelievable world. Unusual noises,
colors, and smells inundated us. Guarding it all from on high
was Old Glory waving atop a flagpole, the sweetest sight of all.
Its stars and stripes had never looked brighter. Tears welled in
our eyes. as we saluted the colors. The U.S. Army with all its
spit and polish, with all its exuberance and gusto, with all its
hospitality and kindness, was there to greet us. As a huge military band played *California, Here We Come*, I tingled with confused excitement. I'd almost forgotten that beautiful tune. The
hubbub was deafening. American friends, American faces,
American music, smiles, handshakes, hugs. Lumbering trucks,
glistening guns, roaring planes, chaotic activity, rapid move-
ments enveloped us. Huddled together into a tight little band
for strength and companionship, we shuffled forward through
the happy bedlam. Was it a dream? They were treating us like
heroes! What had we done to deserve this warm welcome?

But the mad whirl had just started. Funny little cars called
Jeeps sped back and forth hauling officers and men. Despite the
hustle, there was a sense of efficiency in the organized confusion.
Officers issued orders and soldiers snapped to attention.

The sights were hypnotizing. Attractive colors covered everything. Smooth, clean khaki uniforms, bright epaulets, jaunty leather
flight jackets, nurses in white, camouflaged war equipment, and

black shiny shoes caught our eyes. This was a far cry from the drab world of Futatabi.

Orderlies helped us board waiting buses that sped through the ruined streets of Yokohama to the nearby Yokosuka Naval Base. They stopped at a yard filled with enormous tents housing tables, chairs, kitchen equipment and benjos.

A delectable down-home breakfast awaited us. The first of its kind in forty-six months. Long-missing aromas of an American kitchen floated through the air. Fried bacon, ham, eggs, toast, hotcakes, butter, syrup, hot coffee, and orange juice, wafting their special charms, were set before us. We had forgotten such delicious food existed. Some stared goggle-eyed at the stack of hot cakes not sure where to begin, what to do. Shy, emaciated men glanced around wondering if it was all right to start eating. One asked a good-natured G.I. for another cup of coffee—no more Kobe trash! Our shrunken stomachs limited our intake. Finished, we stared helplessly at the steaming food on our plates.

There were hundreds of prisoners sitting in the far end of a warehouse waiting to be processed. We took our places and waited our turn. Men without legs, living skeletons, were unable to talk. Hollow-eyed and silent, they sat like obedient children waiting for someone to help them. Hospital ships lay along side the dock to take care of the stretcher cases.

A portable American toilet, with a seat and soft tissue was a pleasant surprise. What luxury to sit and ponder the mysteries of life. Little wonder the Japs thought Americans were sissies and too weak to fight in the jungles. A comfortable toilet would pacify anyone.

We were bathed, deloused, given a hasty medical check and issued new clothes. Red Cross canteens gave us cigarettes, candy and ice cream. A Hershey bar and a vanilla cone were too tasty to describe.

Someone shoved a ticket home into our hands. Bob Vaughn, with a battered back, had been placed aboard one of the ships for a long voyage home. He violently protested being separated from the PanAm group who was scheduled to fly home that afternoon, thanks to PanAm's connection to the Navy. Even though Bob could barely walk, Gregg pulled strings and got him off the ship in time. The poor guy trembled in pain but was adamant about joining us.

At 4 P.M. we boarded the train for the Atzugi airfield. By the time we arrived, we were lousy again. No matter. Trucks were waiting to drive us to the airport. As the sun sank below the horizon, what was left of Japan and its Greater East Asian Co-Prosperity Sphere was left in the twilight.

At the airfield, the Army fed us again to the music of a swing band. The nostalgic tunes brought lumps to our throats. Toe-tapping *Chattanooga Choo-Choo* and *Don't Sit Under the Apple Tree* made us smile. A group from an outfit called the USO (United Service Organization) sang *Sentimental Journey*, reminding me of our attic hideaway, the junky little radio and sweet Doris Day.

Giant C-54's landed and took off every thirty seconds. Troops and equipment came in, prisoners and sick went out. The efficiency of the American military, the quality and quantity of its supplies, the snap and diligence of its personnel, all were in sharp contrast to the destitution of their defeated Japanese counterparts.

At 7:15 P.M. we climbed aboard a C-54 skyliner, and following the instructions of the pretty stewardess, fastened our seat belts and pinched ourselves to see if we were dreaming. With the four engines echoing defiance, we headed down the runway. At 7:32 P.M. on September 9, 1945, with Mt. Fuji silhouetted in the distance, I said good bye and to hell with Japan. Forty-six miserable months ago I had arrived dirty, hungry, freezing, and hopeless in the hold of the Argentina Maru. Now I was leaving clean, warm, well-fed and happy in a luxurious skyliner. As the lights of Yokohama disappeared from view, just as those lights of San Francisco had disappeared so many years before, I wondered again what awaited me at the end of my journey.

Two hours later, we landed at Okinawa. An awaiting truck taxied us on an exhilarating ride through the woods and fields. Motion, wind, sounds and the aroma of a clean countryside awakened our sleeping senses. Swerving around the curves, it stopped in front of a Red Cross canteen. A smiling uniformed lady served us doughnuts, coffee, cream and sugar. I also had my first Coca-Cola. Its sweet tang tasted like the nectar of the gods. Then off to the prisoners-of-war compound to sleep in my first American bed in nearly four years. Crispy clean sheets devoid of bugs, lice and buzzing insects caressed my aching body. What luxury!

More than 10,000 prisoners crowded the gigantic compound. Americans, Dutch, Anzacs, and British in all shapes, sizes, and conditions. We were delayed for three days while a typhoon blew itself out in the Philippines, so we swapped yarns, read magazines, drank hot chocolate and chewed Milky Ways. It rained steadily but we didn't mind the mud. The military guys told stories of hell holes in the jungles. The Japs had been as cruel as the Germans at Buchenwald. We cringed at the horrible reports. Three days in the chow line three times a day curbed our appetites and tightened our belts.

On the morning of the fourth day, we were awakened, fed, mustered, registered, and driven to the airstrip. A B-24 awaited us, and the friendly crew made our flight to Manila a pleasant one. We dabbled in small talk amongst ourselves.

"There's a subtle thing going on between my nose and my brain," I ventured. "Maybe you guys can tell me if my nose is playing tricks. But there's a difference in the odor between the Japs and the Americans. Their smells must reflect what they eat. Japs smell like boiled rice, fish and soy beans. Americans smell like meat, milk, and potatoes. Maybe we now smell like Japs. Have you guys noticed?"

Grant and Dick agreed. Bob and George were non-committal. Gregg ignored the question. Fred added "Wait till you smell a pretty girl and she smells you. That'll prove the point."

We knew we were lucky to be alive. We'd had many close calls but the closest had come at the end of the war. Investigators found a directive in Prime Minister Tojo's file to all military units to kill all foreigners, including military and civilian war prisoners, in case of an invasion of the Japanese homeland by Allied forces. We suspected this would be the case if the bomb had not been dropped. I owe my life to Harry Truman. God bless him!

Five hours after takeoff, we circled Manila and flew low over Clark field noting hundreds of B-29s, P51s, and helicopters parked and combat-ready. The quantity of supplies seemed mountains high. America was ready to invade Japan.

From the stories about the destruction of Manila, I didn't expect to see much of the city left. Except for a number of bombed-out areas, the city appeared intact. The harbor, however, was a graveyard of sunken Jap ships.

A band greeted us with another rendition of *California, Here We Come*. As we passed through the city to our compound it was obvious that Manila, though injured, was in excellent shape in comparison with Kobe, or Osaka, or Yokohama. Shops were open, restaurants, dance halls and bars were doing a brisk business. In Kobe, everything had been leveled—nothing open, no one shopping, nowhere to be entertained. Kobe, indeed, was a dead city but Manila, had survived.

We stayed seven days in Manila. Again, we were issued new clothes, barbered, bathed, and fed all the coke, candy and beer we could consume. We knocked around the downtown center and took in the sights. It was shocking to see young boys swaggering around with daggers in their belts, carbines in their hands, and cigarettes dangling from their lips, like real tough commandos. We saw our first movie, something about a battle in the jungle. We'd almost forgotten about motion pictures, so this propaganda flick kept us spellbound. Our biggest surprise was finding letters from home, uncensored. We were happy to learn that our families were well. A few guys were overjoyed to learn their wives and girl friends were still waiting. Others didn't realize that disillusionment awaited them. I was glad that I was unattached. I was happy to learn I had a new niece, but saddened to hear that many of my friends had died in action.

Waldo Raugust, a PanAm employee captured on Wake Island,

joined us. A bit thin but still hardy, he had hair-raising stories to tell. The strangest tale of all was his missing the PanAm plane with all the company employees aboard that escaped before the Japs captured the island. Waldo was delivering a wounded Chamorran to the infirmary when the plane, unable to wait any longer, finally took off without him. As a reward for his bravery and compassion, he spent forty-four hellish months in a Jap prison camp.

Transportation was finally arranged with the Navy and we left from Sangley Point in a NATS (National Air Service) Catalina patrol plane headed for Saipan. I thought of Saipy, our little dachshund, and wondered if his new masters were treating him right.

After a two hour stop in Saipan, we took off for Majuro Island in the Marshall Islands group. This tropical fairyland provided steaks and ice cream during a USO show while one of the engines was repaired. Sandy beaches lured us into a warm lagoon for our first swim. We hadn't forgotten how to dog-paddle.

Our next gas stop was Johnson Island, another tropical Shangri-la. Another meal, more ice cream. Each island across the Pacific seemed to be competing in hospitality.

On a short hop from Johnson Island, we flew into Honolulu on September 24. Pearl Harbor never looked better despite the brave men and their ships resting on the bottom. As I stepped off the plane at the PanAm base, a hand clutched mine and a friendly voice said, "Welcome home Jim. You're a hero." I recognized the smiling face of Al Lindsay, one of the fellows with whom I was hired and had left San Francisco more than four years before, he to Midway and I to Guam. Ginger leis were placed around our necks by pretty maidens in hula skirts just as the native girls had done in 1941 as we disembarked from the Mariposa. Photographers knelt and snapped our pictures. Reporters with scratch pads crowded around for their scoop of the day. Then, off to a naval hospital for a quick checkup. After that, a lunch at the Officer's Club and off to the airport at Barbers Point to board the Honolulu Clipper, the same Clipper that had delivered me to Guam in 1941—eons ago.

Arriving in Honolulu, September 1945—PanAm group. Front:
L-R-Al Hammelef, Dick Arvidson, Max Brodofsky, Grant Wells,
George Conklin, Waldo Rauquist.
Back Row: Bob Vaughn, Fred Oppenborn, George Blackett, Jim
Thomas, Charles Gregg, Ev Penning.

The luxurious cabin and upholstered seats gave us a feeling of
importance. The stewards were solicitous and eager to please. Cock-
tails were offered but declined. Hot meals were served from the
galley. We slept fitfully to the soothing hum of the motors. As we
passed equitime point, I knew beyond any question we were heading home to the States. There was no turning back.

A strange feeling gradually engulfed me. It had been seeping
into my subconscious over the past few days but I had tried to
ignore it.

I had mixed emotions about going home.

I felt I was peeking from behind a curtain at the frightening
spectacle of my own homecoming. Feeling confused and unquali-
fied, I was scared to face an unknown future in a strange land.
Besides, this blatant attention was wearing on my nerves. I was
already missing my friends and the simplicity of Futatabi. My

country and I had been separated for four years. I felt inadequate to bridge that separation..

Afraid of drawing their ridicule, I gingerly mentioned this dilemma to Dick and Bob. To my surprise, they agreed with me. They, too, suffered these doubts.

Captain Barrows, an old friend, allowed me to look out the cockpit windshield. The flat horizon, like the horizon at Guam long ago was flat and stationary. I gazed at the ocean below as I had in this same beautiful Honolulu clipper four years earlier on my way out to the tropical paradise of Guam and an exotic future. The friendly waves seemed to beckon me as they had above French Frigate Shoals.

Returning to the cabin, I noticed everyone sitting alone, staring out the windows, lost in thoughts. Grant began straightening his shirt. Blackett retied his shoelaces. Bob kept combing his hair while Gregg tucked in his shirttail for the fourth time. As the plane droned on, we laughed silly little laughs and chattered non-sensically. Brodofsky wiped his forehead and shifted in his seat. Fred went to the bathroom to freshen up. Checking the tilt of my cap, I went back to the cockpit.

After an eternity, a speck of land appeared and gradually took the shape of a mountain.

"That's Mt. Tamalpais." said Barrows matter-of-factly, "Mt. Diablo will show in a minute. They're about a hundred miles away."

I stared so hard my temples throbbed. America was rising out of the ocean. The Coast Range took shape and I searched for the Golden Gate bridge. Suddenly, there it was, a graceful arch of steel, spanning the Golden Gate as it had in the summer of 1941. Only then it was disappearing from view as I leaned on the stern railing of the Mariposa.

We swept low over the harbor. San Francisco, Oakland, Alcatraz, Angel Island, Sausalito, and the gorgeous San Francisco Bay spread out below us, all fresh and clean and untouched by war. The clipper circled and prepared to land at Mills Field (presently the San

Francisco International Airport) bordering the bay's water in San Mateo. Was PanAm's base at Treasure Island off limits? No, the PanAm base had moved to San Mateo. The clipper sloshed to a stop and, with a renewed roar, taxied toward the ramp.

We rose and fiddled with our uniforms again. As the plane entered the lagoon, we saw the waterfront crowded with people waving handkerchiefs and banners. There must have been a thousand of them. As the plane touched the dock and I prepared to step out, a band struck up *Home Sweet Home*. It was too much for me to handle. I ducked back into the cabin too ashamed to cry in front of all those people. Swallowing to hold back the tears, I held the doorframe for support. When the signal was given to disembark, it took all the guts I could muster to be the first off and face that happy throng. When the band played *God Bless America*, the crowd screamed, and my legs started to buckle.

**I was first off the Honolulu Clipper at San Francisco Airport,
1945. Followed by Max Brodofsky.**

The crowd was held back a minute while the photographers
snapped their cameras. On a given signal a surge of screaming
humanity engulfed us. I searched frantically for my mother and
brother but they were not there. I felt alone and forgotten in the
crowd. But I got a vicarious thrill at the squeals of delight as moth-

ers, fathers, sweethearts, and kids flung themselves into the arms of their loved ones. Grant's little girl hugged the sobbing daddy she had never seen. Men and women alike wept openly. No one noticed that I was alone.

We were led to the terminal building. More refreshments, while the photographers and reporters buzzed among us. A PanAm vice-president shouted, "Congratulations! You're back; PanAm and America welcome you."

President L.C. Reynolds told us, "Your accrued salaries await you, take a vacation—forget the past and come back to work when you feel like it."

I spoke to my mother on the phone. Her sweet voice quavered and then she dissolved in tears when I told her I'd be home in a few days. I realized then she was unable to travel to San Francisco. My brother in Oceanside, California had left his phone number with the request to call when I arrived. He uttered a fumbling greeting. The situation probably embarrassed him.

A company van took a few of us to see San Francisco. I was struck by the general familiarity of the place and yet enchanted by the sights and sounds that seemed new and exciting. Buildings painted in beautiful pastels and tasteful colors swept past the window, a sharp contrast with Japan's wooden buildings, an unpainted dull, monotonous gray. The sound of musical bands, the clang of streetcars, the roar of autos, the whistle of cops, and the noise level everywhere rattled my ears. Everybody was frantically going somewhere and doing something. People walked and talked faster. Skirts were shorter and tighter (which we appreciated) and the bobbed hair styles were sleek and attractive. Since nylons were scarce, the gals painted their legs with stocking designs. An ingenious way to cope with the problem. Radios blared the latest hit tunes in a musical style that was heavier on brass and drums.

The lexicon had changed. New words and phrases like "fat, dumb, and happy", made me smile. Acronyms like "snafu" (situation normal, all fouled up), "fubar" (fouled up beyond all recognition) and "tarfu" (things are really fouled up) described life with humorous honesty.

America was at the peak of its power and enjoying it. Factories were turning out war materiel in a flood. New cars were nonexistent because Detroit was making tanks instead. Meat, butter, and canned foods were rationed. The military got first chance at all items. Store windows displayed smiling mannequins draped in conservative clothes. War propaganda dominated the radio, newspapers and movies. Hollywood had turned out hundreds of B pictures to entertain the home front and the troops. *Time* and *Life* magazines filled their pages with stark photographs and chilling reports of the war alongside photos of starlets and Rosy the Riveter. War bonds sold like hotcakes. Everyone seemed to be patriotic and happy. This was America geared for war and I was thrilled to see it.

Returning to the PanAm building, I was given $100.00 as a draw on my salary and a plane ticket on United Air Lines to Salt Lake City, departing in half an hour. The broad, rugged, and beautiful landscape of the Wild West flowed beneath me. Salt Lake City and the Wasatch range looked familiar and the lake seemed as flat as ever.

Darkness was creeping over the mountains as I boarded a bus for Malad, Idaho, 120 miles to the north. We passed Ogden and Tremonton, Utah. As I entered Malad valley, the moonlight gave a soft glow over familiar benchmarks along the highway. I saw the lights of Malad appear ahead. As usual the town seemed asleep— after all it was eleven PM and all decent Mormons should be in bed. Consternation at my late arrival churned my thoughts. Would anybody be there to meet me? If not, how was I going to get a ride out home this time of night? Mother was old and hardly capable of coming to get me. I felt nervous, unable to plan.

As the bus turned into Main street I could barely make out the Co-op store or the Malad hotel. Bannock and Main, the center of town slept soundly and only a few cars were parked near the two saloons. Stepping off the bus with my duffel, I stood alone looking for someone I knew. Nobody. As I stood there on the empty sidewalk a friendly voice yelled a hello. It was my cousin Sarah Larson, our nearest neighbor. She had happened by after some last minute shopping. We embraced. It felt great to see someone from the family.

"Jimmy Thomas, I never even knew you were coming. Your mother's fine. Does she know? Can I give you a ride home?"

"You sure can. I didn't realize I'd be so late."

My place was four miles west into the central part of the valley. On the way, Sarah gave me a quick briefing on the effects of the war and who was killed and who was married. The road hadn't changed and our neighbors were still tilling their farms. But nearly all the young men had joined up.

We turned into the yard. The house and barns were in darkness. Mother and Aunt Stena were asleep. Sarah went with me to the door. My knees were knocking louder than my rap on the door. I heard a shuffle inside. The light in the kitchen came on and Mother, in her bathrobe, opened the door. She let out a scream and gathered me in her arms. We sobbed together before standing back to eye each other. In four years, she had aged ten years from worrying about me and I felt I had aged twenty in the same time.

"Jim, my God it's good to see you. Are you hungry? Could I fix you something to eat? Steen, wake up. Jim's home."

Aunt Stena emerged from the bedroom, rubbing her eyes and adjusting her dress. She hadn't changed a bit. Sarah said goodnight and left us to soak up the moment.

The old kitchen and the wood stove never looked better. Except for the modern telephone, things hadn't changed at all. The table, chairs, refrigerator, and china cabinet were right where I had left them. I inspected every room. All the furniture was in its accustomed place. In the living room I saw the spread-legged table, the wood burning heater, the tall china dresser on top of which Mother used to hide our Christmas presents, the old Philco radio, the divan, the bookshelf filled with our childhood books, and her pedal sewing machine that patched and re-patched our clothing. The adjoining bedroom with its two double beds, separated by a wooden chest filled with letters. The wardrobe closet filled with her deceased children's clothes stood in the corner and a lonely, makeshift bookcase completed the familiar scene.

They were tired so we went to bed. The clean, white sheets welcomed me. Even more welcome was the silence of the country-side, with the occasional mooing of a cow in the distance, the rustle of the shade trees from a friendly breeze. The familiar sounds and smells awakened my childhood memories and crowned my first night in this rustic, little log house where I was born.

Kitchen noises awakened me. Mother's building the fire in the old stove and preparing my breakfast, mingled with the mourning doves singing their welcome, was almost more than I could stand. I heard a tractor and a pickup passing as the country-side came alive.

With my mother, day after arrival home.
Note my G.I. clothing—1945

The smell of bacon, sausage, fried eggs, scrambled eggs, hotcakes, toast and coffee filled the house. Mother was ready to feed me. I ate a little of each but the food, though appetizing and enticing, was more than I could manage. The two ladies were disappointed, almost insulted, that I left their efforts almost untouched.

I escaped from the house and went outside. The old homestead, except for a little more aging, looked like the place I'd left years before. I was surprised to see that Mother had rented the farm and sold all the livestock. But I walked about the empty yards, soaking up the sights, smells and sounds of my boyhood. I will never forget that walk But I felt strange and out of place. A chasm had opened between me and reality that would haunt me for a long time to come.

I was home at last and my life as a free man was about to start all over again.

CHAPTER 41

Adjusting to Freedom

To my dismay, I learned there's more to homecoming than bacon, eggs, and apple pie. As pleasant and appreciated as all the food, and attentions were, I felt confused and out of place in this now strange homeland that I had dreamed about for so long.

Friends and relatives, good people all, came to see me. A mixture of curiosity and concern reflected in their faces. I wondered if they were expecting to see an emaciated wrack of bones or an idiot driven insane from four years of starvation and torture. They seemed almost disappointed to see me looking so well. As good Mormons do, some brought pies and cakes as tokens of love and respect. Others stopped me on the street to shake my hand and welcome me home. The friendly butcher gave me choice cuts without asking for food stamps. Overwhelmed by this outpouring of love, I found it difficult to communicate, to make them understand that I wanted to be left alone to get my bearings, visit old sights, and quietly absorb the pleasure of being free again.

Well-meaning as these good countryfolk were, the inevitable first question was, "How did they treat you?" I wearied of answering the question, and I quickly grew to hate the subject. I wanted to forget it, think of happier things and talk to mother. I wanted to know what it was like in America during the war and learn what I had missed.

Some public recognition was kind and complimentary. Two Mormon bishops competed in wanting me to speak to their congregations. I gave the main address at the Armistice Day celebration and spoke to the audience on the theme of "life, liberty and the pursuit of happiness." They gave me a standing ovation. The Republican Party asked me to run for state senator. I politely refused, since politics definitely was not my cup of tea.

A hidden wall remained between me and those on the home front. We talked a different language. The average person seemed frivolous and shallow to me and I probably impressed them as a dismal bore. I read papers, magazines, and all the books I could find, trying to catch up on the war. I saw scores of wartime movies and laughed at their slanted themes. On the radio, I caught Bob Hope, and Edward R. Morrow. Old friends who were still around seemed like strangers. Many of my fraternity brothers had died in the war, making me feel both sad and guilty. Most of my old girlfriends had joined the WACs, worked in war industries, or married and moved away.

Since I was not suffering from any major body problems, physical recovery came quickly. Regaining lost weight required nothing more than eating Mother's cooking, a pleasing pastime, and I tucked away second helpings. But eating didn't touch the real problem.

Psychologically, I was all mixed up. Disoriented. Everything in Idaho seemed as foreign to me as everything had seemed that morning I caught my first look at Japan outside of the Zentsuji camp. Then, I was adjusting to a miserable prison life—confinement and hunger, compliance and resignation. Four years of Japanese restrictions and regimentation had changed me. Now I had to reverse directions and catch up with the world that had passed me by.

In truth, I was finding it as hard to adjust to freedom as it had been to adjust to prison life. I had to make my own decisions, assume responsibilities, and pay my bills. Four years of confinement had repressed my initiative and fostered inactivity and passive acceptance. In short I was changing gears with a loose clutch.

PanAm gave us back pay at the salary at which we were hired—no raises, no bonuses. Since I was earning $125.00 a month, I got a healthy check for $5750.00—the biggest sum I had ever had all at once. Ironically, since we had left a tax-free island, Guam, and gone to a non-tax-free foreign country, Japan, the IRS decided we must pay income tax. Flabbergasted and furious, we screamed to the company about this ugly injustice. We stirred PanAm into protesting this outrageous demand and after several months of negotiations and a letter to the President, the IRS backed off.

Most of the PanAm internees were disappointed in their new assignments. We felt that the company had changed from the old, familiar, personable corporation it had been before the war. Now, PanAm, phasing out its obsolete Boeing flying-boats for fast, land based Lockheed Constellations, was filling expanded contracts and had already hired hundreds of new employees. Updated technology called for new job descriptions and personnel policies. Progress had passed us by and the new management didn't know what to do with us, for we had seniority but no modern skills.

Hired as an Assistant Station Manager, I was now reassigned as a Flight Dispatcher. That meant shift work—one week "days", one week "swing", and one week "graveyard"in rotation. My life turned into a topsy-turvy world of changing schedules, alternating days-off, and disruptive sleep patterns It was an unnatural life style and I couldn't adapt. The humdrum work routine was mentally debilitating and the loss of sleep taxed my health. I knew I didn't want to spend the rest of my life like this, but couldn't seem to find a better direction.

On a typical day, the airport office was a bustle of noisy ex-GIs, clacking teletypes, and roaring engines warming up for take-off. Between arrivals and departures, we swilled down gallons of bitter coffee, saturated the air with cigarette smoke and listened to embellished GI talk. All the self-proclaimed heroes had a war story and the first liar didn't have a chance. Tall tales of "daring-do" gave me a feeling of inferiority, and a sense of having missed all the colorful action of the war. One guy was a glider pilot who won a medal on D-Day. Another was decorated for shooting down two Zeros in the South Pacific. Another had single-handedly defeated Hitler by marching all the way to the Rhine. One night on "swing,"someone asked me about Japan. I was surprised that anyone would be interested in my relatively dull experiences after all those exciting tales.

To keep their attention, I told them about the bombing of Kobe on March 17, 1945, when more than half the city was destroyed with incendiaries. I told how a B-29 was hit by a Kamikaze and fell in pieces around our camp. They were silent as I told of finding and burying the body of the brave pilot, Major Fitzgerald. My story finished, I returned to my desk.

Stan Pierce, a quiet, pleasant trainee, tapped me on the shoulder. His face was somber but friendly, and his steady eyes were misty.

In a low voice he said. "I was in that raid on Kobe, and Major Fitzgerald was my buddy. We all wondered what happened that night when he didn't return. This is the first time I've heard for sure that he was killed. We were told only that he was missing in action, that's all. Many 'Missing in Action' guys were later rescued at sea so we always held out hope that he was still alive in some Jap prison camp."

"We sent his papers and belongings to his wife after we were released." I replied. "She was very grateful, but it was hard to break the news to her. What a coincidence that you knew him!"

"He and I met in training," Stan reminisced, relieved to find someone who understood. "We flew out to Moffett Field together on our way to Saipan and stayed at my folks' house in Los Altos. My wife and I decided to take him to the Moffett Field Officer's Club for a last fling. Since his wife was back East, I talked my sister Barbara into being his "date." We had a good time and left the next day for the blue Pacific and God knows what."

"What kind of a guy was he?"

"The best, and one helluva pilot. We did four raids together – Tokyo, Yokohama, Osaka and Kobe. By the way, why don't you come to my folks' place next Sunday, for a swim and barbecue. Bring a date. My folks will be glad to meet you. How about it?"

With crossed fingers and a touch of anxiety, I accepted his invitation.

I didn't know any girls except a casual few at PanAm. But I gathered my courage and asked Gail, a friendly airport clerk, to come with me. We followed Stan's map and arrived at his folks' home in Los Altos Hills about 3 P.M., Sunday afternoon. His beautiful mother left off working in her flower garden, to greet us warmly.

"You and your wife might like a quiet dip before the rest of the family comes. They'll be here soon and they're pretty boisterous."

She pointed to the large, inviting pool and bath houses, and told us to make ourselves at home. After setting her straight on our non-marital status, Gail and I changed into our bathing suits and dove in. We were splashing happily about when a beautiful, dark-haired girl in a flowered dress appeared at pool side. I was overwhelmed by her graceful figure and easy manner. Gail, too, was impressed.

"Hi, I'm Barbara, Stan's sister. Welcome aboard," she said with a warm smile.

I finally collected myself enough to introduce ourselves. Needless to say, I was smitten. For all time.

Barbara and I were married six months later, on March 26, 1947. I wish I could thank Major Fitzgerald for his unwitting role of cupid in this ironic coincidence of my meeting Barbara.

Four years later, I felt I'd reached a dead end with PanAm, so I regretfully resigned, leaving behind memories, friends, and *Clipper Glory*. After several false starts, I found a fulfilling profession in real estate finance which I followed for 36 years, retiring in 1987.

Now, in the year 1998, 56 years after rescue, I'm living happily in Mountain View, California with sweet Barbara. We have three daughters and a son who have, collectively, presented us eight grandchildren. The four children, sans spouses and kids, hosted our Golden Wedding Anniversary last year in the La Playa hotel in Carmel, California where we had spent our first night of our honeymoon. My best man, Dick Arvidson and, Pat, Barbara's sister and Maid of Honor, were there to help us celebrate. Stan Pierce,

Barbara's brother who introduced us also attended. Barbara never looked lovelier and as I viewed our progeny around the banquet table—all happy, healthy, loving, and beautiful, I felt immensely proud and fortunate. The circle was complete.

CHAPTER 42

Epilogue

Many felt a let-down from their glorified anticipations of home-coming. Most of the returnees found their families intact and ready to start a new life together, some did not. Some found their wives had spent their ongoing salaries and had run off with a new boyfriend. Others learned their girlfriends had forgotten them and disappeared. One Guam resident learned his wife was a Japanese collaborator. Most everyone felt lost and out of touch. Unable to cope with the changed society and missing their internee friends, some drifted away, some took to drink, and some committed suicide. Internment had left an indelible stain on our characters. The more fortunate made successful transitions—found jobs, got married, and had kids. I was lucky to be unattached so I had no one to please but myself. I went through the motions of adjustment but my heart was not in it. I could not rush things as time was needed to heal the wounds of captivity. Luckily, I found Barbara who helped me think of more immediate things. Like the advise given by R.H. Blyth years earlier, I had to put the past behind and concentrate on the present. It worked but it took time.

At this writing (2001), very few Futatabi internees are left, perhaps a dozen or so. Those I have contacted lately seem happy and well adjusted. All bitterness towards the Japs, in particular, and man's injustice to man, in general, has dis-appeared. When we meet now, it's always fun to recall old times and turn unpleasant camp episodes into humorous anecdotes.

Being the sentimental type, I have held several reunions of the old PanAm bunch at my home over the past twenty years, Of the original eleven, only four of us are left: Bob Vaughn. Grant Wells, Dick Arvidson, and me.

Of other friendly internees, Jack Taylor has retired from an exciting career at Caltech where he worked in the space program, Bill Young dabbled in Idaho politics and became a successful Idaho attorney, Roy Henning became a popular electronic executive. Bill and Roy died a few years ago. Red Rupert ran a successful trucking business which he sold before retiring in Florida. Other roustabouts in the contractors gang continued their careers in various world wide construction projects. I've lost track of most of them.

My PanAm buddies did quite well. Dick Arvidson and I have shared good moments together. He was my Best Man at my wedding fifty-four years ago and I was Best Man at his wedding that occurred in my living room. Dick had a successful career as communications supervisor with PanAm. He is now retired in Oregon.

Grant Wells is happily retired from a fulfilling career in aviation and lives in Vacaville, California with his loyal life.

Fred Oppenborn retired from Aerosiam and died in Bangkok a few years ago. Charles Gregg and Max Brodofsky carved out long careers with PanAm.

George Conklin retired from a career with the Stanford Research Institute.

Al Hammelef died a sad death in Manila.

Ev Penning and George Blackett lived out their lives in their hometowns. In fact, George vowed to never leave Wells, Nevada again. As far as I know, he never did.

Bob Vaughn married his loyal girl friend Ann and went to United Airlines. He retired to help his clever wife manage their real estate investments. He still brags about salting the Skull's bath.

Barbara and I visited Kyoto and Kobe in 1988 as guests of Shigeru Tenaka. a secondary school English teacher in Kyoto. Shigeru had been our house guest a few years before on his visit to Los Altos High School where Barbara worked. He drove us around in search of old prison sites. The Canadian Academy had been destroyed in the bombing. The site now was an archery range in a large park. Only the elementary school across the street remained. Marilyn Monroe's picture was tacked to the new electric light pole abutting the site. Ito-Machi Street was there but the Seaman's Mission had been destroyed in the bombing and a modern office building stood in its place. I walked the length of Ito-machi for one last time, remembering.

**My barracks at Zentsuji Prison Camp near Todatsu,
Japan—June, 1988.**

We found the Zentsuji camp mostly intact, but it was now a driving school for taxis and bus drivers. I inspected the barracks where I lived in 1942. I actually saw the slot where my bunk was located. The attendant gave me a small piece of wood from the building for a souvenir.

The nearby Kobe Athletic and Racquet Club park had been converted to a children's playground full of slides and sandboxes. The bleachers had disappeared long ago. The happy, screaming kids playing on the slides never knew anything about the role their park had played in the war. They didn't even know there had been a war nor did they care.

Old stove room and cistern—all that is left of Futatabi

**Boarded up tunnel at Futatabi Prison Camp—
one of the few remaining landmarks—June 1988.**

Futatabi was the biggest surprise of all. The Japanese in the area knew nothing about its history or location, so we had difficulty finding the site. After much searching we managed to reach a country school in the adjoining canyon. The headmaster was most helpful and directed us through his school grounds. The campsite was a shock to see. All but the store house had been destroyed by fire. The ground was flat and barren. The only landmarks left were the cistern, the store house, and the boarded-up tunnel. Walking around the exercise yard my mind was flooded with memories of R.H. Blyth, Roy Henning, Harold Mason, and dozens of other buddies of long ago. I was sorry that I had made the effort. Thomas Wolfe was right when he said, "You can't go home again."

Kobe itself was one of the most modern cities we saw in Japan. The U.S. Army's air wing can take most of the credit for Kobe's urban renewal, for the entire city had been rebuilt as a result of the bombings. Skyscrapers, streetcars, promenades, and shopping centers had risen out of the rubble. The waterfront had regained its noise and clutter.

Shigeru invited us to speak to his English students. They were polite and respectful. They asked good questions about their counterparts in America. Because of its cultural heritage, Kyoto had been spared bombing during the war. None of his students seemed to know anything about the war. It was as if it had never happened. Only the very elderly remembered and they wanted to forget, so they avoided the subject.

Harold Mason, Dave Hatter and Reggie Price immigrated to America where their daughters lived with their G.I. husbands. It was nice to visit them again. Only Reggie is alive now. I learned that Cliff Price had become one of the wealthiest men in Japan and his eccentricities earned him the reputation of the "Howard Hughes" of Japan. He and Mason had become business partners and formed a lucrative company that exclusively distributed Coca-Cola, Bireley's orange aide, and Lipton's tea in Japan. Cliff, too, died several years ago.

Stan Pardon returned to teaching and continued his happy ways. The most pleasant news of all concerned R.H. Blyth. According to Mason and Hatter, Blyth had become the tutor of Crown Prince Akahito, the heir-apparent to the Imperial throne. Akahito is now the Emperor and Mr. Blyth is dead but his legacy lives on.

A few years ago, I wrote a story about the March 17, 1945 air raid on Kobe titled *Fire From the Sky*. Thousands of subscribers from around the world must have read it in The Retired Officer's Magazine. I've received phone calls and letters from B-29 crewmen living in the U.S. and as far away as New Zealand, Australia, and Europe who took part in that raid. As a result of that article, I have been made an Honorary Member of the 19th Bombardment Association and the 73rd Bomb Wing Association, the two groups that bombed Kobe that night. I consider this a crowning compliment from those brave men who flew through the flak and brought me closer to freedom. I still wish I had been up there with them.

In retrospect, I feel this whole episode in Japan was nothing but a bad dream. As individuals, the Japanese are as honorable and likable as any other race. I have many wonderful friends among them.

Today, my world centers around more important and immediate things, as R.H. Blyth said years ago. I've become philosophical in moments of repose. My grandson asked me, "What is the most important thing in the world?" I said, "There are a lot of things that are important and they are always jockeying for first place. So, it depends upon the situation and the time. There are three things of equal importance to me as I reflect upon my life: good health, a peace of mind, and freedom. I hope you are able to gain all three and I hope I'm lucky enough never to lose them."

A SHORT BIO OF JIM THOMAS

Jim Thomas grew up on a farm in southeastern Idaho and graduated from University of California in Berkeley in 1941. Except for four years as a POW in Japan in World War II, he has worked and lived in the Bay Area for sixty years. Retired, he lives in Mountain View with his wife of fifty-four years and is enjoying a life of self indulgence.

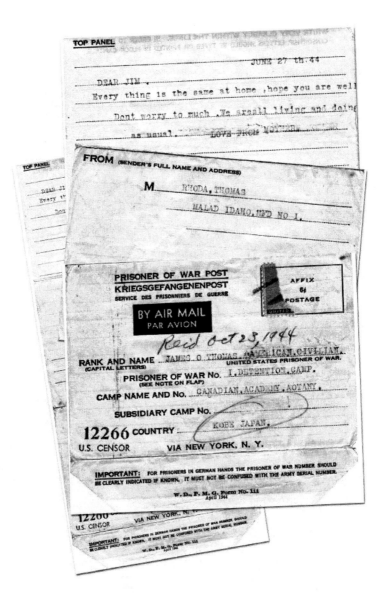

TOP PANEL

JUNE 27 th 44

DEAR JIM

Every thing is the same at home ,hope you are well

Dont worry to much .We areall living and doing

as usual.   LOVE FROM MOTHER

FROM (SENDER'S FULL NAME AND ADDRESS)

M   RHODA, THOMAS

MALAD IDAHO,RFD NO 1.

PRISONER OF WAR POST
KRIEGSGEFANGENENPOST
SERVICE DES PRISONNIERS DE GUERRE

AFFIX
6¢
POSTAGE

BY AIR MAIL
PAR AVION

Rec'd oct 23, 1944

RANK AND NAME JAMES O THOMAS, AMERICAN CIVILIAN.
(CAPITAL LETTERS)   UNITED STATES PRISONER OF WAR.

PRISONER OF WAR No. I.DETENTION.CAMP.
(SEE NOTE ON FLAP)

CAMP NAME AND No. CANADIAN.ACADEMY.AOTANY.

SUBSIDIARY CAMP No.

12266 COUNTRY   KOBE JAPAN.

U.S. CENSOR   VIA NEW YORK, N. Y.

IMPORTANT: FOR PRISONERS IN GERMAN HANDS THE PRISONER OF WAR NUMBER SHOULD
BE CLEARLY INDICATED IF KNOWN. IT MUST NOT BE CONFUSED WITH THE ARMY SERIAL NUMBER.

W. D., P. M. G. Form No. 111
April 1944

CLASS OF SERVICE

This is a full-rate
Telegram or Cable-
gram unless its de-
ferred character is in-
dicated by a suitable
symbol above or pre-
ceding the address.

WESTERN
UNION

R. B. WHITE
PRESIDENT

NEWCOMB CARLTON
CHAIRMAN OF THE BOARD

J. C. WILLEVER
FIRST VICE-PRESIDENT

SYMBOLS

DL = Day Letter

NL = Night Letter

LC = Deferred Cable

NLT = Cable Night Letter

Ship Radiogram

The filing time shown in the date line on telegrams and day letters is STANDARD TIME at point of origin. Time of receipt is STANDARD TIME at point of destination

Received at

KH 48 - EX POCATELLO, IDA. 402 PM 2-26

MRS. RHODA THOMAS,
MALAD, IDAHO.

MESSAGE FROM ONE MEMBER OUR GUAM STATION CREW WHICH HE SUCCEEDED
GETTING TO HIS FAMILY VIA JAPANESE SHORT WAVE RADIO ADVISES THAT
ALL AMERICANS FROM GUAM ARE SAFE HE SAYS GUAM PERSONNEL WERE TAKEN
TO KOBE JAPAN AND THAT THEY ARE WELL TAKEN CARE OF.

CLARENCE M. YOUNG
PAN AMERICAN AIRWAYS TREASURE ISLAND
SAN FRANCISCO, CALIF.

448 PM

THE COMPANY WILL APPRECIATE SUGGESTIONS FROM ITS PATRONS CONCERNING ITS SERVICE

ADDENDUM

The Imperial Rescript

The *Imperial Rescript*, the official opinion of the Emperor, was repeated monthly to remind the people of Japan's noble war aims. Declaring war on the United States and Britain, this document was released by the Board of Information on December 8, 1941. One of the most revealing papers of World War II, I would like to include it here in its respective and incredible entirety as an addendum to this book. Imagine, if you will, its impact on the "uninvited guests of the Emperor" incarcerated at the Seamen's Mission in Kobe.

"We, by grace of heaven, Emperor of Japan, seated on the Throne of a line unbroken for ages eternal, enjoin upon ye, our loyal and brave subjects:4

We hereby declare war on the United States of America and the British Empire. The men and officers of our army and navy shall do their utmost in prosecuting the war. Our public servants of various departments shall perform faithful and diligently their appointed tasks, and all other subjects of Ours shall pursue their respective duties; the entire nation with a united will shall mobilize the total strength so that nothing will miscarry in the attainment of our war aims.

To insure the stability of East Asia and to contribute to world peace is the far-sighted policy which was formulated by our Great Illustrious Imperial Grandsire and our Great Imperial Sire succeeding Him, and which We lay constantly to heart.

To cultivate friendship among nations and to enjoy prosperity in common with all nations has always been the guiding principle of our Empire's foreign policy. It has been truly unavoidable and far from Our wishes that Our Empire has now been brought to cross swords with America and Britain.

More than four years have passed since China, failing to comprehend the true intentions of Our Empire, and recklessly courting trouble, disturbed the peace of East Asia and compelled Our Empire to take up arms. Although there has been reestablished the National Government of China, with which Japan has effected neighborly intercourse and cooperation, the regime which has survived at Chunking, relying upon American and British protection, still continues its fratricidal opposition.

Eager for the realization of their inordinate ambition to dominate the Orient, both America and Britain, giving support to the Chungking regime, have aggravated the disturbances in East Asia.

Moreover, these two Powers, inducing other countries to follow suit, increased military preparations on all sides of our Empire to challenge us. They have obstructed by every means of our peaceful commerce, and finally resorted to a direct severance of economic relations, menacing gravely the existence of our Empire.

Patiently, have We waited and long have We endured in the hope that Our Government might retrieve the situation in peace, but Our adversaries, showing not the least spirit of conciliation, have unduly delayed a settlement; and in the meantime, they have intensified the economic and political pressure to compel thereby Our Empire to submission.

This trend of affairs would, if left unchecked, not only nullify Our Empire's efforts of many years for the sake of the stabilization of East Asia, but also endanger the very existence of Our nation. The situation being what it is, Our Empire for its existence and self-defense has no other recourse but to appear in arms and to crush every obstacle in its path.

The hallowed spirits of Our Emperial Ancestors guarding Us from above, We rely upon the loyalty and course of Our subjects in Our confident expectation that the task bequeathed by Our forefathers will be carried forward, and that the sources of evil will be speedily eradicated and an enduring peace immutably established in East Asia, preserving thereby the glory of Our Empire."

We were to see this Rescript, a hundred times over the next four years. It was their "White Paper", the official word of their Emperor, the heavenly entity for whom the people were willing to die. This was their holy war to smite the lowly Caucasian infidels.

Futatabi Roster

HYOGO KEN INTERNMENT CAMP
FUTATABI KOBE, JAPAN
Sept. 7, 1945 (revised as of today)
AMERICANS FROM GUAM CAPTURED DEC. 10, 1941
No. Name
PERSONNEL CONTRACTORS,
PACIFIC NAVAL AIR BASES, ALAMEDA, CALIF.

* Remain in Japan.	Age
1. AITKEN, Robt. B.	28
2. ANGELL, Frank, M.	48
3. APEDIALE, Thomas, D.	38
4. ASHBY, Woodrow, O.	28
5. BACON, H. Edw., Jr.	29
6. BENDON, Thomas, L.	28
7. BETZ, Paul	53
8. BETZ, Ralph	46
9. BURROWS, Harry, F.	40
10. CAMPBELL, Neil, D.	37
11. CHAMBERS, Leigh, S.	44
12. CLARY, Sr., Eugene, E.	44
13. CORLEY, Nathan, D.	46
14. CRAVER, Chas., G.	46
15. DAVIS, Edwin, L.	50
16. DEVINE, Richard	53
17. DOWNING, Cecil, T.	34
18. DURHAM, WALTER, E.	34

19. EDMONDS, Kenneth, R.   27
20. ELDRIDGE, Clark, H.   49
21. FALVEY, William, J.   33
22. FARWEL, Gurden, J.   59
23. FRASER, Kenneth, S.   31
24. GILBERT, F. M.   32
25. GORDANIER, Wm., F.   29
26. HARDY, Kenneth, F.   30
27. HARRIS, Leon, A.   41
28. HAUN, Harold, L.   28
29. HERMES, Joseph   35
30. HOFFSTOT, Robt. O.   24
31. HUBBARD, Robt. R.   55
32. KINNISON, David W.   52
33. KIRSCH, Robt. E.   56
34. LANKFORD, Lee, F.   58
35. LUCKE, Harley, J.   36
36. MAXIM, Edw. G.*   39
37. MEAD, Herbert S.   29
38. MEYER, Halsey, G.   36
39. MEYER, Kenneth, E.   28
40. MONEYHUN, Chas. E.   43
41. MORGANTHALER, Joseph   49
42. MYERS, Edw. L.   51
43. NEASS, Lawrence, F.   52
44. OCCHIPINTI, Rosario, F.   27
45. O'LEARY, Jas. B.   29
46. PETROVITCH, John, R.   62
47. PLEITNER, Walter   45
48. ROBINSON, Milton, A.   51
49. ROBIRA, Wallace, M.   35
50. ROSKOWYK, Raymond, G.   39
51. RUPERT, Frank, D.   30
52. SMITH, Charles, A.   45

53. SMITH, Roy   52
54. SMITH, Wm.   34
55. STERLING, Bryant, A.   30
56. STICKEL, Zane, A.   28
57. STUBBE, Wm. J.   51
58. TAYLOR, Jack, L.   27
59. TERRY, Jas. I.   64
60. THOMAS, Gomer, J.   40
61. WALLACE, Donald, D.   43
62. WATSON, Mortimer, E.   25
63. WEST, Carl, M.   37
64. WHITE, Alton, R.   30
65. WOODRUFF, Arthur, E.   24
66. WOOLLISCROFT, Everitt, B.   44
67. YOUNG, Jr., R. Herndon   29
THE FOLLOWING DIED DURING INTERNMENT
68. WICKMAN, Harold H.
69. GAHLEY, Martin, P.
THE FOLLOWING LEFT CAMP AUG. 29, 1945
1. CLUDAS, Averill, B.   49
2. NELSON, John, C.   53
THE FOLLOWING WIVES WISH TO TRAVEL
WITH THEIR HUSBANDS
70. Mrs. H. Edw. Bacon, Jr.
71. Mrs. Arthur E. Woodruff
72. Mrs. Zane A. Stickel
PERSONNEL   PAN AMERICAN AIRWAYS CO.,
TREASURE ISLAND, CALIF.
1. ARVIDSON, Richard, A.   29
2. BLACKETT, Geo. L.   28
3. BRODOFSKY, Max   51
4. CONKLIN, Geo. M.   32
5. GREGG, Chas. F.   30
6. HAMMELEF, Alfred J.   42

7. OPPENBORN, Fred, B.   37
8. PENNING, Everett, H.   28
9. THOMAS, James O.   28
10. VAUGHAN, Robt. J.   29
11. WELLS, Grant, S.   35
PERSONNEL - COMMERCIAL PACIFIC CABLE CO.,
22 BATTERY ST., SAN FRANCISCO, CALIF.
1. FODEN, Geo. L.   58
2. HANSEN, Martin   54
3. HENNING, Roy, C.   30
4. MACMICHAEL, Sidney   62
5. O'CONNOR, Patrick, J.   51
PERSONNEL STANDARD OIL CO.,
225 BUSH ST., SAN FRANCISCO, CALIF.
1. HUSTON, Ronald, N.   38
CAPUCHIN FATHERS, 1740 Mt. ELLIOTT BLVD.,
DETROIT, MICH.
1. BENDOWSKE, Fr. Arnold   31
2. DONLON, Fr. Adelbert   47
3. LAFEIR, Fr. Alvin   38
4. LEY, Fr. Felix   36
5. McCORMICK, Fr. Mel   29
6. MARQUETTE, Fr. Xavier   45
7. PELLETT, Fr. Marcian   35
8. STIPPICH, Fr. Ferdinand   45
9. THOMA, Fr. Thophane   35
10. BADALAMENTE, Br. Gabriel   40
11. FEELEY, Fr. Alexander   33
PERSONNEL U.S. CIVIL SERVICE COMMISSION,
WASHINGTON, D.C.
1. LOWE, Enoch B.   39
2. McNULTY, Dr. Stanley C.   35
PERSONNEL U.S. NAVY DEPT.
ENG. BUREAU, WASHINGTON, D.C.

1. ENCERTI, Dominic 35
2. FEAREY, Herbert G. 48

PERSONNEL U.S. NAVY DEPT.
BUREAU YARDS & DOCKS, WASHINGTON, D.C.

1. BRINKERHOFF, Harold K. 41
2. BRUNTON, Foster D. 37
3. FLAHERTY, Hubert W. 59
4. SACHERS, Hans, H. 48
5. WALKER, Chas. L. 63

PERSONNEL ATKINS KROLL CO.,
230 CALIF. ST., SAN FRANCISCO, CALIF.

1. FALL, Fred W. 58

RETIRED RESIDENTS OF GUAM

1. BARBOUR, Jas. 68
2. BUTLER, Chester C. 60
3. COX, Otto, T. 61
4. D'ANGELO, Guiseppe 66
5. ELLIOTT, Hiram W. 64
6. GAY, Elmer L. 72
7. HUDSON, James M. 50
8. HUGHES, Wm. R. 54
9. JACKSON, Arthur W. 65
10. KERNER, Albert 66
11. MANLEY, Albert 65
12. NELSON, Jas. E. 54
13. NOTLEY, Wm. H. 68
14. OLIVE, Euell, T. 48
15. PAYNE, Wm. A. 44
16. SGAMBELLURI, Marcello 65
17. UNDERWOOD, Jas. H. 67
18. VAUGHAN, Wallace 73
19. WOLFORD, Harland T. 55